'I love its honesty and the obvious experience and knowledge woven into it. It also gives an honest and, at times, brutal description of some children's experiences. These children are under-represented in society and academic texts. I applaud the authors in giving them this platform and voice in this way.'

Ruth Lazarus, *play therapist and clinical supervisor at Beacon House Therapeutic Services & Trauma Team and Director of Held in Mind CIC, UK*

A Trauma Model for Assessing Siblings

A Trauma Model for Assessing Siblings delivers a rigorous, trauma-informed framework for assessing and supporting sibling relationships in a range of caregiving settings. Drawing on decades of therapeutic and social work practice, this volume offers actionable guidance, tools, and insights, culminating in a complete assessment model for use in court, care planning, and therapeutic settings. Building upon the foundational understanding of trauma-informed assessments of sibling relationships in care and permanence planning within the authors' other publication, *Foundations, Trauma, and the Child's Voice in Sibling Relationships*, it addresses when and how to separate siblings, when to keep them together, and how to support ongoing contact in a child-centered, developmentally informed way. An invaluable guide for therapists, counsellors, social workers, child welfare professionals and indeed anyone involved in making decisions regarding the placement of children.

Tim Woodhouse is a senior trauma-informed therapist, consultant, and clinical supervisor with over four decades of experience in children's social care, psychotherapy, and assessment. He served for 16 years on the National Society for the Prevention of Cruelty to Children's Child Sexual Abuse Consultancy and helped set up the first children's Sexual Assault Referral Centre at St Mary's Hospital, Manchester, UK. He is the founder and clinical lead of Tiptoes Child Therapy Services, working nationally across adoption, fostering, residential care, court-directed assessments and interventions. Tim is a level III certified sensorimotor psychotherapist, level III Internal Family Systems therapist, Eye Movement Desensitisation and Reprocessing practitioner and British Association of Play Therapists-registered play and filial therapist. He is also a registered social worker and Achieving Best Evidence-approved interviewer, known for bridging relational depth with clinical precision.

Norma Howes is a highly experienced and respected independent child protection consultant, therapist, expert witness, clinical supervisor, trainer, and author with over four decades of work in trauma-informed assessments, therapeutic interventions, and children and families social work. Her clinical specialism spans complex trauma, dissociation, forensic assessment, and attachment-focused therapy within foster care, adoption, and high-risk family systems.

A Trauma Model for Assessing Siblings

The Sibling Paradox

Tim Woodhouse and Norma Howes

LONDON AND NEW YORK

Designed cover image: Getty Images

First published 2026
by Routledge
4 Park Square, Milton Park, Abingdon, Oxon OX14 4RN

and by Routledge
605 Third Avenue, New York, NY 10158

Routledge is an imprint of the Taylor & Francis Group, an informa business

© 2026 Tim Woodhouse and Norma Howes

The right of Tim Woodhouse and Norma Howes to be identified as authors of this work has been asserted in accordance with sections 77 and 78 of the Copyright, Designs and Patents Act 1988.

All rights reserved. No part of this book may be reprinted or reproduced or utilised in any form or by any electronic, mechanical, or other means, now known or hereafter invented, including photocopying and recording, or in any information storage or retrieval system, without permission in writing from the publishers.

For Product Safety Concerns and Information please contact our EU representative GPSR@taylorandfrancis.com. Taylor & Francis Verlag GmbH, Kaufingerstraße 24, 80331 München, Germany.

Trademark notice: Product or corporate names may be trademarks or registered trademarks, and are used only for identification and explanation without intent to infringe.

British Library Cataloguing-in-Publication Data
A catalogue record for this book is available from the British Library

ISBN: 978-1-041-20861-7 (hbk)
ISBN: 978-1-041-20859-4 (pbk)
ISBN: 978-1-003-72460-5 (ebk)

DOI: 10.4324/9781003724605

Typeset in Times New Roman
by Deanta Global Publishing Services, Chennai, India

Norma Howes

Thank you to Tim who has been an inspiration and encouraged me to share our knowledge and write this book together. Also, to his family and mine for their gentle pressure to ensure it was started and completed. Thank you also to all the siblings and their carers who have taught us both so much by allowing us into their lives, thoughts, feelings and the many, too many, paradoxes impacting on them. Thank you to my younger brothers who remember some things as I do, the smiles and laughter as we agree to disagree over some memories adults reflecting back on who was the boss, who was mum's favourite, who fell off which swing and had the most stiches, fall-outs and fall-ins and realise how lucky we are and were to have had and still have each other despite the many paradoxes in our lives. Thank you for reading this book, the thinking and planning you will do, the relationships and insights you will have with siblings whose trauma filled lives, with so many intolerable and misunderstood paradoxes, need now and in the future.

Tim Woodhouse

Firstly, for my wife Kim who believed in this book and enabled it to be written by holding Tiptoes steady at the helm – I know it consumed me, thank you. For our children Ellie and Nia who continue to teach me so much about sibling relationships. For my parents; my mum, Shirley, and in memory of her siblings: Brenda, Margaret, Joyce, Stella, Ralph, Eileen, Jean, and her surviving younger brother Jimmy. For my Dad, Gary, and in memory of his sister Diane, DiDi. For my sister Kirstie and our ongoing sibling relationship. For all the children and families that allowed me into their lives since 1984. They taught and challenged my beliefs about sibling relationships. I carry their memory with me as I continue to endeavour to support others that come after. Finally, thank you to Norma, who has been a lighthouse, helping navigate stormy waters, and ensured safe passage, it's been quite a voyage.

Contents

Acknowledgements	*xi*
About the Authors	*xii*
Foreword	*xiii*
Prologue	*xvi*

PART I
When Siblings Need to Be Apart   1

1	From Mantra to Map: Deciding Sibling Placements	3
2	Contact Matters or Impact Matters: Risks, Rights, and Realities	13
3	Bridges or Battlegrounds: Contact in Context	24
4	Healing, Harming, or Holding On?: Sibling Contact	34

PART II
When Siblings Can Stay Together   45

5	Together by Design: Conditions for Stability and Success	47

PART III
Identity, Healing, and Therapeutic Support   63

6	Hurt-full and Healing Pages: Therapeutic Life Story Work with Traumatised Children	65

PART IV
The Assessment Framework: Thinking, Feeling, and Evidencing Well   81

7 Start Lines and Fault Lines: Timing and Tensions for Sibling Assessments   83

8 No Foregone Conclusions: A Trauma-Informed Sibling Assessments   93

9 Listening before Listing: Making Sense of Adult and Child Narratives   178

10 From Insight to Action: Analysis and Decision-Making   194

PART V
Sustaining the Work: Supervision, Well-being, and Organisational Care   213

11 Boiling Frogs and Full Up Jugs: Metaphors for Vicarious Trauma   215

12 When the Work Gets In: Vicarious Trauma, Clinical Supervision, and Self-Care   224

References   *231*
Index   *237*

Acknowledgements

Our editor, Routledge with particular thanks to Alice Maher, Manon Berset, Anna Moore, and Prisha Revar, our team at Tiptoes Child Therapy Services and all at the British Association of Play Therapists (BAPT).

Inspired by those who taught us, John Briere, Colin Ross, Ellert Nijenhuis, Cathy Steel, Melanie Watt, Janina Fisher, Virginia Ryan, Pat Ogden, and the Sensorimotor Psychotherapy Institute, Anne Bannister, Ann Cattanach, Eliana Gill, Richard Schwartz, and all at IFS Training UK, Rise Vanfleet

Special thanks to Pete Ayling, Di Gammage, Ruth Lazarus, Lorna Hauff, and Martin Calder who believed in this book.

About the Authors

Tim Woodhouse is a certified advanced sensorimotor psychotherapist, social worker, play therapist, and Internal Family Systems therapist who is trained in a wide range of associated therapies. His social work career started in 1984, working with children with disabilities, terminal illness, and developmental issues across, residential, field work, adoption, fostering, investigation, and court assessments before specialising in all aspects of sexual abuse and sexual harm. He worked on the National Society for the Prevention of Cruelty to Children's Child Sexual Abuse Consultancy, helped establish the UK's first children's Sexual Assault Referral Centre in Manchester and was an investigating officer on the Waterhouse Inquiry. He is the founder, and a director of Tiptoes Child Therapy Services, a specialist service for children, siblings, and families affected by sexual abuse, sexual harm, and developmental trauma.

Norma Howes, CQSW, ADSW, DCFS, MSc, has worked as a social worker and child forensic psychologist and is now a sensorimotor psychotherapist and Eye Movement Desensitisation and Reprocessing practitioner. She started her career as a trainee social worker in 1970 in Strathclyde. She is now involved in training agency staff and other therapists on all aspects of childhood trauma, specialising in assessing/treating victims and perpetrators of sexual and physical assault, a clinical supervisor, author, provider of clinical governance and governmental advice nationally and internationally. She has a private practice working with adults and children who have experienced significant harm as children and/or as adults. She values working with both adults and children in how this enables the adults' articulation to help the children and the children's voices to help the adults. She is especially interested in the impact of trauma/abuse/domestic abuse (in childhood and then across the lifespan) has on attachment, the survival strategies needed at the time and how these inform consequent relationships and behaviours (especially between siblings).

Foreword

At the end of Shakespeare's 'Comedy of Errors,' twin brothers, separated from birth, find one another again and celebrate their renewed relationship:

> We came into the world like brother and brother, and now let's go hand in hand, not one before another.
> (Shakespeare, 1594/2025 Act 5, Scene 1)

Despite their different experiences and life paths, they acknowledge their shared identities, seeking mutual understanding as they start the next phase of their lives, with a new awareness of one another. As a twin myself, I loved this quote when I first heard it, but more so following the death of my twin brother some years later, when it connected me with the loss involved in going 'one before another,' and reminded me of how my own ongoing identity continued to be affected by my relationship with him.

This quote came to mind when I was asked to write a foreword to these two books on the sibling paradox. For many of us, sibling assessment touches both our personal and professional lives. Personally, I grew up in a family of 4 siblings and have come to understand over time the significance and potential benefits of these relationships for my own life. Professionally, I have worked with many groups of siblings as a social worker and therapist and contributed to assessments and decision-making about siblings' short- and long-term placement decisions, often struggling with the complexity of these decisions and my own conflicting emotions about them. Such work has included seeking the views of children about their potential placement with family members and siblings, while paying attention to their age and understanding, their individual histories and shared experiences and seeking to represent their views honestly and directly to decision-making forums. Or supporting sibling groups when they have been separated, working to help siblings to say goodbye to one another and to acknowledge the loss and sadness involved. Or preparing children for contact with siblings they have not seen for some time or may not know at all. All of this work is emotionally charged, requiring our skills as practitioners in communication, empathy and exercising professional judgement, alongside our own self-awareness and ability to acknowledge our personal beliefs and values about sibling relationships and how these have shaped us.

These two volumes make a welcome, much-needed contribution to our understanding of a complex area of theory and research and in support of our application in practice when assessing siblings. Reading through them, I was struck by the depth of therapeutic understanding that underpins every chapter and the empathy and compassion with which even the most complex of practice dilemmas are explored. Norma and Tim bring a wealth of experience as practitioners, therapists, and supervisors to their writing, drawing on their considerable experience to inform the key ideas explored within the texts. Most significantly, the books develop and enhance previous practice guidance (Lord and Borthwick, 2008; Beckett, 2021), integrating existing understanding of attachment theory and placement planning with a theoretical understanding of trauma, to present a clear framework that can support practitioners across disciplines when undertaking sibling assessments.

This is no simple task, and the two volumes presented here reflect the complexity of the challenge, through the range of theoretical and practical issues they consider. The first volume helpfully begins with reflections on theoretical coherence and how we can sustain our own intellectual and emotional coherence as we practice within this complex, contested field. The authors challenge us as both organisations and individuals to reflect on the decisions we make and to recognise the constraints that sometimes shape our practice, shifting our focus or diluting our conceptual thinking. At the heart of the first volume is a theoretical presentation of how attachment relationships and brain development can be affected by traumatic experience and how this may affect each child uniquely. Throughout, the child's voice and identity are brought to mind, through research and rich case examples, drawing on the authors' combined therapeutic experience and practice wisdom to demonstrate how theory can be applied to children's experiences both as individuals and within sibling groups. The case material supports the reader to really engage in applying and understanding the concepts being discussed. The final section of Part I focuses directly on listening to and understanding the child through a trauma-informed lens, encouraging us as practitioners to make meaning out of presenting behaviour and conversations with children, to put these into context, while checking out our understanding with the child themselves and honouring their experience and perspectives.

Volume two continues the authors' theoretical framework in more detail, applying their ideas to specific areas of practice issues such as decision-making about keeping siblings together or placing them separately, evaluating the benefits and potential risks of sibling contact, and understanding the implications of life story work within a trauma-informed framework. The authors also present their distinct, integrative model for trauma-informed practice, offering practitioners a template for future sibling assessment. An additional strength of this work is how the experience and voice of the child is threaded through each discussion, urging the reader to consider each child's distinctive developmental needs within the wider decision-making framework. Throughout, the authors sustain the coherence of their own practice model, balancing their analysis through both attachment/trauma-informed lenses, integrating relevant research evidence from a wide range of disciplines and sources to inform their discussion.

Finally, the book returns to core issues of self-awareness and self-care, highlighting the importance of developmental, reflective supervision and the obligations of employing organisations and managers to help sustain staff who are engaged in this field of practice, highlighting the potential risks of vicarious trauma and moral injury for practitioners who work without appropriate support mechanisms.

I feel renewed awe and respect for the authors when I consider the scope and ambition of these volumes. Readers searching for a simple checklist approach to assessment will be disappointed. The texts provide a comprehensive framework for sibling assessment, mirroring the complex, multi-dimensional nature of practice in this field, while integrating complex theoretical ideas and practice examples with humanity and authenticity. The authors acknowledge the potential challenges and dilemmas of sibling assessment with compassion and congruence, offering many helpful strategies to improve and support our understanding and decision-making. As such, they provide an innovative and illuminating addition to the practice literature and a valuable tool to inform our growing understanding and practice in this complex area.

Dr Peter Ayling
University of Worcester

References

Beckett, S. (2021) *Beyond Together or Apart: Planning for, Assessing and Placing Sibling Groups: Good Practice Guide*. London: Coram BAAF.

Lord, J. and Borthwick, S. (2008, 2014) *Together or Apart? Assessing Siblings for Permanent Placement*, 2nd edn. London: Coram BAAF.

Shakespeare, W. (1594/2024) *The Comedy of Errors (Oxford World's Classics)*. Oxford: Oxford University Press.

Prologue

Norma and Tim met in the mid-1990s sharing a belief that children who have lived through developmental trauma needed services designed and delivered with depth, humility, and rigour. The subtitle *The Sibling Paradox* reflected a simple truth in their trauma-informed practice: paradoxes appear everywhere, especially when deciding who should live with whom. A parent can be both a haven and a hazard, a sibling, closest ally and fiercest rival. Naming these contradictions matters. When we map a child's extended chronology paradoxes surface that can help guide planning, rather than distort it.

Before any assessment, practitioners must notice their own starting points, 'siblings should always stay together,' or 'separation is safer.' Either stance narrows vision and reduces possibility, whereas maintaining an open mind invites the full vista and the possibility of opportunities.

Human cognition seeks confirmation of pre-existing beliefs and avoids the dissonance of contradictory evidence. Serious Case Reviews and Public Inquiries, including the Cleveland and Orkney, show how questions can be framed to fit a belief, producing fragile conclusions. Lord Clyde advised a neutral stance of neither belief nor disbelief of views, but being able to hold both sides of a paradox that can withhold scrutiny. Even today, following the collapse of the Carl Beech case, public statements implied officers were trained to believe allegations. In fact, for decades child-interview training has emphasised neutrality. The paradoxes abound: Was adult-focused training different? Were officers not following protocol? Was the commissioner poorly briefed, or expressing a personal belief? Only by acknowledging and exploring these paradoxes can sound conclusions be reached.

Sibling assessments require the same discipline to identify, question, and weigh up the paradoxes lived by children and embedded in our assumptions, research, and statutory guidance. Only then can we make informed, potentially life-changing decisions.

Some repeated paradoxes include:

- Internalised coping/externalised behaviours
- Attention-seeking/attachment-seeking
- Together/Apart
- Best friends/sworn enemies
- Age-appropriate grief/trauma bonds
- Clinging to damaging contact/rejecting all ties
- 'Contact'/'family time' or 'golden time'
- Parents' needs/children's needs
- Prioritising one child's needs/keeping siblings together
- Stability of placement/need for movement or therapy
- Life story work as integration/triggering trauma/dissociation
- Hopes/fears
- Adoption/long-term foster care
- Staying with extended family/starting anew
- Children's needs now/adults' reflections on their own sibling histories
- Lived experience/professional expertise

Engaging with these paradoxes openly and reflectively leads to more ethical and balanced recommendations.

Both authors began as Local Authority social workers and now work in the independent sector. Frontline experience matters as most decisions about children's futures are made there. The context has shifted markedly over 40 years. Local government cuts were already well underway in the 1980s and have persisted, reshaping and cutting services to critical levels. Smaller workforces carry higher pressures and a greater chance of burnout, then require accessible, easily understood and implemented high-quality guidance that aids professionals in gathering, analysing, decision-making, and relaying information that will echo across a child and their siblings' lives.

Social work delivery models have cycled through generic, specialist, patch/area models, long- and short-term teams. Teams have been replaced with 'hot-desking' and working from home. Balanced multi-experienced teams have often been replaced by fluid agency staffing with the undesired effect of inconsistency and change. The context, support systems and the beliefs of the individuals and teams vary considerably, so do their value base and world views. To promote consistency, a clear framework, one that keeps outcomes anchored in reflective practice and current knowledge and not in an individual's untested preferences.

Service divisions: prevention, child protective/safeguarding, investigative/court, placement teams (fostering, adoption, residential), therapeutic services, and leaving care bring different foci and beliefs about 'what works.' Decisions can shift with changes of practitioner or team reorganisations, creating further instability for children.

As Blom-Cooper's enquiry into the death of Jasmin Beckford noted, weaknesses in training, supervision, and allocation have far-reaching consequences. A transparent format for how decisions are made and what support will follow helps families and professionals understand reasons, conditions for review, and thresholds for change – even if those decisions are disputed.

Specialist Local Authority trauma teams have dwindled. Child and Adolescent Mental Health Services provision for looked-after children in some areas has been dismantled entirely and other services reduced whilst facing increased demand. With fewer specialist colleagues or services to consult, practitioners can be left floundering for support with the often controversial and difficult decisions they have to make.

Much training has shifted towards online delivery. There is a paradox here too, as whilst virtual connection increases capacity to see other people, its lack of human presence further feeds into isolation and disconnection. Learning that builds reflective capacity, tolerates, or invites challenge and integrates left-brain knowledge with right-brain empathic attunement is impossible to achieve behind a screen responding to slides and quizzes. The further we move away from creative, experiential, challenging, multidisciplinary, face-to-face human learning, and relationship building, the harder it becomes to render coherent judgments about human care relationships, including siblings – it has to be lived and experienced.

So Why This Book?

Their shared curiosity is not only about the strengths, gifts, and needs of individuals, but about why children and families sometimes present in chaotic, rigid, inconsistent, stuck, dangerous, or baffling ways. That curiosity led them to deepen their therapeutic training across multiple contemporary modalities, whilst continuing to assess and report for Magistrates, County, and High Courts.

This led to undertaking and continuing with training to gain further therapeutic qualifications and current knowledge in this rapidly expanding field. Both now work primarily as therapists and have a joint experience exceeding 80 years. They also assess and report on family functioning for Magistrates, County, and High Courts. A remark about the need for more informed assessments and planning where siblings maybe split and contact needing to be purposeful, became this book.

Increasing numbers of children are being seen whose plans have been shaped by assessments that were descriptive but lacked analysis, where trauma-informed questions were not asked, where behaviours were not understood as distress responses, where contact lacked purpose and structure, where sibling placements lacked a coherent formulation and where multiple therapeutic programmes were implemented without goals, reviews, or analysis of change, regression, or stuckness. Placements threatened by the legacy of decisions that were not reviewed in the light of new information became increasingly commonplace.

The combination of social work and robust therapeutic training alongside professional longevity offers perspective on the pressures practitioners face when making decisions that may shape a whole life. Work with families requires holding paradoxical, competing needs in mind while keeping the child's welfare paramount. Listening carefully to all siblings' wishes and feelings, including when they disagree, or seemingly agree.

This volume aims to deepen understanding of developmental and complex trauma and its impact these have on a child, sibling or adult's capacity to:

- Take in information, process, understand, or present a view.
- Develop a deeper understanding of the limitations of Gillick or Fraser competence.
- To understand what must happen for lasting change to occur.
- Consider wishes and feelings, make the distinction between wants or needs, and use this to inform decision-making.
- Consider the developmental age/ability of the child to determine a timescale for the outcome.
- See the paradox in the 'ability' of a number of young people who can sometimes be seen as having competence and the danger in not seeing the 'sometimes.'
- Recognise a sibling placed with the wrong sibling or with the right sibling in the right or the wrong or the least-worst placement.
- Seriously consider the impact of siblings joining late or being removed early and other changes in the sibling group.
- Avoid arranging contact with no clear purpose, plan, or content.

It also invites practitioners to:

- Weigh developmental age when setting timescales.
- Recognise when siblings are with the right/wrong sibling, in the right/wrong/least-worst placement.
- Consider late entrants and early removals in sibling groups.
- Avoid purposeless contact; define goals, structure content, prepare and debrief participants, and review intervention impact.

This book is neither pro- nor anti-sibling contact. It is pro-purposeful contact, aligned to assessed needs, with content designed to support safety, regulation, relationship, and reflection.

Sources and Stance

The foundations of this book are enduring social work texts, enriched by research on trauma's impact on children, siblings, adults, families, and practitioners; by child development, psychopathology, and neuroscience; and by therapeutic literature that challenges assumptions. Above all, the heart of this book centres on the lived experiences of children and families across eight combined decades: siblings well-matched and thriving; siblings together who should not have been; siblings apart who may have flourished together; reunifications made too early or too late and separations made too early or too late.

This book is not about blame. It will not blame individuals, teams, organisations, governments, or finance. This book is about curiosity and challenge. Challenge of beliefs, views, values, sentiments, and, maybe, even cultural, faith, or other personal identity markers.

This book uses each child's gender pronouns where known; otherwise, language is kept in a non-gendered format. Where quotes are used, the original author's terms are used.

It is hoped this book will become essential reading for anyone meeting children where conversations touch the complex, often paradoxical territory of sibling relationships, together or apart, and those who plan contact. May it support clear, courageous, reflective practice, and help all of us hear what is said, unsaid and not yet sayable in children's words, behaviours, and silences.

Afterword

These two volumes are filled with case examples. They are based on real people from a combined 80 plus years of practice. To preserve the anonymity and confidentiality of service users, all case material in the book has been altered and pseudonyms are used throughout. Where actual case material is used, explicit permission for this has been given. Other examples are composite case material that has been developed. After giving a recent keynote, an attendee came up afterwards and stated that she and her colleague were still working with a family that was given as a case example in the presentation. It was not the family being presented; it just felt like it to the attendee. These case examples will resonate because there are only a finite number of circumstances that can be presented, a lot for sure, but finite.

Part I
When Siblings Need to Be Apart

Chapter 1

From Mantra to Map

Deciding Sibling Placements

Beckett (2021) highlights important points in her updated guide on planning and assessing sibling groups, many of which were emphasised by the Department for Education (DoE) (2018). She identifies several 'hallmarks of high-quality assessments.' They should be, 'Child-centred, holistic, focused on action and outcomes, involve children and families, build on strengths as well as identifying difficulties, are multiagency and multidisciplinary, and are transparent and open for challenge.' The conclusions draw on research into adoption placement outcomes (DoE, 2013). Whilst this evidence is valuable, many children experience multiple placements before adoption, meaning that decisions about who lives with whom, or apart are often made earlier in this journey. What remains absent is robust research on the outcomes of sibling placements in multiple settings: Adoption, Special Guardianship, Short and Long-term Fostering, and Residential facilities. This identifies the need for research on outcomes across all placement types.

The decision to move individual siblings is a unique challenge and a responsibility. For Local Authority childcare social workers, the need to protect children is paramount and may require removing a child from the birth home to a place of safety. That place of safety can range from a connected carer, someone the child already knows, a complete stranger to a relative with whom they share a close and familiar bond through regular contact.

Children who have lost both parents in a road traffic accident are more likely to be placed with a known relative with whom there has been a close familial bond, rather than in an unfamiliar household. This is particularly true if their prior parental relationships and relationships with the known relative have been previously positive. Both parental and relative relationships in these circumstances will have been: 'adequate parenting to highly nurturing,' emotionally stable, empathetic, encouraging, and child-focused care.

The placement decisions for children who have been removed from a highly abusive, neglectful, authoritarian, or permissive family situation with high Adverse Childhood Experiences (Centers for Disease Control and Prevention, 2010) (ACEs) and low warmth hold many more variables to consider. Conversely, an unfamiliar relative may seem a safer option from the children's perspective than the more familiar relative based on the premise that a familiar relative is more likely to

DOI: 10.4324/9781003724605-2

have been involved in the children's family chaos and therefore may be and feel as unsafe as their family situation. Or paradoxically, they may feel safer because that familiar chaos makes more sense and presents less challenge for the children. Another paradox is that it may be harder to trust or connect to a relative because the child believes he/she must have known what was going on but either failed to act or they apparently condoned and did nothing to change what was happening, approved and joined in. These paradoxes may result in the decision to place the children in a less or least familiar situation where there has been no, or limited connection, where emotional, physical, or geographical distance enables a greater sense of security until an assessment on the purpose of and timing of maintaining any family connection is completed.

Cherry, now aged seven, was a toddler when her mother died. This experience was exacerbated by Cherry not being discovered for three days after her mother died as they lived alone. Cherry was placed with her father. He responded as soon as he had been alerted to his separated spouse's death. Cherry and her father lived together for three years until she was aged six. Cherry made clear allegations of recurrent sexual abuse by her father. She was then placed with Sonia, who had immediately volunteered to care for her. Sonia had three grandchildren. The eldest granddaughter, Evie, was the product of a relationship between Sonia's stepdaughter and Cherry's father. There was no biological relationship between Sonia and Cherry, but a half-sibling relationship between Cherry and Evie. The placement, tempestuous and fiery from the start, was constantly on the brink of disruption. On the surface, the relational distance between Cherry and Sonia seemed helpful because it was maintaining a level of connection between half-siblings.

Sonia had something missing in her life. She filled this with a co-dependent relationship with her daughter, Susie. She regularly looked after her grandchildren when Susie was overwhelmed and Sonia was where her grandchildren would run when in conflict with their mother. She filled her house with stray dogs and cats, abandoned caged birds, and other animals. The 'abandoned' Cherry was a seemingly snug fit in this distorted family unit. Sonia and her daughter were inseparable one moment, argumentative and rejecting the next. Cherry's placement with Sonia increased this conflicted relationship. Evie had anorexia, was rejecting and hostile, and whilst she preferred to live with Sonia rather than her mother, she frequently fell out with both and bounced between their houses. Evie hated Cherry almost as much as Susie did. The fundamental flaw in the placement was that Susie could not look at Cherry without having the thought, 'Did Cherry's father do the same to Evie as he did to Cherry?' Evie also could not look at Cherry without being reminded of what their father had done to her and lived in constant fear that Cherry would eventually work that out, or ask her, and then 'out her.'

When assessing placements, it is necessary to actively search for 'not known' information as much as the information already known. The discovered 'not known' positives in this family resulted in significant help being offered and accepted. It took two therapists five years to stabilise the family and overcome the many challenges. Their interventions included individual therapy for Cherry, individual therapy and therapeutic parenting support for Sonia, school support for all the children, individual work with Susie and Evie, and finally parent-child work.

> The structural variables such as the age of children, cognitive gifts such as intelligence, gender or birth order appear to have less impact on children's relationships than the children's individual character, a safe family environment that engenders a 'felt sense' of safety, was structured, organised and met each individual child's need.
>
> (Pike et al., 2009)

Beatrice, Remi, and William were removed from their parents care due to neglect. Thirteen-year-old Beatrice was placed independently into a specialist children's home. Her sexualised, sexually reactive behaviour was extreme. Her impulsive/reactive absconding (hyper-arousal) put her at clear risk of sexual exploitation. Her sexually reactive behaviour and violence were also a risk to others. It was recognised that if she was placed in a foster home, unless it was an exceptional placement, the level of her unmet needs and the dangers from her behaviours could not be adequately supported and very likely lead to multiple placement breakdowns.

The boys, Remi aged ten and William aged seven were placed together. The positive assessment, which resulted in that decision included many of the factors identified by Tucker et al. (2008) and Beckett (2021: 71). They appeared to have a 'positive relationship.' They shared the male foster carer's interest in football. Tucker et al. (2008) cites shared activities as a resilience factor for sibling relationships. There was no 'intense rivalry or Jealousy.' 'Exploitation' between the boys was not witnessed although there were concerns about their relationship with their sister and the risk from their sister. The presence of 'potential scapegoating' was not found. There was no finding of 'hierarchical' behaviour and no 'sexualised behaviour' was witnessed between the boys. They were not 'acting as triggers to each other's traumatic material.'

Neither Beckett nor Tucker invite assessment of, or recognition of, a trauma bond. A trauma bond was not considered between Remi and William because of the apparent positive indicators to their relationship. A relationship, even with all the potential contraindicators to a trauma bond is still not one of the hardest to establish, despite its reputation. When a sibling group has lived in the same trauma-filled environment, its presence must be taken into consideration.

Remi, as the older sibling, was not seen as 'struggling to invest emotionally' any more or less than his younger brother and indeed both seemed to settle well into the routine of the foster placement. The 'age difference' between the boys was acceptable. There were no other 'family placements on offer to either child either together or apart' and neither child had a 'significant attachment to other appropriate families' where placement for one over another may have influenced a split.

Finally, the boys were not split due to the 'size of their sibling group' (Lord and Borthwick, 2008).

Initially Remi and William settled into their placement well and they were able to continue to attend their school. Contact was stopped with their sister because Beatrice was too dysregulated to manage direct contact and the boys were dysregulated with indirect contact. They continued to have supervised contact with their parents that was stressful and dysregulated both boys. When William disclosed that his sister had regularly come into the boys' room when they lived at home and had sex with them, his relationship with Remi became fractured and fraught. Remi had not wanted to disclose. He was effectively outed by his brother and began to exert passive pressure on his brother to retract. William was not emotionally or psychologically strong enough to withstand his brother's pressure, but nor was he willing to back down. Remi became resistant in therapy and rejecting of the carers because while they proactively supported both boys, they refused to join Remi in exerting pressure on William to retract. In their not doing so both boys spiralled.

It was not just Remi who was refusing to accept William's truth; the Team Around the Child (TAC), a type of professionals meeting no longer in use, steadfastly refused to believe that Beatrice's behaviour could have stemmed from her own experience of sexual abuse. For fear of leading, she was not asked about where her behaviours came from. The power of secrets, of unknown experiences, will always be any assessor's greatest challenge. The notion that Beatrice's presentation came from nowhere, was of her own making or not, or was not going to have an impact on her brothers was wrong. Indeed, quashing the view that her presentation signalled whatever she had been exposed to had implications for Remi and William was a catastrophic misjudgement. This lack of curiosity by the TAC led to another hypothesis not being explored: was Remi also trying to stop William talking about Remi's sexual behaviour with him.

Children and young people have different strategies for managing their experiences. It is necessary, therefore, to understand children's presentations in light of each of their siblings' behaviours or the lack of behaviour, which is actually also a behaviour. A decision was made that it would be in the boys' interests to be split. William stayed because he had a reciprocal relationship with the carers. Remi was moved, because whilst the carers supported him emotionally, when they refused to support him in suppressing his brother's disclosures, he began to push them away. A decision which also effectively maintained secrets in the siblings' relationships.

One of the most significant aspects of decision-making is hypothesising about the unknown, how to test and analyse the unknown in a coherent and manageable way. This is not just in initial decision-making about who lives with whom. It is also needed when children have been placed together and disruption seems likely whether or not to promote therapy as a potential catalyst for change, if yes, for how long, or no, how quickly to move children on.

So, what does happen when children who should never have been placed together have been placed together, and the placement is close to disruption?

Carlton, Zac, and Billie, the children placed for adoption with Martha and Ed are an example. They came from a sibling group of six and suffered the loss of their three siblings by this match. Zac and his siblings experienced multiple ACEs, including severe and persistent neglect. They were only removed from their family home after the Royal Society for the Prevention of Cruelty to Animals had removed the family's pets. The children all lacked appropriate supervision and were bitten by the family dogs. The older children were pseudo-parentified and looked after their younger siblings without the developmental sophistication needed to do this successfully. There were parental mental health issues, alcohol misuse, and they lived in a volatile violent family.

At the time of referral for therapy, Zac's behaviours had become so extreme that the adoptive parents were on the edge of making the decision to end the placement. Zac had become the middle child of this new family ensemble and despite the phrase 'middle child syndrome,' the order of children is not the only factor in the outcome of sibling relationships. There are a myriad of quotes and research suggesting it is not without effect, 'I was a redhead and a middle child; both can make you feel excluded. It's like fighting to be included, in the swim of things. After a while you start to develop a bit of a victim mentality, which isn't great for a happy life' (Shirley Mason, member of the famed American rock group Garbage), suggesting that whilst perhaps not key to sibling outcomes, it should not be ignored. 'A "small stressor" (such as being the middle child) on an already traumatised child tends to make a big impact on the brain and body because trauma is cumulative' (Siegel, 1999).

Zac's referral prompted a review of all the issues to be considered to make informed plans for these three siblings.

- Despite all the siblings experiencing ACEs, the impact on each of the siblings will be different. It is important not to mistake internalised coping strategies or compliance for resilience. Any child who seems to be unaffected is more likely to have a different strategy to their clearly troubled siblings who are externalising the impact rather than internalising their distress. A search for any positive, resilience-building factors for each sibling is therefore needed. In other words, 'What did this child experience that the others did not?' Having a clear understanding of each child, their individual characteristics, positive and negative experiences, and their behaviour towards each other is helpful in ascertaining their individual coping strategies. Using an extended chronology for each child will be useful.
- What was the nature of, and the level of dependency in, each of the relationships between Carlton, Zac, and Billie, both individually and in various combinations with the older siblings from whom they have been separated?
- It is known that some of the older siblings took on a pseudo-parentified role and were caregivers to their younger siblings. The lack of trust in the adults who should have undertaken this task, and the loss of these caring siblings may have raised fears about survival. The older siblings will have also felt a loss

of role regardless of whether they were competent or whether this role was 'good' for them or not. Or it may have been a relief to have had this challenging role and responsibility lifted from their shoulders.
- Sibling children who take on the role of caregiver, but are ill-equipped to do this, feel both the responsibility of undertaking it and the negative consequences of seeing their siblings failing developmentally. A child caregiver, realising that no matter how hard they try their efforts are not enough, experiences the painful negative impact on their self-esteem. Two hypotheses need to be looked into: the likelihood of the trauma bond exacerbating their feelings of loss, and, to avoid feeling or acknowledging this pain, the sibling caretaker may then be compelled to fight to keep this role.
- Careful consideration of all the above needs to be taken into account before arranging contact. Then observation, before, during, and after contact will help determine whether both their behaviours are a fight to retain a healthy attachment relationship, a fight to maintain familiarity, or a flight from their own pain and distress. Unplanned contact where there is no plan in place to resolve a trauma bond will almost always, if not always, intensify the bond, resulting in increased distress-filled behaviours, unmanageable feelings of loss, and potentially placement disruption.
- Zac, already a child cared for by another child, struggled with multiple losses when he was removed from his parents' care and moved from being the second youngest to being a middle child. His losses and their impact included: the familiarity of his parents and chaotic family, his older siblings, his toys, any comfort-giving items, the family pet, later losing the familiarity of his first foster placement, losing Billie for a time, losing his role of being looked after by familiar siblings and noticing if he is now concerned whether he will have to take on responsibility for taking care of Billie as well as managing his self-survival in the absence of his older siblings. More difficult would be to determine the impact of his not yet known losses, beliefs, and fears.
- Carlton had suffered significantly in the care of his birth parents and had been admitted to hospital with hypernatremic dehydration, pneumonia, and focal seizures, which led to a long hospital stay. Whilst in his short-term foster placement with Zac, he blossomed, and his development caught up.
- Billie was placed separately, making Zac, in this period of time, the youngest and not the middle child.
- Billie had been placed in a separate foster home on removal from her family immediately after her birth. Unlike her siblings, she was described as 'normal in her development and behaviour,' which may suggest that she was, or that what she had experienced since conception was 'not seen,' not an unusual consequence for the very young. Her experiences since conception suggest she could not have been as described. She was moved to be with Carlton and Zac just days before they were to move to their adoptive placement.
- And lastly, an appropriate in-depth assessment of each child was needed that included their toxic mix of needs and differing presentations across placements,

what information had been gathered and missed, the difficulties in understanding their multiple complex variations of need, implicit developmental messages, and the caregiving and receiving seen in their differing responses in their sibling, care receiving and other relationships.

This placement should have failed, and very nearly did. On being moved into the adoptive placement Carlton and Billie cried and Zac screamed constantly for years. The adopters were at the point of relinquishing Zac and Services were preparing for the inevitable disruption. If it had failed for Zac, the intensity of the spotlight would have moved to Carlton or Billie. It was impossible to see the tremors in two earthquakes when a volcano was erupting in the middle of them. Zac's pain and the power of his outbursts did not mean his siblings were okay or even seen. The children's relationships had been set within the context of a maladaptive environment and therefore their sibling relationships were organised around that maladaptive setting.

This is not a helpful or healthy way for sibling relationships to be nurtured. Each child's genetic make-up, including resilience factors and/or additional needs, temperament, level of exposure to different ACEs in any of their placements, their position in the family, their experience of abuse, witnessing or being aware of abuse or domestic violence, their similarities or differences in ethnicity, gender or any of the other innumerable factors impact on the manner in which they will then respond in their sibling relationships, indeed all other relationships. Until the loss of these negative relationships is resolved, the making and deepening of positive relationships will be impaired.

The Local Authority was never going to find a placement for all six children. It can happen, but it is rare. Even when a placement for a number of children is identified, an assessment is needed, not just of the children but of the prospective parents' experiences too.

It was right that the three older children were not placed with Carlton, Zac and Billie. They had experienced the longest period of neglectful care, but this did not mean that the younger siblings would therefore be more resilient. Billie was a prime example of this. She only experienced care from her parents in utero, and yet showed a similar level of disorganisation and distress as her other siblings. Research shows that in utero the unborn can experience trauma impacting their developing mind and body. It also shows that parental trauma can change a baby's genetic makeup, while trauma during pregnancy impacts the baby's ability to manage stress. Not only did Billie experience trauma in utero, but she also experienced the loss of her parents at one day old.

The younger the child is, the more likely the child is to have enduring and pervasive problems following trauma. Severe neglect in the first years of life can have a devastating impact even if a child is removed from the neglectful environment.

(Perry, 2006)

Billie was placed in a separate placement away from her older two siblings, who had little awareness of their sister. Billie then experienced further trauma on being removed from her foster carer, her primary attachment figure at ten months old, a crucial time in her development when she would be 'experimenting' with separation and learning about object permanence (Wolkind, 1988). She was then placed for less than two weeks with her two older siblings and their foster carers prior to that move. The decision to place Billie with her troubled siblings would be a further risk to her development.

She was clearly exposed to ACEs in utero and was on her way to her third placement in ten months. This placement was the opportunity to avoid delay in trying to find a solo adopter and followed the accepted script; 'siblings better together' despite there being no relationship with her two siblings.

Being placed with her two very stressed older brothers exposed her to both the stresses of their past trauma and their current trauma of uncertainty and loss. There is no doubt that she could have been placed separately. The Local Authority services had made the decision that the sibling connection was more important than the exposure to the multiple moves and the trauma this resulted in.

Carlton and Zac triggered each other. They had a trauma bond. They were equally neglected by their birth parents and were placed with foster carers who were taken by the younger, more baby-like Zac. Carlton was not scapegoated, but by Zac being favoured, their care was inequitable.

Carlton was not neglected. He began to thrive. His care had improved beyond measure, but both children experienced the foster parents' inability to love the children equally and unconditionally. Zac gained weight, too much weight. He was fervently fed by his carers who doted on him. Carlton witnessed the imbalance but was loved and cared for in a manner that exceeded his previous experience. Zac saw that his brother received less and that was painful, but he could not let go of the attention he was receiving because he was safe and Carlton was the threat that could intrude on or usurp his position. This care compounded their previous experiences of their birth parents' chaos and neglect. They needed to have a relationship but, by this point in their parenting experiences, a sibling placement was contraindicated.

These three children, removed from their birth family, aged two years, one year, and two days, spent the next year in foster placements until an adoptive family was found for all three when they were aged about three, two, and one. Even with the buffer of adoption leave, the new family faced a distressing and turbulent transition period. The family limped on for approximately another seven years doing the best they could with three very distressed children and was close to disruption when they were eventually referred for support. Siblings should be placed together? Did what happened happen because these children had not been assessed, or matched, and were then placed together when they should not have been?

The kindest thing at the start of the process is to be objective, take into account the knowledge of developmental trauma and not put children in this position in the first place. Professionals struggle to do that. At the point of referral, there is a need to assess if the parents/carers have the capacity to do what it takes to turn a situation around when they are already saying they have long since surpassed the end of their tether. There is also a need to consider the likelihood of the children being able to make the internal changes they need to make to live a healthy, balanced life with their siblings. Where children have lived so long together in permanence, it can be looking at 'least-worst' rather than the best option – there is often no best option.

The intervention started with an assessment that found that the parents were invested heavily in their children, and whilst exhausted were warm, receptive, open, consistent, caring and able to act on advice. What of the timescales for change? Each individual child was assessed as requiring in the region of three years' intervention, if they lived on their own. When children are a sibling group this creates convolutions that exceed the complexities of individual complex trauma. They are interdependent on, have multifarious sources and interrelations. The work therefore becomes long-term and relies on a commitment to guaranteed funding. It is not uncommon for funding to be agreed and then, with changes in practitioner or policy, stopped. Specialist therapy is expensive. The cost pales into insignificance compared with specialist long-term residential care, the all-too-often only remaining solution for many children in this situation. It concluded that Martha, Ed, Carlton, Zac, and Billie could be worked with.

The intervention started with individual and couple therapeutic and psychoeducational parenting support. Triggers were identified and the couple entered into their own therapy outside of the support being provided. The parenting support was an important, integral component of the therapeutic package and continued for the duration of the intervention, changing in frequency depending on the levels of stress they or their children were experiencing.

The children started their own bespoke therapy. As expected in therapy, they regressed, an indicator that the therapy is actually working, because they started to access the feelings that were the drivers behind their behaviour and learned presentations. As individuals, their response to therapy was different. They healed, or regressed, or changed at different rates on their differing pathways. Therapeutic pathways are never linear. Zac, despite being the child with whom most concern was raised, turned out to be the child who became ready for the next component of therapy soonest, to be joined in therapy with his parents. Having a parent or carer in the therapy leads to the attachment threat being played out in front of the therapist and creates opportunities to challenge inherent beliefs and responses. This process can lead to another regression, a normative response, one which despite warnings and preparation, can be disheartening for families who were seeing significant change in their child.

Billie followed this trend some six months later. The two siblings shared their parents between their two sessions. Having three siblings complicated this process. It was clear from the progress Zac and Billie were making that they were ready for joint sibling and parent work. This resulted in their third regression, by far the worst regression. The siblings were faced with the reminder of their experiences. The behaviours, consequent to their trauma bond, were 'live' in the therapy room. The reason they survived this sibling work was that the work had been done, in the process of the therapy, to widen their window to enable them to tolerate this next step. It was this work that led to a change in the way the children really began to respond to each other because they lived and experienced their parents being able to meet both their needs and began to allow their parents to do this. The previous maladaptive strategies the children once clung onto began to dissipate. To have done this joint sibling work before they had experienced their individual therapeutic process would have been overwhelming and destructive.

Carlton, unlike his siblings, was still struggling in his own individual process. Noticing the difference in his siblings brought doubt, shame, fear of, and feelings of abandonment. This was the turning point that eventually led to the changes he needed to face in his own therapy. This needed to happen before his parents began to join him in therapy and before the final stage of therapy with all the siblings together.

Positive outcomes for complex, paradoxical sibling relationships do not just rely on the right therapeutic service but need a cohesive supported and supporting team around the child and parents. Parents who are able and willing to make the immeasurable sacrifices. This was a positive outcome for a far from positive placement and could so easily have disrupted at any point.

Questions: If the placement had disrupted how, where, and with whom would these children have been placed? How well would the children be doing now if they had not faced the ongoing exposure to their trauma-bonded siblings? A more significant question: Is children's potential sacrificed for their sibling relationship and despite the potential cost or do we sacrifice the relationship? These are complex questions. The outcome of decisions made is often only seen in retrospect. The outcome from decisions not made will never be known.

Chapter 2

Contact Matters or Impact Matters
Risks, Rights, and Realities

The Children Act 1989 imposes a duty on a Local Authority to promote contact between a child who is being looked after and those connected with him. This applies whether a child is being looked after by a voluntary arrangement or as a result of a court order. This duty also states that contact should be arranged unless it is not reasonably practicable or consistent with the child's welfare to do so. The term 'contact' includes not only personal meetings and visits, but also letters and telephone calls.

Regulation 14 of the Fostering Services Regulations places a duty on fostering services to promote contact between a child placed with a foster carer and parents, relatives, and friends unless such contact is not reasonably practicable or consistent with the child's welfare.

The United Nations Convention on the Rights of the Child has two articles that require consideration: Article 3 sets out that the best interests of children must be the primary concern in making decisions that may affect them. When adults make decisions, they should think about how their decisions will affect children. Article 9 states that children have the right to live with their parent/s unless it is bad for them to do so. Children whose parents do not live together have the right to stay in contact with both parents, unless this might hurt the child.

The guidance is clear. It is not an unequivocal right for contact to be undertaken either for the child or the parent where there is doubt that contact may be the conduit for further harm. It is the right of reasonable parents for contact and the right of children and young people where it is deemed to be on the continuum from benign to beneficial and in line with their capacity to decide and their freedom for self-directedness and their ability to understand the consequences of such contact. The test then is what is a 'reasonable parent'?'

Research done by Dartington Group before the 1989 Children Act linked delay and a low level of contact with the low likelihood of children returning to live with their parents, but this is contradicted by later research which found no statistically significant link (Quinton et al., 1997; Sinclair et al., 2004; Barber and Delfabbro, 2004; Scott et al., 2005; Humphreys and Kiraly, 2010; Schofield and Simmonds, 2009, 2011). The earlier research led to the issue of contact being addressed (and provided) as soon as possible in the planning of a child's placement, and still does.

DOI: 10.4324/9781003724605-3

Despite later research, contact continues to be promoted and provided so that no allegation can later be made about prejudicing the court's decision about a return home by delaying or not providing adequate contact. Another common reason is to avoid the costs of a contested hearing when the demands of the parent for contact, which could have been argued were not consistent with the child's welfare, are reulsts in contact being arranged. The assumption was and still is that members of the close family and extended family will have contact because there is a duty on the Local Authority to promote contact. The final words in the text, unless it is not 'reasonably practicable or consistent with the child's welfare to do so' are often not considered or presented evidentially either at the initial hearing or any later hearings. Instead, what is heard about toxic contact is, 'The court ordered this contact.' 'Using 'reasonably practicable' as an excuse would be difficult to argue, especially following the precedents which dismissed cost as a reasonable excuse.

Another consequence of the Act was the introduction of the 'no delay' principle which can result in every effort being made to return the child to their parents' care and do everything that could contribute to making that happen, especially providing contact because of the, later overtaken, Dartington Research. For babies especially this often would mean daily contact for a minimum of an hour, sometimes two or three hours.

In 2003, Justice Munby (Re M (Care Proceedings: Judicial Review) [2003] England and Wales High Court 850 (Admin) 2 FLR 171) handed down a judgment which has a significant impact on contact arrangements when a baby is removed. In this judgment, he said,

> Typically, if this is what parents want, one will be looking to contact most days of the week and for lengthy periods. Contact two or three times a week for a couple of hours at a time is simply not enough if parents reasonably want more.'

This was reinforced by the Kirklees Judgment (Kirklees Metropolitan District Council vs S [Contact to Newborn Babies] 2006 International Family Law Reports 333 Family Division), where the shortage of resources or difficulties in providing this level of contact could not be used as a reason for not providing it.

However, in the President's Debate in December 2010, Justice Munby made two important points. Firstly, his original judgment referred to the provision of extended contact, which includes the phrase, 'if parents reasonably want more,' adding that in making such a decision, the court should take into account the welfare of the child in considering whether this is a reasonable demand from a reasonable parent. Unfortunately, he said should take this into account and not could take this into account. Secondly, in his experience, there was rarely any argument or evidence presented by the parties that the contact could impact on the baby's development or on the reasonableness or lack of this in the parent. If this was done, appropriate contact arrangements could then be made'.

The negative impact on a baby's attachment in the short and long term of daily contact has been researched (Scott et al., 2005; Kenrick, 2009; Humphreys and

Kiraly, 2010; Ward et al., 2010; Schofield et al., 2011). As a result of this research, the Coram Foundation recommended that contact between babies and their parents should be minimal, but sufficient to enable the parent to be a familiar adult in the early months. This would allow the baby to develop secure attachment behaviours with the carers. The staff and time which would have been used for contact can then be used in parenting classes and individual therapy benefitting parents and subsequently their child. The foundation's conclusion is that if the assessment concludes that the baby can return to the care of the parent, the baby is able to transfer healthy, established attachment patterns to their parent, making rehabilitation more likely to succeed; i.e., a relaxed baby with good attachment behaviours who can initiate these with a good enough parent would be better than the baby with disrupted or disorganised attachment patterns, caused by excessive contact, being returned to an only 'good enough' parent, increasing the likelihood of breakdown.

The legal position in the United Kingdom is described as, 'The bedrock of the Pro-contact culture and there being an underlying assumption that children will benefit from ongoing contact, irrespective of any history of violence' (Calder, 2004).

Violence and its impact upon children are not generally taken into account when arrangements for contact are made and where sexual abuse or domestic violence has been a concern, even where not confirmed needs to be considered with great care' (Radford and Hester, 1995). When reading reports of contact in Social Services Department files and observing contacts, evidence can be found of high levels of chaos and distress for the children, and indeed the contact workers, which contributes to the children's anxieties, insecurities, and fears. Feelings of helplessness and hopelessness about reducing or stopping contact, when it is clear the children are experiencing significant harm and the workers are experiencing vicarious trauma, significant harm pervades, often preventing discussion with legal advisors and action being taken.

Helpfully, the Court of Human Rights recognised (Neulinger and Shuruk vs Switzerland (App No 41615/07 [2011] 1 Family Law Reports 122) the need to preserve ties with the family but also that it was clearly in the child's interests to ensure its development in a sound environment. Concluding that a parent cannot be entitled under Article 8 of the European Convention on Human Rights to have such measures taken as would harm the child's health and development.

There is also Guidance on Practice from National Institute for Health and Care Excellence 2015 and Social Care Institute for Excellence 2010, both commenting on siblings being placed together where possible, and where this is not possible, contact should be arranged, again where it is in the child's interests.

It is also suggested that there should be another, more child- and family-friendly name given to this time spent together. Interviews conducted with children and young people came up with 'family time,' 'golden time,' and 'together time.' Some Local Authorities are looking at or have already changed the name on reading these recommendations. Conversely, keeping the word 'contact' avoids confusion and distress by wrongly naming this time together, especially when what is experienced in contact matches none of these words. Until there is a decision about returning home or long-term care or adoption, the word contact represents a legal contract. Where the plan is long-term in care or adoption thought needs to be given to the change of words and any change must be consistent with that plan.

Examples of questions to help make this decision are: To whom does the word 'family' apply? To the people living with and parenting the child or the people the children no longer live with? Does the word 'golden' fit with how the people involved think or feel about and experience the time spent together? If 'family time' are the words chosen by a child placed in long-term care for the time spent with the people who did him significant harm, does this suggest some serious questions need to be asked about the quality of the placement and the sense of belonging there? Butler-Sloss was clear in her finding that contact needs to be consistent and coherent with the plan for the child; then what it is called must be consistent and coherant with the plan. The plan must also determine the purpose and content needed to achieve and match the plan. This must never be a one-off decision but one under regular review.

There are four different levels of contact:

1. **Supervised Contact**: contact which is supervised by professionals with appropriate training and support to obtain information for reports in legal proceedings. Following proceedings, it is to ensure the children are kept safe during the contact. This contact can also be observed by, but not supervised by, court-appointed experts e.g. Children and Family Court Advisory and Support Service.
2. **Facilitated contact**: contact where the professional is present (a contact worker or foster carer) to ensure contact runs as smoothly as possible and produces the best outcome for the children. But this person is not required to supervise as above.
3. **Supported contact**: contact where no supervision or facilitation is required but where children and family members are helped through the provision of venue, funding, or counselling to achieve best outcomes.
4. **Unsupported contact**: contact where young people are able to make their own direct arrangements with family members and where there are no difficult emotional issues for them. Foster carers and social workers need to be told when the contact will take place and any changes which may require a change to supported contact. The three most commonly stated purposes of the contact are:
    - to maintain the bond between the parents and the child.
    - to promote attachment.
    - to avoid a contested hearing.

Contact is almost always supervised by someone from the Local Authority to enable information gathering as part of an assessment, better-informed interventions and/or for use as evidence in court. Sometimes, but less often, the supervision is by a family member.

A review of the literature on attachment, abuse by omission and/or commission, trauma, neuroscience and when working with a trauma model details the impact on the child of less than 'good enough parenting.' It is also useful to read information about the impact on children of less than good enough contact. All of these issues must be kept in mind when planning contact and should help in determining whether or not contact arrangements can actually achieve the often-stated purpose, for example, to maintain and/or create attachment - to whom?.

Care must be taken to ensure any contact with parents who have done the child significant harm does not cause the child to experience a repeat of their lived-with level of fear or distress and consequent trauma, which would inhibit or prevent the possibility of positive attachment to the parent or indeed reinforce a trauma bond or result in an increased use of coping behaviours that could put the placement at risk.

Planning a Contact between Separated Half-Brothers

Archie, aged four, and Freddie, aged three, are half-brothers. They have the same dad. Freddie lives on his own with his single female carer, and Archie lives with a couple. The two boys are loved very much.

A planned holiday for the couple resulted in Freddie's carer offering to look after Archie. This was agreed and plans put in place to arrange contact between the boys to let them get to know each other before living together for two weeks. This would be a play activity in a park if the weather was fine. Freddie's carer said she would draw up a list of things she needed to know about Archie to make the boys' time together, in this first contact and then if living together, are as stress-free as possible for them and their carers. Although half-brothers, they had never lived together. She drew up the following list to discuss when the carers met together for a couple of hours to chat and plan:

1. Agreement on what the purpose was in getting together. Would this just be an introduction to enable the holiday to happen or would it continue in the future?
2. Dates and times when they would meet in the park – for how long and for what activity. Would the carers stay for all of the first time, or leave half-way through? Could this be a park they both knew already? If yes, what did they usually do there or bring there? If no, what was available there already?
3. What would be Archie's likely response to a new park? Was he toilet trained or were there any issues around his toileting needs? How would Archie let her know he needed to urinate or defecate? What changes would there be in his behaviour to indicate this need? Would he manage this himself or need some help during or afterwards?
4. What would be Archie's likely response to meeting up with someone he had not met before?

5. Freddie, no doubt, would want to bring his favourite toy. Did Archie have one? What would Archie's reaction be to losing his toy, Freddie wanting to play with it or try to take it from him? Would he fight, comply, cry? Would they be happy to share or be in competition with each other? And similarly, she had to think about the answers to the above questions in relation to Freddie's responses to Archie.
6. Who would bring any snacks, wet wipes, tissues? It was agreed these would be brought by Freddie's carer, so she needed to know about favourites and allergies. Did Archie take his time to eat and drink or do this quickly? If he wanted more, should this be given or not?
7. How much time should she give Archie to run around? Would he know when to stop and take a break, self-regulate his arousal, or would she need to do this, and if so what behavioural signs would tell her when a break was needed, and what was the best way to help him calm down and relax? How would she tell him to sit down and for how long? What did they do to enable this to happen?
8. What if Archie or Freddie were hurt? What if either ran off and would not come back when called?
9. Could she trust that Freddie would do what he usually did when it was just him and her, or would he play up, seek or compete for her attention, want to fight with Archie, do as he was told or vice versa? What would Archie's likely response be? What strategies had been used to deal with Archie's behaviour? How did these differ from her own way of managing Freddie's behaviour and ensuring his safety? If there were strategies needed, what would Freddie's response be to these differences?
10. When would the carers meet up to discuss success or otherwise, share any further information or changes needed, and decide if the holiday together would work? So much more information is needed about getting up and bedtime routines if the holiday was to go ahead.

These questions needed answers to enable two dogs, both well trained and much-loved springer spaniels, to spend time with each other. How much harder and more time-consuming must it then be when planning for sibling children to meet?

What Is Contact for?

The issue of contact has to be seen from the child's standpoint: is this in the best interest of this particular child? There is a need to recognise and protect the child's right to either embrace or reject contact and avoid further opportunity for violence and repeated victimisation often witnessed by contact workers who feel helpless and unable to intervene to stop what is happening. Supervised contact not properly planned or managed where the child is uncertain whether or not it is safe, because it does not feel safe, will not protect the child from the memories of past violence, increase the potential for allegations being made about harm experienced in contact resulting from confusion over whether now or then which can cause untold emotional damage and prevents the healing process.

The importance of assessing whether or not contact is in the child's interests and how to make this a more positive experience for all requires not just knowledge of attachment and attachment behaviours but also up-to-date knowledge of the impact of stress and/or trauma on the child's and the adult's capacities for attachment. Recent developments in the use of functional magnetic resonance imaging scans show that stress, trauma and fear have a significant impact on the part of the brain used by children and adults to make attachments.

Assessing the need for and planning the content of any contact between a child and their family members can be difficult and will be time-consuming to ensure it is more beneficial than harmful. Assessing the impact on the child is vital and must consider whether there is a risk of causing further harm to the child. It is important to gather as much information on the positive and negative impact of contact on children to help inform any decision-making about contact. Not just from their behaviour during, but also any impact, positive or negative, on their behaviour, neurobiology and physiology before and after contact.

Identifying the purpose of the contact, its content to match the purpose, the training of any supervisor, and regular evaluation are crucial to ensure contact is only stressful and not traumatic. This regular evaluation cannot just be based on the child's wishes and feelings about having contact but, again, must include observation of the child's presentation and behaviour before, during, and after contact.

It is of note that organising and running a family group conference takes hours of work but is generally a one-off. Running a therapeutic group for children or adults on average takes 3–4 hours of work for each one-hour session to determine the purpose, preparation for, planning of content, time to discuss and reflect on impact on each individual, success or failure in meeting the agreed goals, all of which would inform the next session. Each group session requires the same amount of time, 3–4 hours. When so much depends upon evidence gathered in each contact, surely each contact should be given a similar amount of time, ensuring the decision about the purpose is the same as the last or needs to change, ensuring the content continues to match the purpose, implementation of this purpose, interventions needed, how these will be handled and when, by whom and what level of supervision is required, who will meet with each person attending to ensure all are clear about this purpose, whether agreed or not, the rules and time for feedback. Reflecting on and reviewing every contact will then lead to better-informed decisions about contact benefitting and improving outcomes for parents, single children and sibling groups.

It is easy to assume that contact is for family members or those related to each other. One of the factors identified as contributing to a child's ability to manage and recover from the impact of their experiences, sometimes mistakenly called resilience, is that the child has found another unrelated adult or peer who was or is able to give support and care in that relationship. This person/peer and the relationship offered will therefore be very important to the child. This could, for example, be a teacher, a neighbour, a best friend at school, a member of an organisation like Girl Guiding or Scouting, a hobby coach, childminder, school club supervisor, etc. Contact with this person/peer should be considered especially if reception into care has moved the child away from this person to a new area and face-to-face contact is not possible or reduced by the move. Of course, like contact with members of the family, this contact does not always have to be face to face but could be by phone, or virtual means such as online video communication tools, as long as rules about appropriate conversation are clear and adhered to.

Julie and her twin siblings Amy and Mark were placed in separate foster homes, the twins in one Julie in another. Amy was an enthusiastic and popular Brownie. A decision was made the children should live together and a new foster home for all three was found. An application to join Amy's Pack was done online. Julie joined Amy in her Brownie Pack at the beginning of the autumn term. Neither had been given any 'cover' story or guidance on how to explain they were sisters now living together and being brought by different parents nor was the Brownie leader given any guidance on how this could be managed. Initially there was high excitement about being placed together. Both girls wanted to be in the same six (a unit in a pack, each unit named after a fairy or woodland creature). Within weeks there were significant difficulties in the placement. This was evident in how the sisters now behaved in a very competitive way vying with each other for the adult attention they needed and wanted from the leaders. Amy's behaviour regressed to crying easily, thumb sucking and rocking. The foster carer dropped Amy off on her own at the beginning of December telling one of the young leaders aged fourteen whose task was to greet the girls on arrival that Julie had moved to a new placement, and left. Again, Amy was not given any cover story to help her explain to the other girls where her sister was or how to deal with the confidentiality issues around her history and current life. Amy found this bewildering and distressing. Rather than deal with this the foster carer was advised to withdraw her from Brownies without checking what impact this would have on Amy, her friendships within the Pack and the preparations for Christmas in which Amy was playing an important part. Neither foster carer nor social worker initiated any contact with the Brownie leaders before, during or after their time in the Pack. Lessons were learned by all including the Girl Guiding Association and their Safeguarding Advisor.

The issue of contact has to be seen from the child's standpoint: is this in the best interest of this particular child? There is a need to recognise and protect the child's right to either embrace or reject contact and avoid further opportunity for violence and repeated victimisation often witnessed by contact workers who feel helpless and unable to intervene to stop what is happening. Supervised contact not properly planned or managed where the child is uncertain whether or not it is safe, because it does not feel safe, will not protect the child from the memories of past violence, increase the potential for allegations being made about harm experienced in contact resulting from confusion over whether now or then which can cause untold emotional damage and prevents the healing process.

Additional Considerations for Siblings

Attachments with siblings are of secondary and supplementary importance in children's development. To be able to make a healthy sibling relationship, first of all, requires a secure attachment with an adult. This secure base ensures that an older sibling does not feel threatened by a new arrival because they know that there is enough love to go around. The fact that the siblings being assessed for contact, whether in public or private proceedings, will have experienced at least emotional disturbance, if not significant levels of global harm and trauma, cannot be ignored. Where the adult's ability to extend their love is limited, siblings can be competitive for, and sabotaging of, any closeness each has with that adult. Their contact with each other and with any closely related or extended family will be complicated. Generally, it is not siblings who have had loving, caring, consistent, and empathic relationships with each other that are being assessed. Children who have lived with violence and aggression, their attachment behaviours with each other follow a similar pattern, often with aggression and challenge in contact. This then has a negative impact on both children because their focus is on rivalry rather than sharing.

It is imperative to consider the impact on children of witnessing a sibling being hurt or neglected. It would not be unlikely that where there is harm being done to a child in a family, the other children could have been asked, encouraged, or forced to join in or mete out harm to a sibling. Saying no may not have been an option or, where it was an option, not a free choice. The adult may have offered a choice, 'You do it or I will do it,' which significantly complicates the sibling relationship. Learning from watching how parents demonstrate love or punishment or how to resolve conflict often leads siblings to practice those strategies on each other.

Despite later research, contact is still often promoted and provided to prevent any allegation that the court's decision about a return home was prejudiced by delaying or restricting contact. Another common reason is financial: avoiding the cost of a contested hearing when a parent's demand for more contact, because it is believed to be not consistent with the child's welfare, cannot be agreed. The underlying assumption has been, and largely remains, that close and extended family members will have contact because the Local Authority has a duty to promote it. Yet the final words of the Act, 'unless it is not reasonably practicable or consistent with the child's welfare,' are too often overlooked or omitted in evidence at both initial and later hearings. When other professionals raise concerns about distressing or toxic contact, the response is frequently, 'The court ordered this contact.' and as a result, potentially harmful contact continues.

Attachment to the perpetrator is a key component of a trauma bond needed to ensure survival. In common usage the phrase, 'If you can't beat them join them,' is an example of how predictable this behavioural consequence is. Further, as a way of silencing or stopping a child from reporting harm being done, an adult perpetrator will use the threat, 'If you tell you will be in trouble,' when the child has been manipulated to or seen to join in the harmful behaviour. When a child answers the question, 'What stopped you from telling?' by saying, 'I will be in trouble,' or 'He said I would be in trouble if I tell,' could also indicate this has happened. Remember, a threat will only work where the child believes there is an element of truth in the threat. An extreme example of this was the case of three children, ages eight, six, and four who lived with their mother. The mother's 'live out' partner was responsible for the dowsing of a woman in fuel then immolated her on a nearby church steps. The threat using this previously carried out action silenced adults and children.

Some children who are raised in an abusive environment cannot see it for what it is and therefore do not even need to be threatened. One young person, then well into her late teens stated, 'it wasn't the sex that hurt me, that was normal, that was how I believed parents showed love, what undid me was realising that this was a lie, that my parent's had lied to me.'

To threaten a securely attached child that her mother will not love her or would leave her if she tells would never work because she would know nothing would stop her mother loving her or leaving her.

If there was a gap or unmet need in the relationship between mother and child, or something else the child valued, this could then be exploited. It could be a toy, pet, friend, matter of pride, religion, or shame, and may then be more easily exploited. If a harmed child has participated in the harming of a sibling or another child, the threat of being in trouble and being sent to prison would work especially when there is police involvement and or a perptrator has been arrested. Not unlike, in an attempt to reassure a child by saying, 'it's not your fault' and instead asking, 'what makes you think that?' or 'I'm wondering if someone has told you that,' it's not helpful to say 'you won't be in trouble,' but to say, 'what makes you think that?' or 'I'm wondering if anyone has ever told you that?'

It is not unusual for one sibling to be angry with the sibling who is or has been harmed. In the same way, a child is angry with her mother for the violence done to her by her stepfather. As she saw it, her mother did not prevent the harm and failed to prevent the violence, provoked it, or did not say sorry quickly enough.

Common ways of staying safe and coping include resistance, arguing, passivity, or compliance. When a child who has worked out that compliance is the best way to stay safe witnesses a sibling being resistant and arguing with the perpetrator, resulting in harm being done to their sibling, the child blames and is angry with their sibling, not the perpetrator. The consequent feeling of helplessness can add to the angry feeling and blame the sibling for this painful feeling too.

Adults who have been in care and lost touch with siblings often blame the care system or lack of contact for this. When this is explored further, it becomes clear that the sibling relationship was not assessed and because the contact was not properly planned the trauma and distress it caused had behavioural consequences for the children. This led to contact being stopped, placement breakdown, and the subsequent loss of relationships.

Clive, ten, and his two brothers Ben, eight, and Kayden, six, were taken into care because of domestic abuse and physical abuse of the boys by both parents. A maternal aunt was asked if she could care for her nephews. She said she could take Ben and Kayden but not Clive because Clive and her ten-year-old son did not get on. Ben and Kayden were placed with this aunt and her family under an agreed interim order, later a full residence order. Clive was placed with foster carers who described him as a sad lad who spoke about having taken responsibility for the care of his younger sibling by making sure they were fed and had hidden them when violence was happening at home. At the meeting to discuss contact, Clive's carer said that while washing lettuce for lunch Clive spoke to her about his sadness at not being able to wash grass clean for his brothers to eat because he could not hold onto it when washing it under the tap and how it had gone down the plug hole. A decision was also made that the boys should be told their mother had committed suicide at the end of the proceedings and that their father had received a lengthy prison sentence. Maintaining the relationship between the boys by regular contact was noted as being 'very important.' Carers were encouraged to arrange this between themselves as often as possible and agreed to do so. Contact was stopped after three sessions because of the chaos and disruption in the contact, in the placements and schools before, during, and after contact. It was agreed a full assessment was needed on the purpose and content of any contact and future contact would not be based on the previous agreement that it was 'very important'; words which were more to do with sentiment than assessment.

Chapter 3

Bridges or Battlegrounds

Contact in Context

Contact, rightly, has become a primary focus following family disruption as a result of divorce, separation and legal separation, parental death, hospitalisation, imprisonment, war or natural catastrophe causing enforced or chosen migrancy, or most often in our context, child abuse and neglect during proceedings and/or subsequent removal into care. Contact is often considered the bridge which connects the home environment to the new, or alternative place of residence be it in a connected carers' environment or an alternative to home.

If it is a bridge for positive factors such as identity, belonging and familiarity, the promotion of attachments, connection between past, present, and future, it will also be the bridge for the negative experiences, insecure attachments, and further harm. Bridges are a two-way phenomenon.

People often find it hard to remain unbiased, for example, to change from a parental perspective to a child perspective. In addition, in a world desperate to become increasingly formulaic, a production line, there is a search for a 'one-size-fits-all,' 'conveyor belt,' 'mass produced,' and 'one-in-one out,' approach to work such as 'I did it like this in the last situation, it will fit in this situation.' But humans are not factory-produced items, cars off a production line; they are individuals. Professional manuals are sought from the *Orange Book* of the 1990s to the Framework for Assessing Families, to assessing Harmful Sexual Behaviours (HSB/SHB) and a myriad of specialist or unique interventions. These are required because knowledge is not updated. In teams or services, information is forgotten, misremembered, or lost with staff turnover; it becomes harder to know 'who knows what.' The danger of writing a manual or a handbook is they can become rigid, incomplete, or 'battery farmed,' losing the ability to see the uniqueness of each situation from the unique lens of the practitioner.

The starting point therefore must be an assessment (Beckett, 2021) to determine the purpose of contact, to understand what type of, if any, contact should be considered, which could include:

- Maintain relationships and promote attachments (if the child is going to return home).
- Provide the opportunity for looked-after children and young people to stay in touch with their families.
- Provide a child with a sense of their past and help them to connect to the present and the future.
- Promote cultural identity.
- To ease the pain of separation and loss for the child, young person, and/or their family.
- Reduce the sense of abandonment and loneliness.
- Reassure parents and children of each other's well-being, or where their well-being is in jeopardy, to enable that information to be shared appropriately.
- To assess the nature of relationships.
- To answer the question, when is it in the child's best interests?

Ages of Children

The ages of children are often cited as a key issue in the planning for contact, but it is not just different ages to consider but developmental stages and psychopathological challenges.

Infants and Toddlers

All contact is important to consider, but the very young (prebirth to four) are in a time of significant vulnerability to bonding and attachment issues, relationships (Stern, 1977), neurodevelopment, empathy (Gordon, 2009), temperament, attunement (Siegel, 1999), emotional literacy, authentic communication, social inclusion, and resilience versus adversity (Siegel, 1999).

The process of assessment is full of paradoxes: to juggle competing experiences, a child's removal due to safeguarding issues and the consequences of separation through child placement. Contact may be a buffer for minimising separation from the parent but at the same time be frightening for the infant, impacting on their delicate neurodevelopment.

The impact of separation needing speed must be balanced against the timescale for parent/s to be able to make any required changes, via parenting programmes, therapeutic intervention, changes in lifestyle, domestic violence reduction programmes, anger management programmes, pharmotherapy or addiction programmes, and court timetables. As stated by Brown and Ward (2013) one of the most important issues to confront in promoting better outcomes for abused and neglected children is the mismatch between three timeframes: those of the developing child; those of the courts and those of the Local Authority. The needs of the child will always be paramount.

Lucy and Krystal are a good example of the paradoxes of such interventions. Lucy, who had an unstable and seriously debilitating mental health issue, and her rights as a woman to bear a child. Her rights were balanced against her needs, which negatively impacted on her daughter Krystal's welfare and Krystal's right to be safe. The complexity of the conflicting needs and the sheer numbers of agencies involved in presenting the rights of both individuals led to a protracted legal process, requiring frequent and prolonged contact for an infant who was eventually adopted, but much later than she could have been. The balance between ensuring the rights of the parent and the rights of the child not to be adversely affected is a precarious balance.

Bahar was 19 and came from an Anglo-South Asian heritage. She became pregnant, wasn't ready for parenthood or the repercussions of informing her family. So, she hid her pregnancy. During this period, she liaised with a private clinic, an adoption agency and arranged a day off at work. After having achieved going full term, she booked the day off work, pretending to her family that she was at work, went into the clinic for her pre-arranged Caesarean section, discharged herself with the arrangements between the clinic and the adoption agency and returned home from 'work' with her family apparently none the wiser. There was no delay in placing the infant, and no contact because Bahar had stipulated no contact. All was well in the adoptive family until baby Maya became a toddler, where she began to hide. The hiding wasn't seen as a problem until Maya started school, and she continued to hide at school. The power of an ideal pregnancy is well researched. Whilst the nine-month antenatal period is gaining momentum with regards to knowledge about the impact of maternal stress in relation to domestic violence, drug or alcohol use or even depression on the unborn foetus/baby, less is known about the impact of unusual maternal behaviours as in this case. This is important information in helping Maya make sense of her behaviour. There will be a future impact on Maya when she needs to explore her identity and origin. This will be further complicated if Bahar went on to have children later in life that she kept.

Preschool to Latency

A significant issue for this age group without major stresses or trauma, in happy sibling relationships is their brain is still very much under construction. The higher the stresses, traumas, and paradoxes, the greater the struggle to manage construction tasks: integration of the left and right hemispheres of the brain to increase clarity and understanding, integrating the higher cortex with the lower needs and stress-driven reptilian brain, making the implicit explicit, integrating the many parts of the self and integrating the self in relation to the other.

This is complex for children without overwhelming adversity. For those affected by high stress and trauma, separated from the people who had hurt them or failed to protect them, yet have contact with them, a myriad of unhelpful, rather than constructive processes take place: re-traumatisation with repeated impact on neurological wiring, maintaining skewed or insecure attachments, creating split loyalties, maintaining negative self-beliefs, and impacting on the uncertainty of future outcomes that prevent assuagement and self or co-regulation (Siegel and Bryson, 2011).

Saffron was dependent upon her mother, but her mother gave nothing back to her daughter, to her assessors and probably not to herself. During the majority of the assessment, she was non-cooperative, passively resistant and her blank expression, devoid of affect was presented to everyone, including her daughter. 'The less a person reveals emotions in his or her facial expressions, the more somatic symptoms they tend to experience' (Malatesta et al., 1987). However, during an observation of mother–child contact, she was witnessed dissociating repeatedly as she tried to cook for, share a meal, and play with her daughter. At the end of the contact session, the social worker was in their car ready to leave when the mother emerged into the driving snow and headed towards the bus stop. The social worker offered her a lift home, which she accepted after a moment of doubt. She was told it was just a lift and there was no expectation on her to speak. However, the social worker stated that they saw something and wondered if she wanted to comment. The social worker acknowledged her disappearing (dissociating) and wondered what was going on for her. Ada went quiet, sighed, and stated, 'you better come in.' Sitting down in her spartan living room, she spoke freely for the first time. She recalled the conflict, the murder of her family and her subsequent experience of gang rape by the militia, scarred on her inner thighs as a message for future rapists and left for dead. She managed to escape the country but was 'taxed' en route by further rape and further scarring to her thighs. She recalled arriving in the UK, pregnant and human immunodeficiency virus positive, both of which were the result of her rapes. Her daughter was born negative, which was a relief to her, but her medication was failing, exacerbated by the alcohol that she drank to numb herself from the incessant and unrelenting intrusive memories that haunted her day and night. Cozolino stated, 'Those with PTSD suffer from the oscillating dysregulation or emotional arousal when cued by both conscious and unconscious associations' (2006). She was fearful of leaving her flat as twice she had been raped since her arrival, with one occasion again being stabbed in her inner thighs – letting her know that she may be 4920 miles from home, but home is still here. The worst for Ada were none of these experiences, the worst was that every time she looked at her child, the being she most loved in her existence was at the same time the reminder of her losses and her violation.

Saffron was placed in long-term foster care. The foster carers had a birth child, Lena, the same age as Saffron. Saffron didn't know how to connect with her foster family as she had never experienced a connection with her mother. The longer she lived with the family, the more she adapted to this new environment, but the harder she found contact with her mother. As she became more vocal and curious about her mother's behaviour and lack of connection, the more Ada withdrew. Saffron's response to her mother's withdrawal was to become angry with Lena's desire for connection. Ada's past experience, being repeated in not just by old trauma but current trauma in the here and now was impacting on her daughter's emotional well-being and her relationships with others.

Adolescents to Young Adulthood

The older the child, the less likely they are to be involved in family proceedings. This can make sense due to the timescales of such proceedings; the older the child, the more likely they are to be able to vote with their feet and their ability to find survival strategies to aid their transition into adulthood, except for when none of these apply.

The longer a child has spent in a dysfunctional family, the greater the levels of harm they will have been exposed to and the harder it is to separate from their family. Their beliefs about themselves and caregiving/receiving relationships are going to be increasingly more entrenched.

The task of adolescence is to fragment, to filter or shed who they were raised to be and who they will become as young adults. The greater the harm they experienced in their earlier years, the greater the chance that they did not integrate by age four. This means they will not have integrated by adolescence, in which case they are fragmenting from a place of already being in bits. 'Individuation and separation are challenging for adolescents whose internal sense of self is fragmented. Those adolescents whose trauma was chronic or began in early life may continue to rely on dissociative coping, depersonalisation and derealisation' (Blaustein and Kinniburgh 2010).

The young people most likely to be in a position to give their views are ordinarily developing adolescents, but not the adolescents with multiple traumas. Paradoxically, some may come across as competent, such as Larissa and Lila, whose eloquence and cognitive intellect were mistaken for emotional capacity. Not only were the siblings doomed to the wrong decisions being made, they were put in the position of responsibility for those decisions they made.

Disability

Sonny was preparing to leave residential care as he approached his 18th birthday. When anybody asked him his view, he was emphatic in his opinion that he was ready to move on into independence. The fact was he did not have a choice. A decision was made to move him immediately, before his birthday and only a week before Christmas. No time to plan, or shop for the things he would need as it still was not known what type of accommodation he would have. His plan was looking forward to spending time with his older brother who was living in a post-care supported flat. Sonny was still clearly experiencing the impact of the developmental and complex trauma from his childhood marked by abuse and neglect as well as experiencing the changes relating to adolescence. His sense of future was stunted. His plans, in so far as he could make them, was to spend his days smoking weed, drinking alcohol, and playing on his play station with the sibling who had sexually abused him. Sonny had Global Developmental Delay, the cause of which was unknown. The question 'was I abused because he was disabled, or was he disabled because he was abused?' This is a question that has been asked by many people for decades before him (Morgan, 1987; Brown and Craft, 1989). Sonny refuted his abuse, despite his previous police statements, retraction being a common presentation in children and young people impacted by sexual abuse (Summit, 1983).

He was cognisant enough to manage getting by, but had a desperately compromised ability to process and analyse and make sense of risk as an adolescent, and much harder to analyse when one has grown up in an environment where it is hard to see what is familiar was in fact abuse (Garbarino et al., 1987). He was cognisant enough to manage getting by, but had a desperately compromised ability to process and analyse and make sense of risk. Risk is harder to personally analyse as an adolescent, harder still when one has grown up in a particular environment where it is hard to see what is essentially familiar, as abuse.

There is an onus of responsibility to demonstrate that safeguarding plans have been rigorously considered and include risk to others and risk to self, particularly in relation to HSB, child sexual exploitation (CSE), child criminal exploitation (CCE), and County lines.

Contact Post-Family Proceedings

Hunter, aged 14, some 10 years after he had been removed from his sexually abusive, neglectful birth mother and placed for adoption with his two older sisters, demanded contact. Despite significant psychoeducation, therapeutic support and discussion with his adoptive parents and the TAC on the potential repercussions of this course of action and the potential impact on his younger sister, the request was granted but to start with indirect contact.

And the indirect contact his birth mother quickly seizing control, refusing to answer any of his questions, setting her own boundaries on how they would communicate, dictating when, where, the frequency, how, and for how long. She abdicated responsibility and blamed the adoptive parent for implanting the lies that the siblings believed of her and stated that any communication had to be without the adoptive parents' presence or involvement. She was manipulative and showed a disinterest in him but wanted information about his sister. The contact was closed down quickly but not before it had its impact on both children.

The Welfare checklist in the Children Act 1989 states that the wishes and feelings of the child must be considered. Hunter wanted to have contact with his birth mother. Balanced against this is the welfare checklist, which states the best interests of the child must also be considered. Their wishes and feelings are paradoxically not always good for them.

He had four major beliefs and fantasies that were his drivers for contact:

1. He believed that if he could tell his mother the impact her abuse had had on him, she would be remorseful and provide an apology that would enable him to move on. This was unlikely to happen because to make an apology she would have to acknowledge the abuse her children experienced and if she did that she could, likely would, lose the three children she had had in later life, and potentially her liberty.

2. Despite years of therapy, at times he desperately missed being sexually abused. He believed if he could make contact with his birth mother, the harm would recur and his longing for a familiar connection would be resolved.
3. He wanted to check that his three half-siblings were safe. He believed that if he could be present in the household, he could safeguard them.
4. He was split. He wanted his half-siblings to be safe; however, if they were safe, then did that mean his birth mother loved them more than she loved him and his sisters, whom she abused? Or if she wasn't sexually abusing them, then she didn't love them, and if she didn't love them, then they would be in greater danger from the physical abuse and violence. If she was abusing them, he wanted to prevent it, whilst paradoxically wanting to be re-abused himself.

None of these issues formed the basis of a healthy, helpful, or beneficial contact. The question had to be: what will Hunter, or any child, gain from a contact arrangement where there are any, let alone many contraindications? The contraindications included the impact on Hunter's emotional, psychological, psychic, somatic well-being, and his developmental progress.

Questions on Contact

1. What type of relationship would this be promoting or maintaining?
2. Would this promote attachments? If so, what attachment style would it be promoting and with whom?
3. Would it ease the separation and loss?
4. Would the contact be consistent with the plan, would it be coherent?
5. What are the potential, if not actual, results of contact?
6. What factors need to be taken into account for each sibling when considering family contact, parental contact, and/or sibling contact?
7. What would be the benefits and what would be the potential negative consequences?
8. How are the children likely to differ in their views?
9. Is it coherent?
10. What are the pros and cons for contact?
11. If there is going to be sibling contact, what should it look like?

Factors and Actions Which Have to Be Considered to Safeguard Each Sibling

Premature Disclosure (Disclosure by a Sibling)

The sibling group, Beatrice, Remi, and William, are a clear example of premature disclosure. The boys were not having contact with their sister, even before legal proceedings were finalised, due to the undeniable carnage that ensued. Beatrice was the first to unintentionally disclose the sexual abuse of her siblings, described later in the book. It was a disclosure that professionals struggled to accept and ultimately dismissed.

William was the next to disclose that Beatrice sexually abused him. He did not disclose after contact had ceased with his sister; he disclosed after contact had ceased with his parents at the conclusion of the proceedings. He then disclosed that Beatrice had also been having sex with his brother, a statement that Remi indefatigably denied and, moreover, pressurised his brother to retract. The intensity of Remi's behaviour towards William grew to the point that he had to be moved to an alternative placement. Remi was not ready to accept his experiences outed by his brother.

Only when Remi was moved, and William refused to attend contact, which was ultimately stopped, was William then able to disclose his discomfort at his brother getting into bed with him.

Beatrice did not disclose after parental contact was stopped. It was only after she became uncontainable in her placement that she was eventually moved out of county, where after some years she was able to make a full disclosure about her father's repeated and unrelenting sexual abuse of her, and later, how she tried to find solace with her siblings in the only way she knew how: their sexual involvement.

Enmeshed and Chaotic Families

Paul, aged 13, lived in a specialist residential unit for young people with harmful sexual behaviour. He had been placed there having recorded himself undertaking acts of bestiality and had made covert recordings of his foster siblings in their bedroom. His web searches revolved around sex with animals. His four older birth siblings and parents wanted contact. His parents had been the subject of Local Authority children's social care intervention since the eldest was born. The mother was a heavy drug user and had assaulted her partner numerous times. The father was a drug dealer, misused alcohol and had a historic allegation on police file about his attempted rape of a 12-year-old girl when he was an adolescent. Paul had shared a bedroom with the three brothers despite the fact that all the older siblings had been charged with sex offences. He had a stronger bond with his older sister who had also shown sexualised behaviour from an early age (she was four years older than Paul). Paul gave little away about how he feels about anything, but is clear he will return home, even if that is not until he is 18.

Insecure Attachments and Trauma Bonds

Lacey and Eleanor were in a foster placement when they were having contact with their mother during the care proceedings despite the fact that the mother could not regulate the children individually, let alone together. This led to violence and aggression between the children and from the children, which resulted in the mother becoming overwhelmed. The purpose of contact is to maintain relationships, but the relationships were not safely contained. It left the siblings with a lasting memory of an overwhelmed and scared mother and a skewed memory of each other. The final hearing found that the children should not be returned to their mother's care.

Reintroduction of Birth Relationships

Eliza-Fay, aged 12, had been in a positive, stable, and settled foster placement since the age of 7. She was removed from her mother's care. The parents had already separated. Eliza-Fay started having contact with her dad at his request despite a long absence from her life. The care plan changed as a result of this contact, to rehabilitation to the father in a year's time, against wider professional advice. The result was an almost immediate disengagement from therapeutic services where she had been responding well, a change in her behaviour and a breakdown in the placement before the transition to her dad could occur. She was then placed in residential services where she had four subsequent residential disruptions.

The ability to predict the impact of any changes in children's lives, but particularly to care plans is a cornerstone in the assessment process, to know the unknown, particularly when there is fantasy about the outcome. This was a move from a safe and stable relationship to an unknown and untested relationship.

Realisation

When children and young people progress in their placements, their education, their social interests or hobbies, and/or their therapy, there can be unexpected implications which can often catch practitioners and supporting professionals by surprise. Some of these events impact negatively on the young person, sometimes positively on the young person but can be perceived as negative by the parent or carer. These events include:

- Progression in therapy can widen a very narrow pillbox thin to a wide and panoramic vista (Woodhouse, 2015), but this change whilst helpful therapeutically holds a paradox. Whilst the children can see more because they are more available in the here and now it also means that they can see, sometimes for the first time, how far ahead their peers are, socially, emotionally, cognitively, and educationally. This triggers grief and shame and regression.
- When siblings have lived in an abusive, neglectful, or compromised environment from birth, they have no external comparative experience, does a fish know what water is? When removed, they can be thrown into an existential crisis where foster carers and adopters are showering them with presence (not presents), attunement, affection, care, nurture, boundaries, limits, safety, and love. These alien concepts force the child to see the world differently, but siblings will not necessarily see the world the same. What if one sibling experiences these alien positive interactions enough to be able to view their parents' care differently? But what if both don't at the same time, or one not at all?

These concepts may make them view their parents negatively. But if they view their parents negatively, and they were born out of that negativity, then they too must be negative or bad. To avoid the resultant splitting, they translate this new 'good' into 'bad' and throw the positive back. This can lead to placement disruption. Sometimes, however, the young person experiences those positive interactions enough to view their parents' care differently. This realisation can lead to decision-making that stops or changes contact, usually with an impact on others, Larissa stopped seeing her sister Lisa.

- Sometimes contact that has been already stopped is requested by children to restart, not because anything had changed for the better, but a realisation, a 'felt sense' that a need for action had to occur. Hunter thought the answer was that he could obtain justice by seeing his mother.

Chapter 4

Healing, Harming, or Holding On?
Sibling Contact

Sibling contact is one of the most complex, paradoxical, and contested areas of childcare and safeguarding practice. Sibling relationships can help heal, sustain relationships, support a healthy sense of identity and offer continuity, but they can also harm, retraumatise, or entrench destructive sibling dynamics. Unlike parental contact, sibling contact has historically received less attention in policy, practice, and research. Yet its significance is often profound, shaping identity, belonging, and long-term relational patterns. This chapter explores the complexities of sibling contact through a trauma-informed lens. It considers how rivalry, trauma bonds, coercion, resilience and placement planning intersect, and it illustrates these dynamics through case examples drawn from practice. The aim is not to provide a formula but to highlight the careful thought, assessment and planning needed if sibling contact is to heal rather than harm.

Sibling Attachment and Rivalry

Attachments with siblings are of secondary and supplementary importance in children's development. The first factor is the child's relationship with their primary caregiver. To be able to make a healthy sibling relationship requires a secure attachment with an adult. For that to develop, the parent has to be functioning as a reasonably well-adapted person. The relationship that develops means that the caregiver becomes the secure base in which the child can develop a sense of safety and trust. The firstborn then competes with the primary caregiver's partner. When this is navigated well, this sets a positive template for any future sibling relationship. The result is that the older sibling does not then feel threatened by the arrival of a new sibling because the parents' behaviours clearly show there is enough love to go around. Despite this, there is still the likelihood of sibling rivalry as they develop their identity, personality, test boundaries, and explore familial and sibling relationships. This rivalry, when contained, may go through periods of intensity but it does not overshadow the relationships negatively. Where the adult's ability to extend their love is limited, it results in siblings competing for and often sabotaging any closeness each has with that adult. What follows is a similar pattern often with aggression, challenge, and competition. This then has a negative impact not just on

DOI: 10.4324/9781003724605-5

both siblings, but on everyone in the family, because the primary focus becomes rivalry rather than sharing. Ordinarily developing siblings have relationships that wax and wane. They are in a constant state of flux, but within consistent parameters that tend to remain consistent to that relationship regardless of the situation.

The lighthouse metaphor is a helpful way of explaining this dynamic. A narrow beam of light represents love that can only shine on one child at a time. The light then moves on, leaving one child in the dark, fearful in the dark, with jealousy and rivalry seeking to bring the beam back. A broad beam, in contrast, demonstrates that love can extend to more than one child simultaneously. Sometimes, as in the case of Lacey and Eleanor, their mother had so little to give; she needed to reflect the light back to herself to survive. This metaphor can help practitioners, parents, carers, and courts understand behaviours and plan interventions to promote more secure and sharing sibling bonds.

Why Sibling Contact and Why Now?

If contact is going to be considered, there must be a clear rationale for its purpose and that purpose must be child-centred, and child-centred around the needs of all the siblings involved. Structure and routine are important but the paradox is that contact does not have to be a regime if it is not in the child's best interests. Lacy and Eleanor could not manage formal contact in a home environment or a contact centre because they triggered each other. They could manage being out in nature, getting wet building dams in the stream, kicking leaves in autumn, paradoxically being together and apart. They had contact like favourite cousins, not weekly regimented but when the desire came, when an idea popped up, whilst ensuring it did not drift. For some children spontaneity is more helpful than expectations – contact is not brownies or cubs. This method can circumvent the trauma bond, allow many more photo opportunities than staged togetherness allowing the siblings to revisit the experience afterwards, without the intensity of a troubled but developing relationship.

Trauma and the Sibling Bond: Safety and Safeguarding

The siblings, open to social care, whose relationship is being assessed, will have experienced significant trauma and its many paradoxes. Trauma impacts each sibling differently. Externalising children are more likely to receive therapeutic services, while their quieter, internalising siblings are often overlooked. Yet internalising siblings may be equally, if not more, affected by their own trauma and both internalising and externalising by witnessing harm done to a brother or a sister. Consider the siblings of those children whose abuse and murder was outlined in Volume 1. They were often assumed to be fine or unaffected when in fact their needs were profound.

Assessments must therefore consider not only each child's individual impact but also the consequences of witnessing a sibling being hurt, neglected, or killed.

It is not unusual for siblings to be asked, or coerced, into joining in the harm. An adult offers a false choice, 'You do it or I will do it.' Or as one older sibling was told, 'This is your fault. You are stupid. You are not doing it properly. Watch while I do this (rape) to Jay (younger sibling) then you will get it right. You have to get it right for the camera.' Without the option of saying no, saying yes is not consent. Such coercion profoundly distorts sibling relationships. He was not helped by the interviewers in the Achieving Best Evidence (ABE) interview telling him it was not his fault when he said 'it' was his fault, before taking time to find out which 'it' he was talking about. Was 'it' his own experience of sexual assault, what he had witnessed being done to his sibling not just once but again because he did not get it right, what he had done to his sibling, being stupid, wasting time and money in repeatedly getting 'it' wrong, making his dad angry, his mum being shouted at for having such a stupid child, not being strong enough to protect his mum, loving his dad and wanting to get things right so that his dad would be pleased with him.

Alliance with, and attachment to the perpetrator is one of the key components of a trauma bond often essential for survival. Joining in, excusing or blaming the harmed sibling often seems safer than resisting. Anger is then more safely directed away from the perpetrator towards the sibling victim. This mirrors patterns children often observe in domestic violence, where the victim is blamed for the aggression then compounded by the victim saying sorry, often not understanding that sorry was coerced or a survival strategy. These dynamics complicate sibling relationships, whether siblings are placed together or separately, and complicate contact arrangements.

Oliver, aged 8, was interviewed about whether he wished to live with or apart from his sister. When asked if he had any questions, Oliver wanted to know if people who set fires or who did 'sex stuff' would go to prison. The interviewer assumed he was speaking about his father, who had indeed set fires and was accused of sexual assault, and reassured him that prison was the likely outcome. Oliver was in fact asking about himself: about setting fire to his own bed to stop his father's abuse and about his own coerced sexual behaviour with his sister. The misunderstanding prolonged his distress, leaving him terrified of prison and fearful of joining both his father and sister there because his sister did 'sex stuff' too. This example highlights the importance of curiosity before answers, listening carefully before talking, and exploring the meaning behind children's questions.

Without this open mind, it would be virtually impossible to ascertain whether sibling contact was going to be helpful or unhelpful in the siblings' recovery and ensure that it did not negatively impact on their emotional and psychological safety.

Resilience and the Difference between Siblings

Siblings' experiences of abuse differ depending on numerous sometimes paradoxical factors such as age at onset, attachment to parents, duration and type of abuse, severity of violence, number of abusers, peer support, disclosure, and responses including institutional and professional responses. Understanding these variables is essential before arranging contact. What may be healing for one sibling may be harmful to another. Putnam (1997) and Cairns (2002) both highlight how resilience cannot be explained by one factor alone but arises from the interaction of many. Practitioners must therefore assess each sibling individually and in relation to each other, paying attention to both risk and potential for growth.

Obtaining information about all of these variables on the siblings and anyone else who is being considered for contact is necessary to ensure any contact on balance does more 'good' and less harm.

Planning Contact

Sibling contact can, paradoxically both, either or neither, strengthen relationships or retraumatise. Poorly planned contact, without preparation, adult support or attention to sibling dynamics, often results in distress, behavioural fallout and placement breakdown. Adults who later reflected on losing touch with siblings often recalled chaotic, unsupported contact sessions that did more harm than good. Recent research from Coram (2024) explored what was called 'Sibling Time Intervention.' Carefully recruited and trained adults created a welcoming environment, prepared siblings beforehand, structured joint activities and debriefed everyone afterwards. These sessions were experienced positively, but importantly it was not clear whether or not the study involved siblings with or without conflictual relationships or trauma bonds. Where trauma exists, contact requires even greater care. Like parent-child contact, sibling contact must be assessed, structured, and supported to prevent harm and preserve long-term connection. Contact must be in the best interests of each child before it is even considered.

Adults who have been in care and have lost touch with siblings who then blame the care system for this. When this is explored further, and not taken at face value, it becomes clear that the many paradoxes in their lives impacting on the sibling relationships were not appropriately assessed. It was not unusual to find, that where there had been any contact, it was not properly planned, one adult or maybe two or more were unexpectedly present, the content had not been planned, there was no preparation or debriefing, and the trauma and distress it caused had led to behavioural consequences for the children. These led to contact being stopped, placement breakdown, and the subsequent loss of relationships.

Wishing and Hoping Rather Than Assessing and Planning

Clive, aged 10, and his two brothers Ben, aged 6, and Kayden, aged 4, were taken into care as a result of serious physical abuse by both parents. The case papers noted that Clive was a sad lad who had taken responsibility for the care of his youngest sibling by making sure he was fed and hidden from what was happening at home. When he was first removed from home Clive was placed with foster carers under an agreed interim order, later a full care order.

His brothers were placed with a maternal aunt and her family under an agreed interim order, later a full residence order. Their mother died by suicide at the end of the proceedings. Their father received a lengthy prison sentence. Maintaining the relationship between the boys was noted as being 'very important.'

The carers were encouraged to arrange frequent contact between themselves to which they agreed. The case papers made no note of any assessment of the relationship between the brothers, nor whether the correct combination of siblings to live together was the right one. This decision was made on the available placements. Contact was stopped after three sessions because of the chaos and disruption in placements and school before, during and after contact. Later it was agreed the statement that it was 'very important' was more aligned with sentiment than assessment.

Sibling contact must be seen as being just as, if not more, difficult to assess and arrange than child/parent contact. Collusion with or reinforcing trauma bonds need to be avoided and cognitive distortions/thinking errors needed to manage paradoxical, complex feelings must also be identified. More importantly, having been identified they must be worked on to ensure a less damaging and hopefully positive relationship between the siblings and consequently other people in the future.

Assessing and Planning and the Wishes and Feelings of Two Siblings

Mags was 12 when she was taken into Police Protection with her 14-year-old brother Patrick following gang-related threats that put their parents' lives at risk. Their names, anonimised further here, Mags and Patrick, were part of their new identities. The children were placed in separate foster homes, would not see their parents again and would not see each other for at least two years to ensure everyone's safety. An intermediary was appointed to pass information between them, but neither accessed this offer.

Two years later, Mags asked if she could meet up with her brother. Although this raised some additional security considerations, the practical planning of the meeting was no more complex than arranging contact between any two siblings their age. The social worker and her manager drew up the following schedule:

- To meet with the foster carers of both siblings, to check that they were comfortable with contact being arranged and assure them that if it went ahead, the contact would be fully supervised by two practitioners. The young people would not be left alone together, nor permitted to tell others about the meeting, whisper, or take photographs. Contact would be in a neutral place. The foster carers were also asked what potential problems they could foresee, based on their knowledge of the children. Updates on the well-being of both sets of

carers and young people were provided before and after each contact. In total, five meetings were needed to reach agreement.
- To meet with Mags to explore what had prompted her to ask for contact now, her memories of life with her brother, and the nature of their past relationships and friendships. These sessions also considered her hopes and fears, how she might feel if Patrick refused to see her, if they did not like each other on meeting, if he had changed, or if either no longer wished to continue contact afterwards. A plan for the contact was developed, one with clear rules, yet flexible enough to feel natural and not overly structured. Six sessions were needed to achieve these aims.
- To meet with Patrick for the same reasons. Four sessions were planned.
- To meet with each head teacher to inform them of an impending number of confidential meetings, meetings that they cannot discuss and that may trigger the young people. It was requested that they be offered additional support or access to a trusted member of staff before and after these meetings, and requested the schools monitor and report any changes in mood or behaviour during this period of time. Two meetings were held, one with each school.
- To meet with the contact worker to plan the practical and relational aspects of the contact, including travel and escort arrangements, managing toilet breaks, physical contact, phones/cameras, food, confidentiality, and the rules around sharing personal information of the contact or the plan with each other or elsewhere including school. It was agreed that the young people would not wear identifiable clothing such as school uniforms, club clothing, or clothing that held logos such as football teams. Time was taken to anticipate possible difficulties and plan how they would be managed. This required three planning meetings between the workers, two further meetings with their managers, and one to visit the venue. Three contact sessions were scheduled, three weeks apart, after which it would be reviewed.

Twenty-three meetings in total, and three four-hour slots set aside for the contacts. One senior manager commented it would have been easier to say no.

Patrick left the first arranged contact after twenty minutes. He gave no explanation at the time or afterwards and refused to see his sister again. Mags shrugged to appear indifferent, but despite having prepared herself for this possibility, she was deeply upset and needed additional support to reach a point of acceptance and balance.

A year later, on the anniversary of the failed contact, Mags disclosed that both her mother and father were members of a paedophile ring involving her and her brother in the 'activities.' She described the frequent sexual intercourse she and her brother engaged in, something she believed she did not mind because he never hurt her the way others did. She believed it began as a search for comfort and hugs and was not surprised it became sexual. Mags wondered if Patrick saw things differently and if therapy might help him come to terms with his past as it had for her.

She also reflected that perhaps he avoided her because seeing her brought back memories he was trying to forget, which might explain his drinking. She knew he had attempted suicide more than once and recognised his need for help, though he refused to engage in therapy.

The workers who had worked hard to arrange the contact were annoyed with themselves for not including this possibility in their original hypothesis generation. They were somewhat reassured they could not know what they did not know and made sure to include this hypothesis in the future.

Restoring Balance and Purpose in Contact

Dalton was three and his sister Rue was two when they were placed together in short-term foster care. Their brother Dixon, aged one, was placed separately. They had no contact with their two older siblings, Beth and Lucy, aged 12 and 13, who were highly distressed, aggressive, chaotic, uncontained, and disorganised young people in residential care. The grinding neglect was seen; the other abuses they were exposed to were not. Beth and Lucy had regular but not frequent contact. The contact was challenging to manage, and the girls were triggered, raising the states described earlier. This is the type of contact which could be determined damaging. However, post-contact they settled and talked fondly of each other. In addition, planned contact prevented them from absconding to find each other in an uncontained way, a behaviour which ceased when contact was reinstated. They stabilised.

For Rue, the plan was originally adoption, but failing to find a match, she was placed in long-term foster care. This placement broke down when she was aged five due to her unmanageable behaviour, and she moved into residential care. Her brother Dalton was in a separate long-term foster placement, and whilst his behaviour could be extreme, the foster family were able to contain him. Contact between Dalton and Rue was extremely well planned despite the distance, but the depth of their trauma bond, which had not been considered or assessed, left the children and carers reeling in distress from the presentation of both children and was reduced to annual letterbox contact that both children ignored. Dalton, however, looked worried all the time. When his foster mother spoke to him about how he looked, he was able to share his concern for Dixon. No one had considered this sibling relationship because Dixon was so young when the children were removed. All that was seen was Dalton and Rue clinging together and then fighting. There were many concerns about reinstating contact: was it in both children's needs? Was Dalton pseudo-parentified? What if Dalton's already chaotic presentation deteriorated further and put his placement at risk? What if it discombobulated Dixon, who was settled in placement?

Positive Contact: Grace of God or Pure Luck

Sebastian, aged eight, was adopted. He had an unrelated sister, Bryony, aged eight, who was adopted, by the same adopters, a year before him. He had been in placement for five years, and Bryony for six years. They were very close and referred to each other as brother and sister. Both children had birth siblings. Sebastian had three brothers. He was really close to Henley, aged ten, who was also adopted. Contact for them was arranged every three months, rotating between their respective homes. The contact was planned between the families, who were concerned that both boys were missing each other, and decided on contact independently without any protective plan. His two younger brothers, aged four and five, were placed together in an adoptive family. Bryony had four siblings: twins Jemima and Tabitha, aged ten, in an adoptive family, and twins Delilah and Silas, aged six, in a separate adoptive family. All the families had an annual contact camping trip where they spent the week together, it should not have worked, but it did.

There was undeniably a significant amount of luck in this situation, but there are factors which help to understand it. All the adopters were described as emotionally literate, supported couples with wide networks. The adopters talked to each other and challenged each other rather than blandly agreeing. This accepted stance kept them reflective and supportive without becoming enmeshed. Even with so many children, there were enough engaged adults to supervise and create a sense of safety. They organised around activities, walks, food, and play. Being outside in nature is restorative. They utilised the available space, paddled, built dams, walked in the rain, splashed in mud, climbed trees, swung from branches, hid in haystacks, spent time with animals and breathed. This is sensory, physical, emotional, and again, together but separately at the same. apart.

Positive Final Contact: Saying Goodbye

Georgina aged seven and Jessica aged six, removed from their mother on the grounds of neglect, were placed with their maternal aunt. Their two younger sisters, twins Harmony and Melody aged three, were placed in short-term foster care.

The plan was for Georgina to stay with her maternal aunt and Jessica to be placed with her cousin, the maternal aunt's adult daughter, and for Melody and Harmony to be adopted. The plan was accepted, although the aunt was consumed by grief and self-blame for not being able to keep all the siblings together. She knew she did not have the capacity and was able to vocalise this when she was approached to take them.

Georgina and Jessica had a strong sense of siblinghood, identified as sisters and due to the previous support of their aunt had been buffered from the impact of their mother's struggles. Having already spent much of their time together with their aunt prior to removal, their relationship with Harmony and Melody had not developed to the same extent. When adopters were found, the already reduced contact between the twins and their older siblings moved to final contact planning. The carers were prepared. Georgina and Jessica would remain in direct contact because the aunt and daughter lived in close proximity. It was acknowledged that this change for Jessica would not be without repercussions for both children.

The carers were also prepared and knew what made it necessary to to stop contact between Georgina, Jessica and their twin sisters. Preparation is empowerment. The carers were then informed of, and invited to discuss, the very detailed plan. The carers needed to be supportive of the plan for it to be as successful as it could be.

A location and room for the final contact, the date and the time were booked in advance. It was a neutral venue; it was unfamiliar to all of the children and was away from the Local Authority offices, contact centres, schools, and nurseries, which all had an essence of other purposes or experiences. It was agreed that the contact session would be videoed to aid analysis and future recommendations to support the children.

The children's social worker wrote a bespoke story about a sibling group called 'The Four Teddies,' who had to say goodbye. The story addressed belonging, adversity, resilience, transition, grief, loss, moving on, and the unknowns. The story was shared with the carers, and the metaphor was explained. In addition, a book of photos of the children, foster carers, connected/kinship carers, adopters, and the birth parents was prepared to help assist conversation about the upcoming change in a more concrete manner to sit alongside the story. Finally, the social worker had prepared a brochure that displayed a photographic step-by-step guide through the building to the room where the contact would be, where the toilets were, who would help if help was needed, and who would be there. There was a clear individual child-friendly itemised plan of the structure of the contact, toys and games that would be played and the snacks and refreshments that would be available.

The social worker then had individual sessions with the siblings in the presence of the carers and utilised both the book and the brochure. The role of the adults was to be the children's support, to meet their emotional needs and to observe the children's reactions. That night, after the children went to bed, the social worker held a therapeutic parenting support session to process what the parents and social worker had seen, to share feedback on the children's reactions and how they had settled that night. The adults were then to read the book and brochure regularly with the children until the contact session.

The final contact was attended by all the carers and the twins' adopters. It was run by the children's social worker, who was supported by a colleague, a familiar person to the children. During periods of free play, Georgina and Jessica mostly played together and sometimes included their younger siblings. Harmony and Melody mostly played together and occasionally sought out their older siblings. The contact was calm, but with waves of sadness from Georgina, Jessica, and their aunt. The tears and sadness were acknowledged, and the group was well contained.

Georgina and Jessica identified as sisters. They had been supported in their recovery, boosting the positives in their relationship. They were sad to say goodbye to Melody and Harmony, but they felt more secure in the knowledge they would be going to the right placement for them. The adopters supported a letterbox scheme that enabled annual letters and photos between the children. This was successful and kept the door open for the possibility of future relationships in their adulthood.

Understanding and managing behavioural consequences can be a challenge. The fundamental concept in a trauma model is that the behaviour is not the problem but the answer to the problem. Therefore, trying to stop or change a behaviour without understanding that this is the answer and not the problem will be singularly unsuccessful. If it appears to be successful, it will need to be assessed to check it has not been replaced with another more acceptable answer. Only resolving the problem will result in the behaviour successfully changing.

Sibling contact is complex and demanding. It requires the same, if not greater, level of planning as parent-child contact. Practitioners must be alert to trauma bonds, distorted beliefs and conflicted emotions that shape dynamics. When contact is poorly planned or sentiment-driven, it risks retraumatising children and destabilising placements. When carefully assessed and supported, sibling contact can preserve, rebuild and sustain relationships of lifelong significance. Applied practice requires holding paradoxes, balancing caution with hope, and supporting children, carers and professionals in the messy realities of sibling life.

Part II

When Siblings Can Stay Together

Chapter 5

Together by Design
Conditions for Stability and Success

Assessments will conclude whether sets of siblings should stay together or be separated, and on occasion, these decisions will be 'pro et contra,' or hold as many advantages as disadvantages. Decision-making can become split, leading to delay, intra-team or inter-agency disputes, or conclusions are reached for children to remain together, be that the best, least-worst, or are ncontestable as a result of court instruction outcomes.

Sometimes siblings should stay together simply because it is the right decision. There are no normative family environments that state this is what a family looks like. There are preconceptions, value biases, and social norms or stereotypes which can lead unhelpfully to making a judgement about what is or is not acceptable.

Because It's the Right Decision

Families disrupt, break apart, change, and morph all the time as a result of separation, divorce, death, new relationships, new step-siblings or half-siblings or siblings living with relatives such as grandparents with often and rightfully no social intervention. Families who can work out their separations amicably, mutually and with the children in mind. The outcomes range from successful, through anxiety-provoking, to stressful and sometimes traumatic.

Within this experience, the sibling relationships are often rich in indicators that suggest resilience, positivity, security, empathy, internal locus of control, and signs of integration in all of the children. This finding, however, does not mean, even with the best assessment outcome possible, that the children will not need therapeutic reparative interventions. It is known that some children impacted by high stress or low-level trauma will still require ameliorating support to reach their true potential and safeguard their future. The more concerns identified, the greater the need to have the appropriate provisions provided at the earliest opportunity.

Here the focus is not on those families but on those children who are known to have been through state intervention, and as such will have experienced losses, high levels of stress or trauma.

Daisy, aged four, and Reece, aged three, were full siblings. They were removed on the grounds of neglect by omission (as opposed to commission). This was due

DOI: 10.4324/9781003724605-7

in part to their parents' limitations, which bordered on learning disabilities which despite ongoing support, over time, did not improve their parenting capacity.

The parents' vulnerability raised concerns regarding the potential for exploitation by unscrupulous individuals within the community. While services were actively managing this risk, such incidents were becoming increasingly frequent. Subsequently, the children were removed and placed in a stable foster placement aged three and two respectively before being placed into their adoptive placement a year later.

Daisy externalised, and Reece internalised (for the most part). Daisy was seen to present in two starkly different presentations; both loving and confrontational, which could be seen as both ordinarily developing behaviour for her chronological age, and/or fragmented. The symptoms or markers that indicated this was more concerning lay in her hyper-vigilance and her need to control. She was described as clingy, but also guarded and controlling, particularly in relation to the female carer. She would struggle to regulate and had, on a few occasions, failed to self-regulate or be co-regulated that led her to leave her Window of Tolerance (WOT) and become aggressive and occasionally striking out at her female foster carer. This behaviour suggested an ambivalent attachment style. Despite this, the foster carers, with an emotionally literate and progressive outlook and manner, were able to support each other in managing Daisy's distress.

However, in school she presented as an internalised child with low self-esteem but conversely also happy and carefree. She achieved academically and enjoyed all subjects.

Analysis

Positives

The foster carers were very experienced in terms of:

- The number of years of proactive caring: They had not just undertaken their role but both foster carers attended training regularly, actively utilised consultation within their own agency and with the commissioning agency when available. They undertook clinical supervision and had personal therapy when they felt internal issues were clouding their judgement or beginning to overwhelm them.
- They worked in partnership with birth families and managed contact issues. Whilst being able to maintain a focus on the children they provided a service for and to be a protective buffer where needed. Equally, they worked well within a multiagency network, passing on relevant information to social workers, psychologists, psychiatrists, paediatricians et al. and being open to being contacted. They kept accurate, concise, accessible records and ensured that the children met all their medical, emotional, educational, and social needs.

- They had a working grasp of attachment, child development, psychopathology, developmental and complex trauma, and additional needs.
- They had worked successfully with male and female children of a variety of ages, heritage, faith, ability/disability, and sexual identity.
- They had cared for siblings, had a good understanding of individual needs, the complexity of the sibling interface and how siblings required a complex level of understanding. They were also able to contribute to discussions and carry out plans for contact with separated siblings.
- These were capable and supported foster carers.

Negatives

There had been no concerns throughout the carers' service.

Local Authority Interventions

The children had come to the attention of the Local Authority just after Daisy's birth when both the midwife and health visitor voiced similar concerns. The parents were struggling to meet her needs as a result of their own limitations. The authority responded with family support which stabilised the family. They needed ongoing support and managed to meet (just) good enough parenting.

Their ability to cope, however, deteriorated with the birth of Reece. The demands of having two children, as most parents will recognise, are not simply doubling what you already had but increase the demands beyond that of one and now juggling two children, two developmental levels, managing meeting two sets of needs, giving love, nurture, reassurance, support, as well as basic needs within a sibling setting. The sibling relationship creates a new set of demands in addition to the childcare of a solitary child. The couple floundered. One thing the family had was a consistent social worker, a rarity in the current climate of social work becoming a career rather than a vocation, where reliance on agency staff erodes consistency and belonging. This social worker remained a knowledgeable resource.

Services changed from being scaffolded to resourced, to supported, to 'propped up,' and finally carried as their ability to cope declined. Interestingly, part of the problem became the number of agencies involved trying to prevent the family from failing. More is not necessarily helpful when families have to negotiate increasing numbers of relationships and a greater chance of misinformation, conflicting, or incorrect information. The family were supported through the assessment and court proceedings that eventually led to the children's removal into care.

Contact

Contact remained weekly following the children's placement into foster care. This is not an uncommon arrangement but is one that maintains stress and uncertainty. The children's care plan was to move into adoption where contact would cease, but contact is often maintained in case there is a delay in family finding and the adoption process concluding. This is a paradox. The decision is not to return home, but the purpose of contact is to maintain relationships in the event that they will. This brings to the fore, as discussed in previous chapters on contact, the differences between fostering and adoption settings. In fostering, contact is often an ongoing theme that can maintain relationships despite being apart. The benefits are that the future remains open to change and reunification by keeping relationships, identity, and belonging alive. However, it can also provide opportunities for families to bring their chaos into the child's new family, maintain control, and be potentially unhelpful to the child's future chances. Within the adoption context, contact is often ended before the child is placed. This can make the child feel safer with a greater chance of developing a secure attachment as a positive result whilst losing a sense of identity at the other. There is a danger that individual views on contact can cause professionals to look for information that confirms their often-subconscious confirmation bias in setting outcomes based on their beliefs or judgements rather than being open to the verifiable impact on the children. It is a stark fact that more children in foster care continue to have contact when they shouldn't and children in adoption don't have contact when maybe they could. Whilst the latter is changing, it is also less reliably supported.

The children required decreasing ammounts of contact tot enable them to manage without contact later. An abrupt end, after all, is also traumatic, even in situations where contact is beyond unhelpful, traumatic and dangerous.

Assessment and Matching

The children's needs were assessed by the same social worker in conjunction with a social worker from their adoption team to try to strike the balance between a child-centred view of the children and the sibling relationship as well as the impact level on how adults would manage meeting these children's needs.

The adopters that became the match were selected, assessed and trained by a 3rd sector agency that had a history of positive, proactive, and robust assessments in both family finding and matching. The skills of the agency mirrored the skills required in all childcare work that included:

- Robust policies, procedures and protocols in both these areas.
- Up to date and ongoing commitment to staff training in new, research and evidence-based practices.
- They had good staff retention that provided a consistency of support to the people who used their service.
- They had a proven track record in outcomes. Multiagency working and collaboration, as well as working in partnership with others.

- They were neither child focused nor adult focused and therefore had the capacity to consider the information in front of them and argue the pros and cons of assessment and matching outcomes.
- They had integrated adoption and child support and where the needs exceeded their expertise, they were able to utilise services around them to bridge any gaps in their provision.

The Children

Daisy

Resilience

- She had experienced the consistency of parents despite their inconsistency.
- Consistency of social worker.
- Consistency of nursery and education support.
- Consistency of placement.
- Consistency of her brother's presence.
- Was building her capacity to voice her concerns. She wanted to be called Daisy rather than Daisy-May, a name only her parents call her.
- She had good relationships with her grandparents, but their ailing health was preventing them from supporting their grandchildren.
- Daisy had been supported to understand her transitions with a journey book. This is not the same as a Life Story Book; rather, it is a piece of work that helps children to understand, process, and integrate a specific component of their life within the constraints of their development, chronological age, and trauma experience.
- She had a working understanding of the things that went wrong in her parent's care and a capacity to communicate that.
- She has been building a bond with her social worker and foster carers.
- She enjoyed and excelled at school. Her ability to pay attention, listen, hear, process, analyse, create a narrative, store to memory and retrieve information suggested that academically she was proficient.

Adversity

- Had experienced developmental trauma as a result of neglect by omission. Daisy was loved by parents who did not have the capacity to meet her needs.
- She had an insecure ambivalent attachment.
- She demonstrated some fragmented behaviour (presented somewhat differently at home and in school).
- She cannot stay in her current placement because the plan was for permanence within an adoption framework.
- She struggled with transitions.
- She had issues around safety and trust.

- Despite building a bond with her carers, this did not rectify her insecure attachment.
- Her academic prowess was positive resilience or a negative resource? What wasn't known was how much of her achievement at school was a result of her avoidance of relationships.
- She had not yet received therapeutic services to help ameliorate the impact of her experiences.

Reece

Resilience

- Being a year younger, he experienced less time with his parent's neglect, but unlike his sister, did not experience his parents 'just managing' parenting his sister experienced.
- Is demonstrative with loving actions to both his carers and his sister.
- Is described as having a calm and/or laid-back disposition at the same time as reacting negatively to limits, particularly to a 'no' and challenging his sister when she encroaches on or tries to control his play.
- Like his sister Reece was seen as bright. An additional attribute was his sense of humour and comical turn of communication.
- He utilised his body in play: climbing, jumping, swinging, running, spinning, being in water be it pools, rivers, or rain.
- He wass in good health with no underlying conditions found.

Adversity

- He had not experienced 'good enough parenting' by his parents.
- Was thought to copy his sister's behaviour.
- Is he compliant?
- Was described as having a calm and/or laid-back disposition at the same time as reacting negatively to limits, particularly to a 'no' and challenging his sister when she encroaches on or tries to control his play.
- Information relating to Reece described Daisy and Reece 'biting, hitting and punching each other,' which did not appear in his sister's reports, despite Daisy being seen as the more aggressive of the two children.

The Sibling Relationship

Resilience

- They had lived together from Reece's conception.
- The first year of Daisy's life, whilst continuously on the edge of neglect, largely had her needs met with parental support.

- The family were being held by services. This helped Daisy cope and have some preparation for her brother's arrival.
- The children both had a level of academic prowess enabling them to relate to and achieve together.
- There was enough difference between the children's presentations. They could both shine in their own right.

Adversity

- Daisy had to cope with the conception and birth of her brother with no processing.
- Her brother's arrival coincided with the deterioration of her care by her parents and her parents' decline.
- There were conflicted feelings about the children's behaviour towards each other that ranged from positive at one end of the continuum to aggressive and confrontational at the other. The children's relationship very much mirrored the descriptions of both children, suggesting that they were at the very least reacting towards each other from a template of an insecure ambivalent response.
- Daisy had some level of pseudo-parentified responses to her brother. A presentation that prevented her from having a responsibility-free childhood. This impacted on her brother's desire for autonomy and his need to work his own issues out.

The Adopters

Resilience

- The couple were stable in their relationship.
- They had come to terms with their childlessness and had professional therapeutic support when thinking about their future options.
- They had supportive family networks on both sides.
- They had negotiated childhood and early years with some stress, occasionally high stress but no significant traumatic experiences.
- They had family and friendship groups both with and without children.
- They experienced good health.
- They responded well to the assessment process. They were open, gave clear examples, were reflective and willing to learn. They were capable of participation, sharing what they knew and what they didn't know.
- They demonstrated that they were a resilient and resourceful couple who were open to support and advice.

Adversity

- They both had known family members who had experienced trauma and had some insight into the impact on the individuals, their presentation and recovery, giving them some practical and experienced level of trauma.
- They had both experienced and survived loss and grief – but the losses were nonetheless losses.
- They had never parented.
- They had never parented a developmentally challenged child, let alone two.
- They couldn't possibly know the implications of parenting a child who has experienced developmental trauma.

The Match

Resilience

- The adopters met the children at an open day and were then able to see them in the context of a reasonable phrenetic environment and experience how they coped or were challenged by this situation. It gave them a chance to see the children's personalities, relationships with each other and their carers, and their strategies to cope with the environment.
- It gave the agency an opportunity to ascertain the adopter's levels of insight, reflectiveness, communication style, warmth, compassion, and empathy. This led to discussions with the agency about the children's current needs, backgrounds, life experiences, attachment implications, therapeutic parenting implications, and the outcome of any therapeutic interventions.
- They seemed to want to understand Daisy's boisterous and stubborn behaviour and their high energy levels.
- The couple were financially stable, and the adoptive mother was able to take a year's adoption leave.
- Contact would cease.
- Adopter support was planned by both the child's social worker (for continuity) and the third sector agency social worker.
- Therapeutic support was identified, secured, and planned for both the children.
- The children's experiences had not led or seemed not to have led to a trauma bond. The children appeared to have enough positives in their relationship to build on their recovery from their adversities.

Adversity

- Both children had experienced ACEs as a result of neglect and numerous state interventions. They lived the same experience, so the children will remind each other of their lived experience.
- The children would both be changing placement from a familiar stable foster placement to an unknown, new adoptive placement.

- Whilst the adoptive father was able to take some adoption leave, it was restricted to three months.
- Daisy was going to have to change schools.
- Reece was going to have to change schools.
- The carers would be moving from being childless to having two children in their care: two children with a history. This would be the children's third parenting experience. They were children with trauma; they were children with beliefs about caregivers from a 'loving-neglect' experience and what that meant to them.
- The children would bring with them strategies to cope with parenting, with sibling relationships, which may be the same behaviours, different, or a mixture.
- The children would experience further grief and loss.
- Contact would cease.

Outcome

The placement worked because the foundations were in place. All the assessments coordinated enough so that the unknowns, negative or conflicting information could be addressed because they were identified prior to the final decision. The balance was between the harm the children had experienced and their genetic resilience (where the fulcrum lies under the balance between resilience facts vs adversity) was good enough. In addition, there were plans in place to address the deficits and build on the strengths, the likelihood of a successful placement outcome was greater.

The success of placements is in the balance of the levels of ACEs times the number of placements and carers capabilities times the ability to challenge information that doesn't make sense and look for reparative and supportive services to be ready prior to placement.

Because They Are Already Placed, to Move Them Would Be Equally Detrimental

Sometimes a case is allocated to a worker where the decisions have already been made. This is often the case in therapeutic provision but may equally be a social worker inheriting cases reallocated following a change in social worker.

Hunter, Faith and Charity should not have been placed together. They had been removed on the grounds of neglect, and the children's levels and range of ACEs were not disclosed by the children until after they were placed with Hope and Butler.

Adversity

- The children's experiences had been hidden by their birth family, and any attempts in the court-mandated assessments by the social workers, psychologists, children's guardians, psychiatrists, and others did not enable the parents to share the extent of their harm or enable the children to disclose their experiences. This is not unusual.

- The children only had one foster placement. The carers were boundaried and effective in managing the children on a rather austere level but lacked emotional warmth and reciprocity. Their rather pious outlook also restricted them from seeing the children's sexualised behaviours.
- The foster carers had been in their role for decades. The organisation they worked for was not progressive and did not challenge outdated practices. The view was that if people had been doing the job for years, then they were competent and should be left to 'get on with it.' There was little training, consultation, supervision, or support either offered, requested, or taken up.
- The children's presentation led to services failing to see them as having separate or unique needs, which led to a lack of understanding of their individuality as well as what issues, demands, beliefs, or expectations each child brought to the sibling relationship. This also impacted on professionals' ability to have a clear view of their relationships.
- The children's experiences led to complex developmental trauma, and the relationship was without doubt a trauma bond.
- Hope, the adoptive mother they were placed with, had, it turned out, experienced similar complex developmental trauma the children she adopted had experienced. Hope's experiences led to behaviours that kept her in a cycle of harm and adversity well into her adulthood. This information was not disclosed, remembered and/or shared until long after the children had been placed. Butler, the adoptive father, could not cope with watching Hope struggle and started to avoid coming home blaming work committments. The children not only should not have been placed together but should not have been placed either individually or together with Hope.
- Because Hope would prioritise her children's needs, this sometimes impacted on her health. Hope developed a chronic condition that had periodic acute phases. This health condition, may have resulted from her stressful result of her stressful life experiences and subsequent lifestyle, caused her body high physiological and biological stress, and or the stess of caring for 3 highly traumatised children. It was a condition exacerbated by any stress.
- Hunter had become pseudo-parentified and believed that it was his job to care for Faith and Charity.
- The children were sexualised and this sexualisation led to sexual reactivity that continued into placement.
- Hunter internalised until his overwhelm became unbearable and he would externalise. He had an external locus of control, was incongruent, avoidant, and dissociative. His attachment was insecure ambivalent and insecure avoidant that led to disorganisation. He managed his emotions through control, appearing to be obsessive-compulsive disorder (OCD) and autistic in his presentation.
- He demonstrated scatological behaviours, both urinating and smearing. He left faecal matter around the house. At school, when he managed to attend he hid under tables, in cupboards, behind curtains to be out of site wherever he could manage to be.

- Faith, in a similar fashion to her brother, internalised until she was asked to do something that would result in extreme externalising reactions that put her at high risk of further sexual harm and sexual exploitation. Faith could not cope with the simplest tasks and found self-care overwhelming. She would not let her adoptive parents care for her. At school she was confrontational and noncompliant.
- Charity was reactive going to school, and if she made it into school, her behaviour was missed by teachers becausee she looked engaged, smiled, and nodded but she was absent internally.
- Charity smiled and nodded at all the right times and was immaculate in her presentation. She was compliant and polite. She used, 'I don't know, what, what do you mean?' as stock responses that resulted in adults feeling bemused, befuddled, at a loss and eventually giving up. None of the adults in her life had been able to see, paradoxically, she was trying not to be seen.
- The children's single greatest trigger was each other.
- Hope's single greatest trigger was her children's sexual reactivity. Butler's greatest trigger was his wife being triggered.
- The parents' emotional drift from each other was in danger of destabilising their relationship.

Resilience

- The placement success was dependent on the fact that Hope was such a voracious and ardent supporter of her children that her own needs would become secondary. This is a negative positive.
- Hope's life revolved around supporting the children to ensure they had a better start into adulthood than they had had in childhood and that they had a better childhood than she had. This was a negative positive.
- The services that supported the family created a solid TAC.
- The belief in the children and their adoptive parents was based on evidenced change and progress despite the risks and stress within the family.

Outcome

If the children had been moved none would have managed a family either together or individually, and the outcomes in residential care would have been bleak. This was a high-risk family where services had to accept that progress was going to be slow and was dependent on continuity across all involved services. The therapy moved from individual sessions to attachment-based child-parent, to sibling, to family-based therapy. Hope was provided with personal therapy and therapeutic parenting support that started at two hours a week and gradually reduced to fortnightly towards the end of the intervention. Hope and Butler were then able to start couple's counselling. This helped them see the different stresses on their lives and enabled them to disentangle the children's issues from the issues in their relationship. The cos of the intervention, whilst expensive, pale into insignificance when compared to the cost of residential facilities and the cost to society from the outcomes in adulthood had their ACEs not been ameliorated.

When Families Are on the Cusp of the Balance of 'Good Enough' When 'More Than Good Enough' Is Needed

Inevitably there will be times when children have been placed in a family who are seen to be good enough. Tanya's family is one such example. In many respects, this situation mirrored that of Hope's situation, but with profound differences. These differences included:

- Sometimes it is easier to have two parents than have a single parent. This situation can allow the opportunity for respite for each of the parents. However, it can be harder if the parents are not absolutely consistent this can result in replicating the chaos the children experienced in their birth family.
- Both Tanya and Hope had withheld information about themselves either by omission, commission, or dissociative amnesia during their assessments. Both were eventually able to say that they had withheld information. The difference was that where Hope had been able to share her experiences, process and analyse the experiences and eventually move on, Tanya remained stuck, unwilling, or unable to share the experiences she alluded to, leaving her prone to being triggered by her children.
- Like Hope's children, Tanya's children should not have been placed together. The placement of another sibling with whom they had no previous contact was disastrous and demonstrated that relationships and placements based on birth line are not enough.
- The parents' relationship was stressed; they had no opportunity for personal space and therefore no opportunity to recover.
- Tanya was ambivalent about support.
- They made life-changing unilateral decisions without considering the potential consequences.

The children required more than good enough parenting in individual placements as a result of their experiences.

Because the Children Say They Want Something, Such As to Stay Together

Listening to children is like learning a language; it's an art form and one that should leave the listener full of questions rather than answers. There appears to be a rigid view when it comes to policies, procedures, research, and guidance. The Children Act is often misquoted in this and not just in the placement of children.

- Hunter felt safest when he was with his sisters and wanted to be near her. Faith complained she had no space from him. Charity did not wish to be apart from Hunter, but she needed space to pursue her own interests and be on her own. Hunter was terrified of who he may be without his beleived purpose to belooking after his sisters.
- Hunter repeatedly demanded to be sent back to the birth mother who neglected, physically and sexually abused him. It is less likely a child who is aged seven or aged ten will be reunified with parents who have made no demonstrable change, but it is a regular practice for older children. When children start to vote with their feet or are older in age, even though it is known that nothing has changed within the family. When this happens the child is likely to be hurt or start hurting others.
- Don was aged seven when he was first referred to therapeutic services. There had been a history of sexual behaviours impacting on both children and adults around him. This started when he was just three years old. He needed a service but he wasn't safe. He he was still living at home with a mother who was clearly unable to prevent the behaviours he presented or help services understand their source. He was referred again when he was ten and the behaviours were increasing, but this time the referring agency agreed to fund an assessment. The assessment undertaken found he was both at risk and a risk and that he required reparative services as soon as possible. However, while Don was at home he wasn't safe and therefore therapeutic services were contraindicated. When he was aged fourteen, he raped a child which resulted in him being placed in a specialist unit. He engaged well and progressed, but he wanted to continue to see his mother, the person who gave him mixed messages, couldn't protect him and couldn't contain him. He wanted contact so contact was agreed, and that contact destabilised the placement. Aged sixteen, he started to abscond and where he went was to his mother's house. He desperately wanted to be at home with his mother because this was familiar and familiar felt safe, not because it was safe. Eventually, he was simply allowed to stay at home with his two sisters, where his sexualised behaviour once again escalated.
- Joe was referred to therapy at the age of 14 as a result of serious sex offences. His older brother, who had also previously been convicted of sex offences, had undertaken therapy. Joe undertook therapy for his harmful sexual behaviour (HSB) within the framework of a two-therapist format, an accepted protocol of 'best practice' in situations such as this. He complained to his social worker that he felt restricted by having two therapists and worked better with one therapist: a format he had been used to previously before that therapy had been stopped. The previous therapist stated there had been no therapeutic movement because Joe was exceptionally controlling, and it was hard to track the sessions due to the smoke screen Joe created. During the last sessions with the two therapists, he smiled and stated that it didn't actually matter how many therapists were in the room he achieved his goal. The notion that children and young people can be charming and/or manipulative is hard to accept, but

- these behaviours protect the self from a different belief and/or prevent others from being implicated, or for fear of reprisal should information be shared. Joe was also implicitly stating that part of him wanted the intervention because he turned up every week.
- Satya lived in a foster placement. Her older two brothers with whom she was previously placed stated that they wanted to return home to their father. This was heard and responded to. Whether this was an appropriate outcome for the boys isn't known, but for Satya, it planted a seed that you can be heard and what you say you want will happen. Aged 17, with a chronic eating disorder, significant self-harm, and a compromised pro-social background, she announced that she wanted to stop therapy and move into semi-supported lodgings. What she was actually saying was: what will happen when I'm 18? Are you strong enough to contain me? Do you know what I need? Are you even aware of what I'm struggling with?

Professionals absolutely must listen to children. However, listening to children does not necessarily equate to acting on what they ask or say. There is a need to learn about what their wishes actually mean, what fears they are based on, their expectations and their sense of familiarity. It is unfortunately way too common an outcome that services do the opposite of what children need by acting on what children say they want. This becomes increasingly complicated when siblings say they want different things.

Because There Are No Other Placements

It is recognised that sometimes there is no suitable placement available for a child, or a child and their siblings. The larger the sibling group, the greater the chance that this will be true. However, this doesn't just relate to sibling groups but also to individual children. Sometimes 'hard to place' children are placed with those recruited foster carers or adopters who had just made the level of good enough. As stated previously, good enough is adequate for the majority of birth children. However, the children placed during social intervention often have had such a distorted childhood with multiple ACEs and a dearth of their needs met. Often, all the things that children should have experienced, they did not receive Maslow (1954) and experienced all the adversity and harm they should not have had (see ACEs). This experience of unmet needs, what was missing, plus multiple harm, what was done, then requires not just better than good enough parenting, but parenting plus, plus, plus.

For adopters the relief of becoming a parent can't be minimised. The stress of wondering whether it will ever happen can compromise prospective parents' ability to hear about how children's experiences, what was done as well as what was missing impacts on their behaviourswhen placed. Perhaps they may hear it but may struggle to process and analyse the implications.When these families have a child, and later are are willing to accept another birth child, like Tanya or another unrelated child such as Emma being placed with Jacob, the combination of experiences becomes almost impossibly complicated.

The pressure on practitioners to find a placement can often result in a placement at any cost. This, of course, is replicated in therapy; for example, a child who has experienced a lifetime of ACEs at 16 is referred for therapy, in the expectation they will overcome all of their trauma before they turn 18. Expectations need to be based on the evidence of information available and not just the information sent. A child not being placed with a sibling may sometimes be the better option. Therapy starting when the network is not committed, similarly so.

Foster Carer Is Adamant the Siblings Should Remain Together, Despite the Negative Assessment

Sometimes a professional or carer's view may take precedence over other conflicting views. Clem aged six, Chloe aged five, and Ciaran aged three were in their second year together in a foster placement. This followed removal from their parents as a result of neglect, physical and sexual abuse, domestic violence, and emotional harm. The specialist assessment recommended that Ciaran be placed in a solo adoptive placement, Clem in a solo long-term foster placement with two carers, and that Chloe be placed in a solo adoptive placement. The recommendations were based on the children's levels of need and presentation towards each other and their carers. Despite the fact that many of the concerns had been endorsed by a number of professionals, the emotional impact of separating siblings was in itself a hurdle. The loudest voice overpowered sound analysis. The foster carers were desperate for the youngest two to remain together despite their own experience. This did not provide a positive outcome.

Avoid a Contested Hearing Also Known As, 'Kicking the Can Down the Road'

Busy departments may be influenced by parents who may agree to a care order in respect of their children on the proviso that the children are placed together, or with certain carers, or with certain contact conditions or a range of other such wishes. While this can be seen as a tempting alternative to a long-drawn-out court hearing it often leads to children being placed in challenging situations or placements that cannot stand the test of time.

Someone Else in the Extended Family Can Take a Sibling. This is seen as better whilst They May Not Be Living Together it is seen as the Least-orst Option

Finally, there are also situations where there is a temptation to place the children, or part of the sibling group, in placements because a family member or loosely related individual has the physical capacity to provide them with a home. The potential issues are multifarious but include.

- Lacking emotional or geographical distance from the birth family or may be more entwined with the family than is evidenced.
- The family may be triggered by information the children disclose about their experiences with their birth parents.
- They may find it hard to maintain distance or contact over time.
- That the children believe that as they are family the same experiences will recur and therefore never feel entirely safe.
- That the children may trigger any birth children in the placement, or target them, which may then destabilise the placement.

Part III

Identity, Healing, and Therapeutic Support

Chapter 6

Hurt-full and Healing Pages

Therapeutic Life Story Work with Traumatised Children

A Brief History

Therapeutic Life Story Work became popular in the 1960s but didn't gain traction in texts until the early 1980s when social workers had to negotiate the labyrinth and minefield of undertaking this task with very little supporting literature. This period of time was heavily influenced by BAAF's training (1984) and practitioners such as, Violet Oaklander (1978). She used many creative exercises to help see the child's life experience from their perspective by drawing out what they knew, did not know, were confused about, left out, made up, or dissociated from. In addition, John Bowlby, Ken Redgrave (1987), Pat Owen and Pat Curtis (n.d.), Mary Walsh and Madge Bray (1997) were other influencers in the field. During the late 1990s, it began to appear in governmental research (DoH, 1999: 22). This was one of the tasks social work students were often required to undertake as part of their competencies. This meant that the least qualified, least experienced people with the least training or supporting literature were tasked with an intervention that could have far-reaching implications for the child or young person. A task that needed to be undertaken with the care, compassion, and robust support (Rose and Philpot, 2005). Often the information provided can fill gaps, challenge and/or confirm previously held beliefs, but it can also discombobulate a stressed child and traumatise further a child with a history of ACEs.

Consider Martin in Volume 1. At what point would he need clarification about his sister, her death, and his mother's part in her murder? Is this a role for therapy, life story, direct work, or something else? If he was to be told, who would undertake the task, what planning would be needed, where would it be undertaken, who would be there, who would transport him and/or others, what tools would be used and how would he and his carer be supported to manage the information, pre, during, and post sessions?

The 1980s had some helpful benefits. Social work teams, already suffering the effects of governmental cuts, were largely more balanced. Agency staff were rare, teams were more stable, and those teams were more likely to be made up of knowledgeable practitioners, who had been in practice for years, mixed with new staff and students who brought fresh ideas and challenged the status quo: a tenet of

DOI: 10.4324/9781003724605-9

model coherency. This dynamic of stable, experienced people with new staff enabled the team to feel held (McMahon, 1992), creating a balance of continuity and innovation whilst containing anxiety and stress. Then in turn, they were more able to contain the children. Further, the level of supervision was higher and there were more colleagues available to draw upon for advice. Therapeutic teams were rare. Whilst some Local Authorities had them, most were either within CAMHS or those third sector providers.

The Implications of ACEs and Trauma on the Child

Training to do this task is of course important. It brings together a wealth of information accumulated over those decades but also needs to actively draw on the impact of trauma ACEs and how both will impact whether or not the time is right for this intervention and if yes, how the intervention should be undertaken.

During the Waterhouse investigation (2000) into North Wales children's homes, a retrospective investigation that led to the need to interview those children, now adults, who were in the care system in North Wales. Many of those affected were struggling as adults. Those affected were overrepresented as missing, or found in cemeteries resulting from a foreshortened future due to health issues, overdose, alcohol misuse, or overwhelm leading to death by suicide. They were also found in mental health institutions, openly homeless on the streets or the hidden homeless, sofa surfing or in the prison system. Whether they were in these situations, or those getting by, many struggled to remember. Often, they could not accurately remember faces and names, who was caring, who was ambivalent, who knew what was going on, and who was dangerous. It is now known that trauma, discussed throughout this book, can compromise beliefs, understanding, identity, health, behaviour, responses to triggers, memory, and recall. Redgrave's view that, 'Most of the children who are needing family placements or have been rehabilitated to their own families, or who have been adopted, are not in need of "treatment,"' (1987) predated this knowledge.

Supporting the Child to Understand the Process

There is greater awareness of children masking, internalising, avoiding, presenting as chameleonesque, being compliant or dissociating. These presentations can result in missing the child's needs. Because the Waterhouse inquiry highlighted memory gaps in those children, the service at Tiptoes provides a personalised brochure that is given to the child prior to therapy. It contains an image of the building, contact details, and the work that will be undertaken with the child. It has an image of the therapist/associate, and then a photographic walk-through of the building, the room/s that will be used and the routine that can be expected. This is kept by the child, family, and/or social worker to aid future recall should it be required. It is a powerful gesture and symbol of safety because it suggests the process starts with openness and transparency.

The lived trauma experiences of every child or sibling being provided a service will have resulted in some complications with their history and identity (Fahlberg, 1994) which will therefore need some level of Therapeutic Life Story work to resolve. The only likely exception to this would be if it was a planned agreed removal from parental care at birth, and the mother had experienced a trauma-free pregnancy where she was also free from any difficulties that caused ongoing stress or trauma, and there has been only one placement with no parental contact. It would be safe to say that even if assuming, in the very unlikely event, that this trauma-free child does not experience any trauma events as they grow up, they will still need to know about their birth family, their heritage, the reasons for their removal or being autonomously relinquished, and will need, no doubt want to know, about their family of origin and their own Life Story to developmentally determine, construct, and then reconstruct their identity. (Levy and Orlans, 1998 in Rose and Philpot, 2005: 25). Even this child, with access to all the necessary information needed who has developed the ability to self-regulate their feelings and arousal, will find this a challenge. The child perhaps may at times find doing this work distressing, interesting, confusing, or reassuring, but hopefully, by undertaking it, confirm their identity, history, and deepen their sense of belonging. Any practitioner undertaking Life Story Work with any child will require significant support to not just hold the child emotionally but also hold their somatic or physiological and cognitive responses.

Gaining Consent

Consent has been discussed throughout this text, and the same issues apply here. There is a need to consider whose responsibility it is to consent to this work. Competence to understand the implications of being in receipt of information or receiving information and how this will impact on all involved, especially any siblings not yet ready to undertake this task.

The Chosen Practitioner and Support

There is no doubt a child with a trauma history will need a practitioner who is trained or very experienced in doing this type of intervention and who also has access to their own supervision and support (Wrench and Naylor, 2013). The pitfalls of an ill-equipped practitioner occur when, 'The lack of therapeutic training and personal therapy puts them and the child at risk of feelings emerging within the practitioner or child that are then distorted (transference and countertransference or projection issues) that may lead the work into tricky territory.' (Aldgate and Simmonds, 1988). The TAC, i.e. where no TAC all other professionals involved in the child's life, must also be aware the work is being done and can provide any support which might be needed. This need for an awareness of the pitfalls, the impact on the child, the skills and sensitivity of the practitioner has long since been known, 'It is unfortunately all too easy to press destructive and unwanted information onto a vulnerable child who is just developing a personal identity' (Zeitlin,

1983). A working knowledge would include a knowledge of the child's trigger responses (internalising or externalising), their ability to stay present (Noticing Present Moment Experience or Dissociation), ability to self-regulate or be socially regulated and practice strategies which enable the practitioner to support the child to remain in their WOT.

Consider who is the best person to undertake the task. If it is the child's social worker, the child's history may already be knwn and already there may be a familiar relationship. This relationship may be complicated by the social worker's other roles: investigation, assessment, safeguarding, gathering of wishes and feelings, direct work, their relationship with birth parents and others, removal into care, changes of placement. These roles can cause conflicted feelings, fear, confusion, anger, distrust and may impact on the safety and efficacy of any Life Story Work. If it is a therapist, the relationship may be strong and safe but creating a document which may be seen by others could be confusing if it rails against an already agreed confidentiality cotract. The therapist may also be able to support the child to regulate strong emotions, manage dysregulation and help counter limiting beliefs. Whoever undertakes the work, either familiar and known, loosely associated by role, unknown or introduced, will have to consider pros and cons with care. It will help to create safety and trust by utilising a therapeutic model by providing a regular and dedicated weekly session, day and time (Rose and Philpot, 2005; Wrench and Naylor, 2013). A suitably experienced and knowledgeable supervisor/mentor/advisor should be identified and available for planned support as well as additional consultation, if required. The need for clinical supervision is often met with conflicted feelings by services both advocating for its need and paradoxically missing its importance, failing to prioritise it, not providing an adequate level of provision, or providing it with an inadequately qualified or experienced supervisor, or indeed denying it.

Where the sessions take place is an important factor (Rose, 2017). It can be one of the hardest factors to decide. If undertaken in a Local Authority office, it may remind the child of removal or of parental distress. Being delivered at the therapy centre may cause confusion about the difference between this work and previous or ongoing therapy. At school, with its lack of anonymity or confidentiality, may cause confusion about the boundaries of education or the lack of space to process what can be highly emotive information. It is also a place where friends may be overly curious, peers make the child feel different, and bullies target those perceived as weaker. The home environment, whether it be birth, foster, or adoptive, may feel safe because it is familiar but can mask harm. It may feel new or strange and unsafe even when it is usually safe. It raises the question: where will your parents, carers, or siblings be? and will being physically closer to them hinder the ability to process?

It would be very different to undertake Life Story Work with a child with no trauma history compared to a looked after or adopted child. It is important not to underestimate how complex and time-consuming doing it with a child with a complex history of trauma (Types 1, 2, 3, and/or 4) and multiple separations would be. This work is important, but it is also lengthy and time-consuming, which puts pressure on already under-resourced agencies and overwhelmed practitioners. Due to the threat of, rather than the support of compliance inspections, there has been a rise in this work being undertaken by untrained, inexperienced or unqualified practitioners who are speedily deployed to do it within a tight timescale to meet the needs of regulators and inspectors, rather than the child.

Perhaps this is one of the reasons so many of these books are taken apart or destroyed or not valued or feared by children. During research about the impact of making and having a Life Story Book, the following conversation with a seven-year-old about his previously completed life story book took place. He had been reassured before the conversation started that the book was not going to be seen, or its contents discussed, just some questions asked for his views on having completed it.

Researcher: 'Are you remembering I will not be asking to see your book?'
Child: His eyes widen, his back straightens, his hands clench. He is reassured, emotionally regulated, and he agrees to continue before the next question.
Res: 'Where is your book kept?'
Child: 'Will you tell my social worker where it is?'
Res: 'That sounds like you are a bit unsure about your social worker finding out where it is. Is that correct?'
Child: 'Yes, she said to keep it in my bedroom but …,' he looks away.
Res: 'Sounds to me that the book might not be in your bedroom, is that right?'
Child: 'Yes, when it was in my bedroom every time I went in there I could see it and ….' Lost for words to describe the impact on him, he shuddered and looked down. He looked around and at the door as if checking no one, perhaps his social worker, was listening.
Res: 'Well, I wonder where that book is now?'
Child: 'Susie (foster carer) said to put it in the kitchen, but every time I went in the kitchen, I could see it, so she said we would put it in the loft and get it down before your social worker visits. We can put it in your bedroom while she is here.' Smiling, he added, 'She said we would keep this a secret. You won't tell my social worker, will you?'
Res: 'I'm wondering how we could sort this out because it sounds like a lot of worries and maybe even some secrets being kept.'
Child: Nods.
Res: 'Have you any ideas what I could do to help?'
Child: 'You could take the book with you for your research.' With this suggestion, he visibly relaxes and smiles.

The question of whether to tell his social worker remained unanswered at that time, neither confirming nor denying, to avoid premature assurance or provoking unnecessary fear. The tick box on the record of his reviews has been marked, noting that Life Story Work has been completed.

A conversation then took place with the foster carer about the decision not to tell the social worker, and how this could confuse the child about when secrets were acceptable or not. What would have been more helpful would have been a conversation with him about his fears, and, by resolving these, with his social worker, either at the time or soon afterwards, he would not have carried the pressure of keeping a secret or worrying about the social worker finding out. It was unlikely to be resolved in a single session because it also required exploring how his fears were linked to his developmentally inappropriate belief that others, such as the social worker, had 'special powers,' for example being able to hear conversations through walls and doors. This magical thinking reflected the developmental arrest he experienced at about four years old, when his physical and emotional development was disrupted by significant harm. The foster carer also spoke about how difficult it was to help him to make his own mind up about anything, noting his attentiveness to what others wanted. Whilst she understood that his compliance might have been a way for him to stay safe, she found it frustrating and recognised it also increased his risk in other situations.

Life Story Methods

Life Story Work cannot have a one-size-fits-all approach. All children and young people differ so much in their needs. Much life story work has been criticised for being carried out as a routine procedure for children in care, without sufficient sensitivity to the timing, pacing, and depth of the work, (McMahon, 1992). People also often assume that what comes out of Life Story Work is a life story book. The reality is that what may look like a life story book for one person may leave another cold. Where one individual may need a physical outcome be it paper or virtual, others may not wish for or desire anything so concrete.

Life story 'books' have covered a spectrum of possibilities. These include, and still are the most popular 'Journal' type formats. Importantly, these journal type books should not be scrapbooks, which could signify a judgement that their life stories are 'waste' or 'incomplete,' although the latter may be true.

PowerPoint type formats are increasingly popular. They can hold a variety of mediums: text, pictures, scans or photos of work completed, cards, letters, videos, music and can be copied and shared. They can also have information added later more easily and can therefore become a lifetime journal. The ease of sharing can also be problematic. There is less control over who is able to view them, and the format can be associated with school, college, or work.

Less popular, but nonetheless important are those who have put their stories together in other creative ways, through artworks, including drawings, paintings, and 3D art. One young person put her life story to music. She didn't want a visual record. Others to poetry and occasionally some want no record at all; just the process of sharing with another human in a connected and empathic way was enough.

Creativity is a sign of core. Core requires a level of integration, another sign that the child is recovering from their traumatic past. Creativity is also a sign of engagement in the process, which should be celebrated, encouraged, and recognised that the child is finding some free will in a healthy and adaptive way.

None of these formats are right or wrong, and yet commissioners can be very suspicious of the process where the individual wants no record of the process; and yet the latter makes the most sense for someone going through a deeply therapeutic process, or the child who still fears a record of the past may put them in future danger. Another concern is the number of commissioners who request a copy of the work. Thought needs to be given to what can be shared, how the child or young person may feel about this, and their ability to give informed consent or deny the request.

Planning and Preparation before Doing This Work Is Needed

The practitioner needs to have the capacity and time to plan, research, timescale, and timetable all the work required. Don't underestimate the time needed, expect it will be months, so include holiday/sickness and unspecified absenteeism for the practitioner and the child. The planning is likely to include how to gather information from Local Authority files (Rose and Philpot, 2005), reports, and information from other agencies, such as schools, health, police, and probation, and then to and actually obtain it. Also to consider potential inclusion of, and interviewing or meeting birth parents, family, friends, foster carers, adopters, and/or residential units. The planning may also have to include visiting or exploration of previously lived in homes and towns, hospitals, place of birth, nurseries, churches, schools, or colleges attended, or even interest groups and places for hobbies, interests, or clubs. Many children undertaking the task want to make trips to see some of these places, either with or without their caregivers. These trips require a level of research, risk management, and thinking about how the young person could react.

The child's personal and family file must be thoroughly read (McMahon, 1992; Wrench and Naylor, 2013) and a new, comprehensive, and trauma-informed chronology of the developmental impact of the child's experiences completed i.e., the usual chronology used for any court proceedings is not enough.

Managing the Child's Regulation and Ensuring Safety

Discussion is needed with current carers, school, contact workers, birth or first parents, indeed anyone who was or is involved in this child's life about the planned piece of work for their views on whether or not this is the right time for this work to be done. Any worries or concerns they have should be acknowledged, taken seriously, acted upon and shared because others may harbour the same concerns. Time needs to be incorporated to provide the opportunity to allay these concerns or reservations and to agree to delay the intervention. These discussions should then be recorded to assure the Reviewing Officer for the next review and report this to Office for Standards in Education, Children's Services and Skills if required. This is not just about whether or not this is the right time for the child. It is to self-prepare to undertake the work and also prepare the parent/carer and/or school to support their child through this process.

Having identified any difficult or complicated aspects of the chronology a schedule is prepared for the order in which to work on them i.e., not all the difficult bits one after the other. When the time comes to work with those difficult aspects, consider the medium best utilised to manage this (Burnell and Vaughn, 2008). The life story needs to include the celebrations, the positives, the resilience, joy and fun experienced. Whilst for some these experiences are so absent that the positive may be solely that the child survived childhood. This dearth of positivity is rare; with exploration, the child may find something which kept them going. One young person's memory was the warm amber glow of a Belisha beacon at a road crossing outside his bedroom window.

The information will highlight the child's parent/s carer/s being the cause of their harm by omission or commission, information that they may have avoided facing, cannot recall or dissociated. It is not helpful to repeatedly hear parents being blamed or shamed. Doing this could impact on their view of themselves, their self-esteem, self-worth, and identity, but neither can it be ignored. Therapeutically, one message developed was born out of Sensorimotor Psychotherapy and the 'magical stranger' intervention. The way it is used is to allow distance but simultaneously maintain a connection by saying something along the lines of: 'I don't know why your mum/dad did those things to you/wasn't able to protect you, because I wasn't there. I do know that every little girl/boy/young person deserves to be loved, celebrated, nurtured and kept safe (the missing experience).' Then add/or go straight to (role dependent) 'But I am glad that your mum and dad met (or others as indicated), because if they hadn't met, they wouldn't have had you and the world would be a sadder place without you.' This creates a 'coat hook' on which the child can hang a sense of worth and celebration despite the incest/abuse, levels of violence and neglect experienced. Their creation can be celebrated without the negative connotations being avoided or becoming a source of incapacitation.

When the information gets tough, and the process is hard for the child and therapist, Bannister (2003) would always say, 'Small steps are faster.' Ogden et al. (2006, 2015) say, 'titrate,' and Tiptoes Child Therapy Services hold the maxim, 'You have to go slow to go fast.'

Life Story Work and the Sibling Paradox

Tia and Max are a classic example of how life story work can be required for one young person but their sibling is not yet ready. To withhold the process for Max, the older child, may mean he then accesses their case files and is exposed to the full reality of their experience in an unmetabolised or unsupported manner. To proceed with the process before Tia was ready would expose her to the information in an equally unmetabolised and unsupported manner because Max would be unable to resist sharing his newfound knowledge with her.

Tia was actively engaged in her therapeutic process and whilst finding it hard, was desperately trying to make sense of her experiences. Max, however, was ambivalent, engaging, disengaging, challenging, and struggling to commit to facing his reality. The least therapeutically prepared, Max, was pushing for information whilst the child who was engaged, Tia, knew she was not ready.

Max was an erudite, intellectual, and convincing young man but emotionally illiterate. His sister was engulfed by her emotions, school phobic, socially isolated and less able to verbalise her views consistently and cogently. Both children were controlling in their own ways but, Max, with a charming-manipulative character strategy had the voice that overshadowed his sister. The information he would receive would have the greatest impact on his sister. He would then have the power to share, or not share that information, when he chose.

An A to Z of Ideas for Successful Therapeutic Life Story Work

Allocated practitioner is trained and has the capacity and time allowed to plan, research and timescale all the work required. Take care not to underestimate the time needed, expect it will be months, so include holiday times for you and the child.

Benefactor (clinical supervisor/mentor/advisor) is identified and available for regular planned support and impromptu consultation when required.

Child's file is thoroughly read, and a new, comprehensive, trauma-informed chronology of the developmental impact of the child's experience is completed; i.e., the usual chronology used for any court proceedings is not enough.

Discussion with current carers, school, contact workers, first parents, and indeed anyone who is or has been involved in this child's life about the planned piece of work for their views on whether or not this is the right time for this work to be done. Any worries or concerns they have acknowledged should not be ignored but taken seriously, and time allowed to allay these fears or concerns, or agree if the work needs to be delayed pending consideration of those concerns. These discussions are recorded for the next review and recorded within agency policy.

Every difficult or complicated aspect of the chronology is identified and a schedule prepared for the order to work on them i.e. not all the difficult bits one after the other. Just because a plan is made, it should have the flexibility to change should it be contraindicated.

Find out from the child what information is already known about their history and their understanding and acceptance of this.

Gather and collate all the information from discussions to schedule the work and supervision dates.

Hold discussions with current carers, school, contact workers first, or other parents/carers, indeed anyone who is involved in this child's life about any aspects of concern and the role they each will have in supporting the child through these topics or periods of time.

Identify the presence of siblings in placement together or elsewhere who could be impacted by this work. Any problems or issues should be identified, discussed and, if not resolved, then considered with safeguards. For example, when a sibling also needs life story work, is it done together or apart, with the same practitioner or a different practitioner? Where one sibling is not ready, the danger is that the other shares the information or can be used as leverage. What are each sibling's views on content? Will the child doing the work share it with their sibling?

Just ask the child where to start: now, before coming into care, birth? This does not have to be chronological. Seven-year-old Martin could not be asked where he wanted to start. He needed to be told about the death of his 'unknown' sister before any Therapeutic Life Story Work could be completed because it was the lynchpin for his removal, non-removal, abuse, identity, and fear. Without facing this awful truth, he would not be able to be fully present, such was the power of his trauma over his cognitive ability. This makes the Life Story Work a social intervention and a therapeutic process.

Keep the document, information, and allocated time safe, this helps the child feel safe. Consider any confidentiality issues around the content, who this should and should not be shared with from your own and the child's perspective. Physical life story books have often been the first target for a child in distress. A child who has responsibility for the care of their life history; for example, accessible in their bedroom, who then becomes discombobulated and rips up their book not only has to manage the loss of their book but also the belief that it was their fault it was lost. Conversely, when it is not available, it can be readily forgotten. Mason, aged 7, the 13th of 14 children to be removed was placed in his 6th foster placement. When the placement broke down and he was being picked up, the foster carer in a fit of pique bellowed that Mason did not even have a Life Story Book and if he had, she could have gone through it to help him understand. The five books he had were in a box the foster carer had put in her attic for the duration of the placement and had never looked through.

Language that is both age-appropriate and considered carefully prior to working on difficult aspects of the history with the child. No questions are asked starting with word why (blaming), or the word did (leading). Remember too the usefulness of changing the word should, they should have looked after you better, to could, they could have looked after you if they had (what would have been needed?).

Meeting with the child and their parent/carer or support with the child to explain the purpose of the therapeutic life story work. In this meeting, issues of confidentiality and content will need to be agreed. Who this should and should not be shared with from the practitioners, adults, child's and the commissioner's perspective. Discuss where it will be kept during the intervention and when the work is completed.

Need to work out what will be said to the child about the purpose of the life story work.

Omission may be the signal that a child is not ready to undertake the work, is not safe enough, or does not feel safe enough to undertake the work. This may include the child not having any questions, showing fear, disinterest, or overcompliance with the idea of the process.

Putnam's Child Dissociative Checklist is a helpful tool to help identify the level of dissociation the child is using in different areas of their everyday experiences. Research consistently notes the level of dissociation used is consistent with the level of trauma being experienced or has been experienced. An elevated level of dissociation may be a contra-indication for doing this work. The reasons for this level should be identified and resolved if possible. If the work needs to be done now, then at a minimum, the practitioner must be trained, skilled, and experienced in working with a dissociative child.

Questions the child is likely to ask need to be considered before the work is started so that meaningful and appropriate answers are prepared beforehand.

Remember to find ways to support the child or young person to share their ideas on what will be needed and work out together how this can/will be obtained.

Share the work schedule with the child, checking whether the child has, or is likely to have, other commitments.

Timing and time. Create a rhythm to the work. Regular session times enhance a felt sense of safety and trust. Where difficult information is raised, the child needs to know when they will be seen again. The rhythm of therapy is a helpful template for this; the same day, the same time, the same place, the same person all give the message that this child is important, that they matter, that the power of this work is understood and that the practitioner is strong enough to help them contain and process the information.

Understanding the implications of the Life Story book format cannot be overstated.

Value the child's views, their questions, their work and the time put in. Respect and acknowledge their resistance and anger. These may be a sign that this is not the right time.

What equipment will you need and will obtaining this be a joint enterprise with the child to build and reinforce ownership of the book?

X is the unknown quantity, the risk factors that may occur as a result of doing the work (or not doing the work). It may induce further disclosures, trigger the child to exit their window of tolerance, create unwelcome interest from dangerous people from their past, cause a rift between siblings where one wants information about their past and another is desperate to keep the 'not knowing.' To remain vigilant to the dynamic when one sibling knows, either all the siblings know (whether they should or they should not) or one sibling feels they have a secret, which is unhealthy in its own right, may further compound other secrets they may have had to keep.

You are clear about the confidentiality of the content, who this should and should not be shared with from yours and the child's perspective, discuss with the child where it will be kept, explaining and/or exploring any reasons for any disagreement, for example a best friends may not always be the best friend. But you are also clear that when disclosures have to occur, and they do, that the parameters of confidentiality are different.

Zero in on enjoying the collation of the book together. Together where this is the right thing to do, or apart when the child wants to do it themselves or needs the practitioner to do it on their behalf.

This very challenging piece of work is part of a number of components needed to help children understand and manage the consequences of the harm done to them. Harm which caused biological, psychological, and neurological changes. The failures to protect, organisational requirements, and placement changes. Their coping survival strategies positively required but currently are too often viewed negatively now.

Specific and general life challenges are made the more challenging when there are siblings. Siblings who are often referred to as a 'group of siblings,' and then in planning how to meet their needs are offered interventions as a group, not in planned group work with the inherent predictable aspects of group work, but the same intervention, sometimes with the same therapist on the same day, without the vital, necessary individual assessment to meet their own unique individual needs. This detailed assessment of need must also include when, and sometimes if, life story work is needed.

Siblings will also require:

1. Consideration of individual or sibling intervention.
2. An explanation for each sibling of the reasons for making a book which includes their sibling but is not being done with them.
3. A plan on how a sibling gaining information that may severely impact another child will be managed.
4. Practice in how to share extremely sensitive information prior to having to undertake the task.
5. Which components of the paradoxical information, if any, can be shared.
6. To know if, when, and how the information will be shared by and between the siblings.
7. To know if not to be shared now, how this will be managed and by whom.
8. Help to decide where the books will be kept.
9. To know who will have access to them.
10. Explanations and plans put in place to deal with any competition between the siblings about their choice of shape, colour, size, and content of their book.
11. To know if or how individual practitioners with individual siblings will share with each other and how they will use the history, explanations, and repercussions.
12. How information not known or acknowledged about parentage now, with the rise of DNA testing, television programmes and social media, given a three-letter abbreviation, NPE, Not Parent Expected, will be dealt with.

Hurt-full and Healing Pages 77

Table 6.1 Trauma-Informed Chronology Once completed the knowledge, skills, temperament and experience of any future or current carer or parent can identified and resourced.

Date	Child's Age	Impact Event	Expected Behaviour	Actual Behaviour	Intervention Offered at Time	Developmental Impact	Intervention Needed Now
16 July 24	Conception	Mother raped by partner following her threat to leave.	Mother traumatised and fearful of decision to continue or terminate relationship and pregnancy.	Decided to continue the relationship.	Mother advised about impact on baby. Assessed to see if taking advice seriously or ignoring.	Unknown	Does child need to know circumstances of conception and if so how to explain it?
2 December 24	5 months into pregnancy	Mother admitted to hospital with threatened miscarriage following beating	Seek safety in Refuge, end the relationship.	Mother returned to live with partner despite advice from family and friends not to.	Mother advised about impact on baby. Assessed to see if taking advice seriously or ignoring.	Baby sharing mother's chemical arousal on brain development – amygdala enlarging, size hippocampus reducing. Baby hyper-aroused in utero.	Support and care for mother – education about impact on baby of her fear and distress. Assessing risk of couple's behaviour to parent.

(Continued)

78 A Trauma Model for Assessing Siblings

Table 6.1 (Continued)

Date	Child's Age	Impact Event	Expected Behaviour	Actual Behaviour	Intervention Offered at Time	Developmental Impact	Intervention Needed Now
2 March 24	Son born	C section needed.	Mother concerned for impact on baby first and then herself. Stays in hospital for time advised. Listens to advice about lifting etc and seeks help when needed.	Discharged herself from hospital leaving baby behind because partner had not visited.	First safeguarding meeting. Concerns of agencies involved shared with parents. Plan in place if further violence reported. Offered parenting classes and focus on baby's care needs. Health Visitor and family worker to monitor and report concerns.	Difficult to settle, hyper-aroused, fidgety, not suckling well, weight dropping.	Baby hyper-aroused, difficult to settle, attach. Interventions now informed by this early impact.
31 July 24	5 months	Mother announces 9 weeks pregnant.	Concern about managing baby and pregnancy. Planning how to do this.	Delighted to be pregnant, hoping for a girl. Distracted by pregnancy and ignoring baby.	Continue with plan agreed. Midwife and General Practioner to monitor and report concerns.	Baby feels loss and abandonment. Exacerbates difficulties and need for affectionate attention.	Mother told about impact using lighthouse metaphor.

(Continued)

Hurt-full and Healing Pages 79

Table 6.1 (Continued)

Date	Child's Age	Impact Event	Expected Behaviour	Actual Behaviour	Intervention Offered at Time	Developmental Impact	Intervention Needed Now
2 February 25	11 months	Sister born	Challenges baby sister for mum's attention.	Only for 3 days then described as lovely and quiet.	None. Concern raised for baby's feeding difficulties.	Attachment difficulties/ separation anxiety, issues later with trust, safety, and arousal.	Dad to give more time to baby to release mum and parents share care more evenly.
4 September 25	18 months	Father dies following fight in pub	Notices absence of parent. More affection and reassurance seeking from remaining parent.	Sleeps more than usual. Has to be woken for food. Mother describes him as a very good toddler.	Mother offered phone numbers for Cruise and Samaritans to help with her distraught and very present grief. Nothing in notes about the children.	Mother says he is like his Dad and is violent towards her rejecting her when she tries to cuddle him. Concerned he has attention deficit hyperactivity disorder (ADHD) and dyspraxia because he is a very clumsy child – keeps breaking his toys and laughing.	Physiotherapist advice on reducing size of enlarged hippocampus, hyper-arousal and self-regulation by consistency and games. Family worker to focus on stabilising environment, supporting mother and to find any evidence of another partner.

(Continued)

Table 6.1 (Continued)

Date	Child's Age	Impact Event	Expected Behaviour	Actual Behaviour	Intervention Offered at Time	Developmental Impact	Intervention Needed Now
						Diagnosed as dyspraxic and mum asks about ADD/ADHD.	

An example of a trauma-informed chronolgy. Norma Howes

Part IV

The Assessment Framework
Thinking, Feeling, and Evidencing Well

Chapter 7

Start Lines and Fault Lines
Timing and Tensions for Sibling Assessments

This may sound like a question with an obvious answer: at the beginning, but where is the beginning? This chapter will explore some of the case examples presented throughout this book to identify the pros and cons of when siblings should be placed together, opportunities and missed opportunities.

It is necessary to consider children's needs before they become siblings. This may also sound obvious, yet children are often left in dangerous situations because the risk is overlooked, minimised, missed, or assessed through an over-optimistic or parent-centred lens. Risk is also heightened when the child is younger, has additional needs, communication difficulties, or a disability. Risk is fluid and dynamic, shifting positively or negatively with changes in family makeup, mental health, illness, or harm.

Assessments must include what a sibling is, may be, or may never be, and when a sibling is expected but not yet born or where the existence of a sibling becomes known.

The following examples illustrate the need to consider not only the information available about the siblings but also to ensure that sibling assessments are conducted alongside any other necessary evaluations.

An Only Child

Krystal

Lucy was a 27-year-old woman living with her parents as a result of her vulnerability and inability to successfully negotiate independence due to her diagnosed and unstable schizophrenia. Her parents had argued for her to be given birth control medication, but she would not or could not comply. She was not in a relationship, but her vulnerability exposed her to the nefarious actions of others. She was clearly at risk of exploitation in a whole raft of ways.

Local Authority assessments began when suspicions were aroused that Lucy might be pregnant. Whilst her parents were supportive and loving, they could not contain her during florid episodes or keep her safe when she sought independence and autonomy, something she was not always able to negotiate due to a lack of capacity. Adult Social Care Informed Children's Services of the suspected pregnancy. The package of support offered was unprecedented in scope and provision, yet even though it was parent-centred it still could not meet her needs. By focusing so heavily on Lucy as a parent-to-be, the assessment failed to consider how the child's developmental and attachment needs would be met. Lucy remained in denial of her pregnancy throughout, resisting antenatal care and increasing the risks to both herself and her baby. The argument for her baby, Krystal, to remain in her care was discounted, but the likelihood of Lucy becoming pregnant again was noted as tragically high. This raised the question of how any future children would be placed if her mental health did not stabilise. Little thought was given to Lucy's vulnerability as an adult in her own right. Future considerations needed therefore to include the impact on Lucy of losing her daughter, the impact on Krystal losing her mother and grandparents, and the possibility of losing a future relationship with birth siblings.

A Sibling-Bereaved Child

Martin

Martin was a seven-year-old boy. His mother was diagnosed with schizophrenia and bipolar disorder. The Local Authority requested that play therapy be undertaken to ameliorate the impact of his chaotic parenting experience. A meeting was held to collate the information, make recommendations, and start any other possible interventions required.

The information gathered confirmed that Martin had experienced significant neglect as a result of his mother's unstable condition. This left him with an insecure attachment (probably avoidant) impacting on his sense of safety and ability to trust, which led to control issues. He clearly required a therapeutic service. There were also very clear indicators that he was not safe:

- He was living with his mother, the person he most needed to trust, who either would not or could not keep him safe as a result of her unstable parenting.
- Because she was vulnerable, like Lucy in the previous example, she was unable to see any negative intention in others and was again targeted by men with malintent, raising the risk for Martin.
- The most astounding factor uncovered was that she had committed filicide by drowning Martin's nine-year-old sister in the bath during a rare, but obviously, a particularly severe psychotic episode. This happened two years before Martin was born. He was raised 'not knowing' about his sister.

The Local Authority removed him and placed him in foster care. He settled very quickly. He was now safe and began to feel safe in his female foster carer's presence, and he soon started therapy. There was an ongoing debate about whether or not he should be told about his sister. The argument for this information to be shared with him included the following factors:

- He had the right to know that he had a sister.
- He could not possibly be unaware of her existence, and the failure to acknowledge this will convey a message to him.
- In the unlikely event he did not already know of her existence, the chances were he would find out in an unplanned and therefore potentially more damaging manner: through social media, a school friend, or by someone who wanted to use the information for malintent.
- He also had the right to know in a carefully considered way that his sister was killed by his mother. However, the Local Authority disagreed, believing the information was too much and too psychologically damaging.

Martin returned home from school one day saying a school photograph had been taken. His foster carer asked him, was it a whole school photo, a class photo or an individual photo? He stated, 'Oh no, it was just me and another girl. The teacher took it.' The foster carer felt this was odd, especially because she knew the other child was also in the care system. She reported the incident to the school and the Local Authority. It soon became clear that the teacher had been 'let go' from many schools for similar behaviour and there had been no real consequence for his actions.

This incident created a conduit of change for Martin. He began to express his needs to his foster carer. One day he complained of having a sore bottom. His foster carer suggested she put some Sudocrem on it. Taking him up to the bathroom, she took the cream from the medicine cabinet. Seeing the cream, Martin asked, 'Should I put my head down the toilet while you do it?' This immediately struck the foster carer as strange. She explored the question carefully until he said, 'That's what Dave (his mother's partner) made me do.' She stopped asking questions and told the social worker and the police. A strategy meeting led to the decision to undertake an ABE interview which enabled Martin to disclose the following:

- His mother's partner, whose existence Child Protective Services were unaware of, was a registered sex offender, and had been sexually abusing him.
- This man had been keeping Martin quiet by assuring him that if he told anyone about the abuse, his mother would do to him what she had done to his sister.

Martin had been living in fear. He had endured an abusive situation for an extended period of time and clearly needed reparative services without sabotaging any criminal proceedings. There was now no argument against him being told the truth about his sister in a manner consistent with his age and development. This would enable him to piece the information together, grieve the loss of his sister, understand his mother's health, his missed and actual experiences, including his loss of safety.

These two examples clearly demonstrate the need to consider not just the information available but also to wonder and hypothesise about what else is to be ascertained that is as yet unknown. The importance of context when assessing the conflicting and paradoxical needs of all children, especially when assessments will be simultaneously undertaken, is very necessary.

Placed Siblings

Becky and Tom

Becky and Tom were placed in an Independent Fostering Agency (IFA) provision. A sibling assessment must consider the circumstances and context in which each child is living and how they experience it. Each caregiving situation has its own unique and potentially skewing factors. Becky and Tom clearly required a sibling assessment long before the placement came to its terrible, but inevitable, tragically messy ending. There was little point in only assessing the children when it was clear that the foster carers' relationship and individual presentation also required assessing.

Although the couple had been approved as foster carers, both the assessment and subsequent Panel approval had been unable to identify pre-existing relational and personal difficulties. Even if the relationship issues had developed later, their individual traits would have been present. This raises a difficult question: What could be done when issues that are overlooked or unseen at approval emerge later? The dilemma lies between a failing placement for the sake of stability or moving the children because of problems rooted in the adults' presentation.

This situation required assessment of:

- A further, separate assessment of Emmett and Cicely.
- Their relationship and capacity to change.
- The foster carers' behaviour towards the children and the impact of their scapegoating and favouriting behaviour on the children individually and together.
- The skews in the children's relationship resulting from their formative experiences and the environment in a foster home which lacked the essential elements of safety.
- The children's own needs and how these would be balanced against the required sibling assessment.
- The sibling relationship to be able to decide if either Becky or Tom could stay in placement or leave or could both children stay together in the current placement, or would they need to be placed together or separately in another placement or placements. If being placed separately, what contact arrangements would be needed.

A review was also needed of the management system to look at the tensions between the roles of the supervising social worker and the children's social workers and the management ethos. Differences in the ethos of all management teams needed to be understood and determined when several were involved: Local Authority, Central Government, Third Sector, or Independent Agency. The danger here was that the supportive structure around the family was beginning to mirror the family's crises. When the structure of the supporting service is struggling to remain objective, clear, supportive, and emotionally literate, any service offered will struggle to achieve an effective outcome.

No assessment was undertaken. As Cicely's constant finding fault with Becky continued, so Becky's behaviour continued to deteriorate. As her behaviour deteriorated, Cicely's complaints increased. As Cicely's complaints increased, so her relationship with her husband deteriorated. The foster carers spiralled. Their adult birth children targeted the problem as they saw it or needed to see it, Becky. As Becky felt scapegoated (and was), so her behaviour escalated until the foster carers finally served notice and she was removed.

Tom was left in the placement. Again, no assessment was undertaken to determine whether or not he should be with his sister or in an alternative placement. His behaviour deteriorated. Tom's earthquake, previously overshadowed by his sister's volcano, was now able to be felt and noticed. Tom was scared that he was going to be rejected. This fear presented as anger. His anger escalated as Cicely began to blame him for her deteriorating relationship with her husband.

Lacey and Eleanor

Lacey and Eleanor were beautiful little girls (this is not a subjective statement; it is often a factor that can become a block to seeing the child's actual needs). They were placed in foster care together despite a sibling assessment clearly laying out the evidence to demonstrate living together was not going to be in the interest of either child. Nobody could envisage these two little girls not living together even though their behaviour when living with their mother was extreme and dangerous. This behaviour was repeated in the contact centre and resulted in their mother becoming overwhelmed and sobbing on the floor during the contact assessment. The girls had developed a trauma bond. This meant that the person most likely to remind them of their experiences was each other. Yes, the mother was overwhelmed and incapable of parenting effectively, but Services placed too much onus on the cause of the children's behaviour being the mother's chaotic lifestyle, rather than the resultant trauma bond from the mother's lifestyle.

The sisters were placed together in a foster home with a very experienced couple who had a history of success. The female foster carer stated that they had worked with adolescents who presented criminal behaviour, harmful sexual behaviour, with young children who had multiple and complex needs and with the kinds of challenges from children's presentations. Yet, she described these two- and four-year-olds as the most challenging children they had ever cared for. Within months the carers were on their knees. Another sibling assessment was undertaken, and Lacey was moved into an alternative foster placement. Within three months of this move the carers served notice on Eleanor who was moved to another foster home. By the end of the same year the original foster carers separated. The children were not the cause of the separation. The stress of caring for the children who were unresponsive to their love widened the already present cracks in their relationship.

Tia and Max

Tia was placed into adoption with her brother Max, who was six years older. His 'job,' as he saw it was to care and protect his sister. He experienced the worst of his parents' behaviour and endured this for the entirety of his first four formative and crucial years. Upon arrival at the adoptive placement, he kept the new parents away from his sister. The level of violence and aggression he directed towards his new parents was extreme. The parents loved their children, even though all they experienced was rejection, hate, and venom. Tia did not feel safe around her brother. His taking care of Tia was by his fighting. The danger he saw was their new parents' outpouring of unconditional love that only further fuelled his fear. The parents were scared of their son's behaviour and Tia was scared of her parents' fear and her brother's hatred of them.

An assumption had been made that they should be placed together, but no assessment was undertaken to see if they could or not. As Max grew older, his violence increased. Tia became increasingly reclusive, refusing to leave her bedroom. The couple ran out of hope and took the decision, rather than formally disrupting the placement, to pay for Max to attend a private boarding school. Max thrived there academically because there was no attachment threat. His attachment style remained insecure. His hatred of his adopters festered. With Max out of the house, Tia emerged but remained school phobic. She was verbally hostile to the parents, yet she clung to them. She rejected the adoptive mother and dominated the adoptive father, ridiculing him, yet fearing his absence. The ambivalence and avoidance she presented were palpable and often deteriorated into disorganisation. Her fear could never resolve because every holiday Max would return with his anger and resentment. He felt he had been rejected to the boarding school, that paradoxically he loved. Tia knew that her parents could not keep her safe from the brother who had 'kept' her safe.

As her brother moved towards adulthood, his desire to know about his birth family increased, and Therapeutic Life Story work became an overriding need for him. The problem was that whilst Max was ready for Life Story Work, his sister was not. If Max did not receive the work in a planned and coordinated manner, he was going to receive it in an unplanned and uncoordinated manner as soon as he turned 18, or through social media. Either way, any information he received would be passed on to his sister, and his sister, by not being ready for it, was going to be more affected by the information.

This is not an unusual scenario for siblings who should never have been placed together. It was a situation where it was evidently clear the children should not have been placed together. An assessment was not initially undertaken. Placing them together met the agency's agenda of keeping siblings together. A sibling assessment to separate or place together would have given everyone greater insight into the children's relationship and given the social worker evidence to apply for resources to further support a family in preparation for and during the early years of one or two placements.

Hunter, Faith and Charity

Hunter, Faith and Charity were removed from home on the grounds of extreme neglect. Had a sibling assessment been conducted at the same time as the comprehensive family assessment, it would have made it possible to see that:

- Hunter, Faith and Charity were incongruent. Their outward affect, smiley and happy, did not connect with their inner feelings.
- Charity internalised her feelings and presented as compliant.
- Faith bounced between internalising and externalising when overwhelmed by her feeling.
- Hunter externalised his feelings and presented as compliant towards adults.
- Hunter took on a pseudo-parenting role for his sisters and answered for her. Charity complied with this. Faith did not.

The image presented by the children was incongruent, enmeshed, with skewed roles and an unhealthy relationship. What was being seen by Services was two very young, physically good-looking and charming children. No consideration was given to whether or not these children should be separated. Charity was seen as relying on her brother, even though a child should not have to rely on a child for survival, and Hunter was seen as having a role in caring for his sisters, even though no child should feel responsible for the care of another child. The more Charity complied the more resistant Faith became. A trauma-informed sibling assessment would have informed whether or not the children could or could not be placed together.

The outlook of Services was over-optimistic. The children's behaviour was not considered through a trauma lens.

The children were placed in short-term foster care together. The single foster carer noted that all the previously mentioned behaviours still applied in her care. In addition, she noted that before and after contact the children clung together. The female foster carer believed the children were frightened when seeing their mother, but paradoxically, their behaviour during contact did not support this view. The contact supervisor recorded they appeared to respond reasonably well in the interactions with their mother.

The children shared a bedroom. They were seen to be inseparable and appeared to rely on each other. This further supported the view that they needed to be together. This effectively reinforced the children's view that they needed to rely only on each other for their felt sense of safety.

The children were then placed in an adoptive placement with Hope, Butler. A trauma-informed sibling assessment before this happened may well have concluded they should be placed together but could also have identified the skews in their relationship and how these would need to be resolved. Also, any additional training, information, and skills the adopter would need pre- and post-placement.

Hope and Butler had successfully completed their assessments to become an adoptive parents. Hope could not tell the assessors about her own sibling experience because she could not tell them about her experience of being parented or how both had negatively impacted on her life. She was asked if she had siblings and what her relationship with them was like now. This was not an assessment of how they were as children. To understand Hunter, Faith and Charity's needs in placement required looking through a trauma lens when assessing the parents. If Hope's and Butler's lenses were 'off', then it was crucial to understand what caused this and to identify any issues which would impact on their parenting of the children.

The adopters kept the children together in the same bedroom because being together was the overwhelming belief expressed by Services. It was not long before Hope discovered that her children were not just engaging in sexual activity, which could not be mistaken for exploratory play, because they were having intercourse with each other. Another point where a sibling assessment could have been undertaken but was not.

Sexual behaviour would trigger most parents. It triggered Hope more than most because it was an instant reminder of her own abusive childhood that had increased her vulnerability to the CSE that followed. None of this history was disclosed during the adoption assessment because she could not see it or recall it, but she was enabled to in the safe, calm time offered by the children's therapist. This had implications for her relationship with Butler.

To repeat, there are many reasons people do not disclose such painful and damaging experiences. Part of the problem is that interventions, especially assessments, have become increasingly formulaic. The governmental book on assessing families, *Protecting Children: A Guide for Social Workers Undertaking a Comprehensive Assessment*, nicknamed the *Orange Book* (1988) was cast aside and replaced by the *Framework for the Assessment of Children in Need and Their Families* (2000). Whilst the Framework was by far improved in its complexity, structure, information and layout, it missed the one thing the *Orange Book* did well: how and what to ask when information gathering. Sadly, the guidance needed from handbooks and texts has become self-limiting evoking, 'It was not on the list,' a crutch, 'I cannot do this without the book,' restrictions, 'Keep inside and do not look outside the box.' In striving to create consistency, a good idea, and haste, not always a good idea, the one thing a Handbook cannot give is how to make the necessary relationship. It is within this relationship, that takes time to build, that sharing is enabled by building trust and a sense of safety.

Brenna

This impact was evident in a conversation with Brenna, an adopter in her 50s with two adopted boys. Brenna presented as angry, critical, abrupt, and cynical. She had been supported with therapy for her boys alongside therapeutic parenting support for herself. The therapist providing the therapeutic parent support acknowledged that they were stuck. All the information required had been imparted in as many ways as possible, but Brenna was not shifting. Brenna then accepted the recommendation she needed her own therapy.

In the first session, Brenna engaged in her therapy with unusual speed. In the second, she disclosed a history of child sexual abuse, and in the third, she was concerned about her behaviour towards her younger brother when she was aged three. She disclosed her limiting belief that she was born for sex. Despite the therapists' most tenacious attempts, this would not shift. A different approach was needed.

In session 4

Therapist: 'Can we try an experiment?'
Brenna: 'What is the experiment?' (cautious)
Therapist: 'I am going to say something. What I am going to say may elicit an emotion, a thought, a physical sensation, a memory, a combination or something else' (inviting curiosity)
Brenna: 'What are you going to say?' (mistrust)
Therapist: 'This is really hard for you, it seems you are telling me that it's hard to trust and you cannot make an informed decision without as much information as possible' (reassuring, externally regulating her back in her window of tolerance)
Brenna: Nods.
Therapist: 'I understand that this is hard. My job is not to hurt but help. However, therapy is painful and so I cannot guarantee that what I say will not hurt. My intention is not to hurt. Whatever happens next, we can think and feel through any responses to what I say' (further stabilisation)
Brenna: 'Ok then, do it.'
Therapist: 'Even though you are worried, you are letting me know it's ok to continue despite your reservations?' (further connection with safety)
Brenna: 'Yes.'
Therapist *'You can stop me at any time' (ensuring control remains with Brenna)*
Brenna: 'Ok.'
Therapist: 'I know that you had been hurt in a sexual way by your grandfather and that should not have happened, and this has had long and lasting negative consequences for you.'
Brenna: Nods. (looks cautious)
Therapist: 'Even though you were hurt so often by grandad, for so long, and no one was willing or able to stop it…and it felt like it would never stop …'

Brenna: Wide-eyed and focused.
Therapist: '…you have had more days not being abused than you have been abused'… (watching Brenna's somatic and emotional responses notes she looks angry)
Therapist: 'I can see I got that wrong. I know it feels like the abuse has not stopped, but that stopped when you became an adult and got away from Grandad' (acceptance)
Brenna: 'It never stopped even when Grandad no longer had access to me.'
Therapist: 'I want to understand. I'm sorry I got that wrong, but I wasn't there in your adulthood, so I don't know what happened next.' (compassion without shame or blame)

Brenna went on to describe an adulthood of multiple rapes, infidelity, and working in the sex industry. All of this felt like it was out of her control and informed her beliefs about the intentions of all males. Unlike Hope, who was triggered by her children, Brenna's belief system was skewed and influenced how she interpreted her sons' behaviours. She saw intentions in their behaviours that were not there. A sibling assessment of her boys would have been equally useful but it would have to take account of Brenna's beliefs about the intentions of all males. How would she see her boys as they grew and developed into adults?

This chapter has highlighted that without a trauma lens being utilised, despite best interventions, opportunities will be missed when it would have been possible to undertake the correct intervention at the optimum time, or make the decision to separate siblings to circumvent or prevent further harm to each individual or the sibling relationship. This means a sibling assessment can be undertaken at multiple points and does not need to be triggered by an event. Transitions are particularly useful times; placements in chaos and the threat of disruption are not. The chapter also shows that sometimes children's behaviours are triggered by the adults' experiences and therefore multiple concurrent assessments may need to take place at any time. This is model coherency.

Chapter 8

No Foregone Conclusions

A Trauma-Informed Sibling Assessments

The careful consideration of the needs of children and young people, shaped by the individual experiences of each sibling, is of paramount importance. Their self-beliefs, perceptions of caregiver motivations, and responsiveness are complex, and additionally more paradoxical having experienced multiple ACEs. Consequently, perspectives on relationships, both with others and among themselves, are intricate and challenging to understand fully. The task is to approach this paradoxical complexity in a manner that enables services to assess and address their unmet needs effectively, enhance their skills, resilience, and self-efficacy, mitigate past trauma, and make trauma-informed decisions regarding current and future placements, whether with or without their siblings.

With so many paradoxes, issues and dilemmas, how then can the material be gathered?

A Guideline

1. Filter, process, and organise gathered information into a coherent, accessible, and trauma-informed accessible framework.
2. Fact finding. Construct the assessment using an extended trauma-informed chronology.
3. Differentiate and create hypotheses from assumptions that are neither overly positive, optimistic, nor pessimistic, and avoid sentimentality of personal bias whilst remaining mindful of any other inherent bias.
4. Establish what was done, what it did and what was missing for each sibling and family member in order to answer the 'so what next?' question.
5. Triangulate and cross-reference information gathered from the multiple sources, from the child, siblings, family, educational settings, other care providers, therapy, and psychometric findings.
6. Assess the information gathered – the 'So what?' bit.
7. Draft the report, in detail, with the pros and cons of placement/s together or separately with recommendations.

DOI: 10.4324/9781003724605-12

8. Identify what is needed to ensure, whether the conclusion is together or apart, and provide the services needed to ensure, as far as is possible, there is a successful outcome.
9. Timescale for follow-up and review.

In this and in any assessment being undertaken, the importance of beginning with an open mind cannot be overemphasised. Too often there is an already predetermined view of what the outcome should be. This leads to significant errors being made. This then results in even more serious consequences because crucial information has not been looked for. It has, of course, then not been included or if the omission was noticed it has been minimised or dismissed because it did not fit the pre-determined outcome or mindset of the assessor or organisation. This is especially important when, at the time of writing, the belief and therefore the focus or predetermined outcome is that siblings should be kept together. There is no reason to disagree with this stance as a good starting point, but only if the assessment is done with an open mind, open hypotheses and the detailed questions listed later are asked, and more importantly answered. Only then a conversant, trauma-informed decision can be made. This will reduce the traumatic impact of the decision in the short, medium, and long term not just for the children involved, but also for their parents, carers and workers.

Appropriate support and therapeutic services should be implemented in a timely manner to ameliorate harm and prevent further trauma. Sometimes therapy is delayed from a misguided view that the children are too young or need to acclimatise. Or the vaguer, 'it's not the right time.' It is known that the sooner ameliorative interventions are provided the better the outcomes. Further trauma can result from relying on luck, hoping the decision was the right one, supporting a placement which should not continue, by causing emotional devastation when being separated from a much-loved supportive sibling or conversely emotional damage by keeping siblings together when they should not be.

An example of another assessment needing an open mind is in suspected or actual domestic abuse. Too often, there is a lack of hypotheses and a mindset fixed to achieve the most common conclusion, that because it is true men are usually the perpetrators, then men must **always** be the perpetrators and that victims can never be at fault. This view was advocated in the Freedom Programme and was strongly presented on Women's Hour on BBC Radio 4. This closed mindset runs the risk of at least inadequate, if not completely wrong conclusions when failing to fully assess who is the victim or the perpetrator of the violence.

The victim is never at fault? However, simply making that statement does not help an assessment. Consider, for example, a woman who has had three violent partners before her current relationship. Her children, her partner, and even she herself may describe her behaviour as 'provocative.' This is not an exercise in victim-blaming, but an attempt to understand the complexity of trauma. What early relational template led her to be unconsciously drawn to violent men? What in her development created a bias towards the familiar, even when that familiarity was unsafe? It might also be asked: when living in an untenable environment, why does she respond with 'provocative' behaviour or better still, what is it that makes her provocative? One hypothesis is that, knowing violence is inevitable, but not knowing when it will happen, she subconsciously seeks to control the situation. By provoking the incident, she reduces the uncertainty and anxiety of waiting, because the violence has now occurred. In this formulation, the violence was always going to happen; the unbearable part was not knowing when. This can then bring about a false sense of agency, a feeling of being incontrol, an acceptance of self-blame and absolution for the perpetrator and subsequently a real sense of relief. The tension of waiting can then subside and the relationship continue.

The same questions must be asked of the victim and the perpetrator. When did they learn that violence was an acceptable way to deal with relationships or problems? How did they come to believe that harming women was effective or satisfying? What was their relational template that shaped these beliefs? What was their relationship with any siblings? Did this result in either or both being a victim or perpetrator with a sibling or siblings.

Equally important is what the siblings were learning as they witness these dynamics. Where were they when the violence occurred? How do they make sense of who is responsible? Do they see their father figure as a victim of their mother who does not do as she is told, whether serving dinner on time or meeting his clear expectations? Do they believe that their mother should have 'learned' by now that compliance prevents anger, and therefore her failure made her responsible? If she insists on saying, 'He loves me and I love him,say sorrry and it's my fault,' do the children internalise the message that violence equals love or indeed love equals sex? Do they begin to believe that being violent with their siblings is a legitimate way to resolve disputes? And do they ultimately accept that the victim must apologise, thereby concretising a distorted belief that blame lies with the person being hurt?

Another example arose when watching the news coverage of the then British Prime Minister, Boris Johnson, visiting a school. As he walked to the front of the classroom, one little girl in the front row became giggly and squirmy, clearly overwhelmed and, in that moment 'out of her window' of tolerance, by this famous person being in her class.

An immediate viewers reaction was, 'Oh boy that is not ok.' Hypotheses followed:it was not ok because the child's behavioural response, which was filmed and shown on national television, showed a physiological reaction, over which she had no control. It highlighted her vulnerability and potentially a sexually reactive response to previous harm.

That realisation triggered a cascade of reflective thoughts:

- *Where did that thought come from?* (self-reflection).
- *If Boris were predatory, would her behaviour signal that she was a vulnerable child that he could target or groom?* Jimmy Savile, for instance, was known to exploit exactly such vulnerabilities.
- *But surely, she could not 'fancy' him because I certainly don't.*
- *And yet, why would she not?* If we consider the impact of being precociously sexualised and how that warps and alters expected developmental norms.
- *Uninformed self-reasurance followed that there was no way he would respond in a dangerous way, followed by a visceral shake of the head,* because most adults when faced with unusual or vulnerable behaviour, do not take advantage.

However, if Boris had noticed and been concerned, his responsible response would have been to share those concerns about the vulnerability he had witnessed.

Consider a future scenario in which an investigation takes place into that girl's allegation that Boris had assaulted her or had started to groom her. In such a case, would her behaviour be considered alongside his? This would not be in order to blame her but to understand how her vulnerability could have been exploited. One task for the assessor would be to explore her previous experiences, those that may have created this vulnerability, and identify the interventions to safeguard her, regulate her responses, and build resilience against future risk.

Another danger is that assumptions could prevent her needs from being seen. If it was assumption that 'no one could possibly find him appealing or attractive,' it might not even have been hypothesised that her behaviour, as a result of sexual reactivity, could present as 'flirtatious.' In this case, it would be an important indicator of stress-related sexualised behaviour that could be missed. While intervention should rightly focus on the adult perpetrator, there is a risk that her needs are missed.

Later if she were to say it was her fault and that reassurance was given to her that 'it was not your fault,' the message would be necessary but not sufficient. It probably will not reduce her sense of responsibility or guarantee her future safety. One young person described being sexually assaulted multiple times by multiple adults. She said she knew all adults were only sexually interested in her, and rather than wait for the assault she would initiate the assault with a smile or teasing. In doing so she could have a sense of control over **when** she was assaulted, because she knew from experience she had no control over **if** she would be assaulted.

This parallels how some children in domestic violence situations may believe that initiating violence gives them some control over the inevitable. In both cases, shifting the blame to themselves can create a false sense of agency and control where genuine control is almost always absent and coercive control dominates.

Two adult sisters, Donna and Paula, one of whom had moved by choice 200 miles away from the town they grew up in and by choice lost touch with her sister and their extended family. Paula, the sister who remained was in a violent marriage resulting in safeguarding issues being raised on her behalf and separately on her children. After months of what Paula felt to her was pressure from the children's social worker, she agreed to Donna being contacted as well as the Local Housing

Authority where Donna lived, to see if she qualified for 'local connection' housing in that area. Paula and the children were then moved to an area where they knew no one except her estranged sister. The trauma both sisters had experienced whilst growing up was the reason Donna moved so far away. Their estrangement should have raised the hypothesis that their relationship might be a strained or difficult one; therefore, how willing or able would the sisters be to give or accept support from each other? Predictably, the sisters could not even look at each other without being activated and reactivating their unresolved, profoundly distressing childhood memories. The result was an inability to look at each other, let alone support each other. Paula's migration back to her hometown could then be explained and understood. Instead, she was blamed for returning, was viewed as having made a 'lifestyle choice' by returning to her violent partner and her unwillingness to engage with services resulted in her children being removed from her care.

A six-year-old girl was removed from her parents' emotionally and physically neglectful care. She was placed with foster carers whilst her three-year-old brother was hospitalised for failure to thrive. The foster carers asked for help in how to reassure her it was not her fault her brother was in hospital. She was constantly saying it was her fault and the carers constant assurance that it was not her fault was to no avail. Instead of telling her it was not her fault, she was gently asked to explain what made her think it was her fault. Her answer, 'No matter how hard I tried I couldn't stop the grass going down the sink.' Gentle prompting enabled her to continue, 'I knew my brother was hungry. I could see the rabbit in the garden eating grass. I couldn't find anything for him to eat so I collected some grass. I ate some in the garden. I knew it should be washed so I climbed up to the sink to wash it but it all went down the plug, I couldn't catch it and there was none left. The social worker told me he was in hospital because he did not have enough to eat.' The importance of changing the beginning of 'why questions' to 'what questions' and to reflect on anyone's belief about fault cannot be overstated.

In all the examples, the importance of a trauma-informed assessment with no blame, no shame, empathically curious and open-minded questions about behaviour is just as important as those asked about the behaviour of all members of the family to ensure a positive, safe outcome and future for them all. Just as, if not more important, when assessing whether or not siblings should be placed together or separately, and determining what the plan for and content of any contact.

Assessing the Information Gathered – the 'So What?' Bit

Information in reports often contains only narrative; i.e., vast amounts of information, but little or no analysis of the implications or consequences for the short-, medium-, or long-term well-being of doing the right thing, the wrong thing, or indeed of doing nothing. Undertaking analysis is perhaps technically the hardest component of the work required. Not the least because it is essentially a lonely singular task. It does not only have consequences for the child, their siblings, and family but also for the assessor both professionally and personally. From the *Orange Book* in 1989

(Assessing Children in Need and their Families, HMSO), the enquiries into events in Cleveland (1987) and in Orkney (1991) *The Lilac Book* in 2000 (Framework for the Assessment of Children in Need and their Families, HMSO 2000) and more recently in *Beyond Together or Apart* (Beckett, 2018, 2021) where each contains over 100 pages on information gathering but at most only one or two pages mentioning the need to assess and analyse the information gathered, there is significantly no guidance or proforma on how to do this. For example, in the *Lilac Book* with 4 lines on page 10 and 7 lines on page 11: Analysis: The next section (of the assessment) is for practitioners to analyse the significance and consequences of the needs, strengths, and difficulties identified in the assessment. 'This is a key stage in the assessment process. Practitioners should consider the inter-relationship between each of the domains of the Framework for the Assessment of Children in Need and their Families. For example, a child's difficult and demanding behaviour, stemming from a lack of attunement from their depressed parent, may be a major contributory factor to a parent's depression, which may in turn lead to the home environment being neglected and increased demanding behaviour from the child. It will be helpful to list key protective and stress factors in each domain and indicate how they relate to those identified in the other domains. It is important that strengths as well as difficulties are identified. Parental and family strengths should be built on and used to inform the plan. When analysing the information gathered, practitioners should also evaluate the impact on the child and family of any services already provided.'

Hence what has been titled the 'so what?' bit, which joins with the need for hypotheses generation, in effect it is the same thing, because it is fundamentally about what the future could hold. It will raise further questions. It will never be 100% correct. Human beings and their relationships can and will be joyfully and frustratingly paradoxical and unpredictable. Professional credibility is put at risk by committing to paper information and opinion, thus making tangible something that will remain fluid with changeable relationships and high-risk-filled outcomes, over which there is no predictable pathway to success. What does not work is known, or maybe more accurately to say what could or should not work is known, but paradoxically it then it does. No doubt there will be the need to continue to read and search for that missing definitive variable, the one which could lead to a successful sibling relationship or could predict failure.

Assessment Components

Part 1: Self-assessment of Fitness to Undertake a Sibling Assessment

1. Fitness of agency

    Can the agency currently contain, emotionally hold, and supervise practitioners to undertake the assessments? This will not be part of the individual's assessment but will ensure that every practitioner is able to reflect in a congruent and coherent way. If the service or agency is not safe, how can their practitioners be safe? (Table 8.1).

Table 8.1 Fitness of Agency

Ethos/Support	Fitness of Agency		
	Style/Frequency		
	Positive		Of Concern
Intervention Outlook (Dove or Hawk)	Balanced	Interventionist	Non-interventionist
Team meetings	Monthly – Quarterly	Weekly*	Annual/Triannual/Never
Case management	Monthly – Quarterly	Weekly*	Annual/Triannual/Never
Clinical supervision	Weekly, fortnightly Monthly*	Continual*	Annual/Triannual/Never
Case Consultation	As required	Micromanaged	Never
Personal therapy	Supportive or provided short-term or when needed	Ongoing	Never or critical
Training	Looks for need/desires	Overwhelming	Absent, not valued
Culture	Cohesive and positive	Toxic, negative, micromanaged	Individualism, absent, fragmented
Improvement plan	Supportive	Overwhelming	Absent
Management style	Flexible, consultative, and democratic	Autocratic, rigid, paternalistic	Laissez-faire, inconsistent, absent

* Where more frequent supervision or support is required then this is of course a positive factor. Context is important in understanding any data. Examples where more regular support maybe needed include; students or the newly qualified, those with high or complex caseloads, those on an improvement plan or those going through a period of crisis.

2. Fitness of the Practitioner

   Can the Practitioner currently contain, emotionally hold, and provide a safe service to both the child/young person and the parent/family in order to undertake the assessment safely and effectively? This again will not be part of the individual assessment but will ensure that every practitioner is reflecting on their situation in a congruent and coherent way. If the practitioner is not, or does not feel safe, how can their practice be safe? (Table 8.2).

100 A Trauma Model for Assessing Siblings

Table 8.2 Fitness of Practitioner

Fitness of Practitioner (self-report vs observed)

Ethos/Support	Style/Frequency		
		Positive	Of Concern
Intervention Outlook (Dove or Hawk) Team Meetings	Balanced Aware of pros vs cons of separating siblings.	Interventionist Tendency to react and split siblings.	Non-interventionist Tendency to maintain the situation by ignoring concerns or utilising every service to keep siblings together.
	Attends with an agenda, contributes, safely challenges, positive outlook, altruistic, cares about self, colleagues and team, has a sense of energy, shows a range of coherent emotions.	Takes up space, toxic presentation, hijacks the agenda, controls, manipulates, coercive, cares about self, undermining, creates cliques, passive aggressive, hostile, secretive.	Avoids, frequently late, emotionally absent, unprepared, relies on others, ambivalent, inconsistent, manipulates, cares about self/no self-awareness, passive aggressive, emotionally overwhelmed, or underwhelmed, secretive.
Case Management Supervision	Understands the purpose, contributes, safely challenges, has a sense of need, attends with agenda, aware of skills and learning needs. Can accept constructive criticism, praise and implements suggested or agreed decisions, feeds back progress.	Actively resistant, confrontational, negative, manipulates the agenda, ignores instruction, says yes but means no, presents as insightful or has intermittent insight, case files usually up to date, can be subjective or misleading.	Passively resistant, fails to bring agenda, glib, sentimental, lacks passion, says yes but fails to act or forgets, over-reliant on supervisor, lacks insight, case files not up to date or lacks analysis.
Clinical Supervision	Understands the purpose, contributes, is aware of projection, transference and countertransference, safely challenges, has a sense of need, attends with agenda, aware of skills and learning needs. Can accept constructive criticism, praise and implements suggested or agreed decisions, feeds back progress, can tolerate thoughts around personal therapy needs.	Actively resistant, confrontational, negative, manipulates the agenda, disingenuous, ignores instruction, says yes but means no, presents as insightful or intermittent insight, case files usually up to date but misleading or vague, can be subjective or ambiguous, rigid beliefs.	Passively resistant, lacks self-awareness, fails to bring agenda, glib, sentimental, lacks passion, says yes but fails to act or forgets, over-reliant on supervisor, lacks insight, case files not up to date or lacks analysis, inconsistent, ambivalent, disingenuous.

Table 8.2 (Continued)

Fitness of Practitioner* (self-report vs observed)

Ethos/Support	Style/Frequency	
	Positive	Of Concern
Case Consultation	Seeks and prioritises support. Committed, positive outlook is infectious, not put off by a challenge.	As above. Disguised compliance, can be high energy in the moment, can have strong verbalised beliefs but does not follow through. Negativity can be a theme, gas lighting.	As above, lacks motivation, bland responses, picks up the words, phrases of the consultant, plagiarises, copies and pastes from previous reports, write ups, takes the line of least resistance.
Personal Therapy	Knows and can accept that when their ability to function moves from periods of stress to overwhelm and find themselves triggered by their work, can seek out therapeutic support.	May not talk about their experience of therapy or whether they have had it or not. May harbour the thought that they do not need therapy or experience therapy to provide therapeutic support to others.	Has never had therapy, or only had the minimum therapy as required by their training. Is unaware of their needs, in denial or minimises their situation.
Training	Has an attitude of lifelong learning. Understands the need for professional development and updating practice. Will seek out further professional qualifications as well as learning associated models with continuous professional development. Supports and encourages others, mentors, promotes and shares learning with the team. Curiosity about character strategies and parts in supervision. Training, time space and future consultation put in place.	Careerist as opposed to a calling or a vocation. Training may be an means to an end. Less likely to be orientated around enhancing the lives of others and more towards status, role or income. In training they may take over, hold back or present as positive and only give negative feedback. No curiosity. Wry smile on reading about topic, such as parts and continued working without change.	Does the minimum. Sees qualification as a means to an end. Talks about what they intend to do but do not necessarily follow through. May fail to attend training days, twilights, etc. May fail to confirm attendance and turn up or confirm and not attend. Reflections may lack substance, depth or passion. May be ambivalent or avoidant. May swing from overly positive or continually negative. Dismissed Parts and character strategies as not relevant to role. Manage without so will continuum as before.

(Continued)

Table 8.2 (Continued)

Fitness of Practitioner* (self-report vs observed)

Ethos/Support	Style/Frequency	
	Positive	Of Concern
Culture	Is passionate about their job or role. Want people's lives to be enhanced, be that the people they provide a service for, their team and colleagues or themselves. See the benefits of their team, their building and their purpose whilst also being able to be a critical friend. Point out weaknesses but come up with improvements or seek out others to help come up with solutions. Ultimately, they want to be there, work together and find solutions.	Is passionate only about their own advancement. Teams and agencies are merely steppingstones rather than wanting to leave their positive mark. May be manipulative, seek to create subgroups that create toxic energy. Rather than desiring to create change in an organisation, they seek to undermine it. May present as keen advocates, but this is not maintained. Agree to decisions but passively or actively undermine them or refrain from carrying them out.	Mood hoovers, energy suckers and negative energy harbingers. May present as reasonable but don't want to do any more than the minimum. Will complain about change, without wanting to know or hear the reasons for change. Did not show up to any of the meetings or discussions and did not read their emails, want it repeated after the event. Everything is begrudged, a chore, an irritation or a burden. Do their work, but it feels like work. May be over-reliant on others or practiced incompetent. Passive or 'plays the victim.' Blames others. Sulks, fails to accept responsibility. May complain, fail to change, rely on other people, be over-reliant or opt-out. May lie. May repeat the same mistakes, 'coast' or even behave in ways that result in dismissal, putting the onus of responsibility on the employer.
Improvement Plan	Everyone makes mistakes, learn, move on. Everyone goes through periods of difficulty when this may impact on their work to some degree. People who present as balanced, thoughtful, self-reflective, accept advice and strive to do the best they can do rarely would end up in this situation, those that do, or those capable of change will accept responsibility (and where the rest lies with the agency) and undertake the remedial work required.	May leave the agency. May show disguised compliance, may say 'yes' but mean 'no.' Passive resistant, actively resistant. Blames others to avoid responsibility. May 'go-along-with' recommendations. But not 'own' their concerns. May be manipulative, lie, be superior or entitled. They may shine when observed, but this may be only surface change.	

Table 8.2 (Continued)

Fitness of Practitioner* (self-report vs observed)

Ethos/Support	Style/Frequency	
	Positive	Of Concern
	Ability to Engage: Self-aware, enters the relationship with authoritativeness, sensitivity and humility. Attuned to power differential. Aware of anxiety, resistance, anger and other overwhelming feelings. **Ability to Connect:** Is interested, open, curious in the person, their experiences and how they view the world. **Ability to build Rapport:** Demonstrating empathy and empathic attunement. Holds the ability to accept the way that the client sees or views their world. Can meet the client with eye contact and can reflect feelings with posture and non-verbal responses.	**Ability to Engage:** Over-confident, authoritarian, may utilise veiled threats, they may use parents, carers, teachers or others as leverage or even placement or educational security as influence. **Ability to Connect:** May rely heavily on their own experience. May purport to say they know how the client feels. **Ability to build Rapport:** May utilise their own interests that the client may share such as music, sport, art, or genres of TV or films. May overuse emotions that the client is not feeling, smile too much or over emphasise a reaction to feelings. The danger is that empathy is lost, and attunement is more grooming in nature.	**Ability to Engage:** Lacking in confidence, lassaiz faire, apologises, over-explains. Struggles to self-regulate or see the impact of their own anxiety. May use tension reducing behaviours **Ability to Connect:** May rely too much on the examples of others. May ingratiate themselves **Ability to build Rapport:** May be prone to sentimentality, be overly, but not congruently 'nice.' Have no respite in eye contact or avoid eye contact. May overuse body language or fail to mirror with attunement but no empathy.

(Continued)

Table 8.2 (Continued)

Fitness of Practitioner* (self-report vs observed)		
Ethos/Support	Style/Frequency	
	Positive	Of Concern
	Ability to develop Therapeutic Alliance: Is reliable, consistent in their approach. Is clear about professional boundaries and can respond compassionately to limits. Is prepared by having a good understanding of the client's experience. Has created a safe space where the client comes to have faith and trust in the practitioner to emotionally hold and contain them and their feeling of a lack of safety. Is able to accept rather than agree with the clients view of the world. Does not rush or pressure the client, but is not scared to address difficult, complex or challenging issues. Is congruent and coherent in their presentation, responses and manner. Is clear about the parameters of confidentiality, sharing information and what information goes into reports and reviews. Is able to tell the difference between a healthy relationship, compliance and creating dependency.	**Ability to develop Therapeutic Alliance:** Controlling, authoritarian, overly educative. Lacks humility is rigid and creates compliance. Overemphasises behaviour rather than understanding the behaviour. Limits access to resources or tools. Often 'knows best.' Lacks trust. Works too quickly, maybe impatient or intolerant. Overuse of psychometrics and lacks creative interventions. Over diagnosis of developmental psychopathology and/or neurodivergence. Is overly opinionated, certain or sure. Can be unclear using 'psycho-babble' and technical terms.	**Ability to develop Therapeutic Alliance:** Being unboundaried or unable to respond to therapeutic limits. May be inconsistent, unreliable. May show fear of behaviour rather than see the fear behind the behaviour. May appease the client to avoid certain feelings from being welcomed into the therapeutic space. May be too quick to change intervention style or be overly influenced by a controlling or fearful client. Lacks trust. Can work too slowly or be avoidant. Overuse of tools that have no empirical or cathartic value. Lacks the ability to account for attributing developmental psychopathology or neurodivergence. Lacks confidence or evidence. Can be unclear about what to share often confusing themes with process material.

*This can apply to therapists, social workers, foster carers, adopters, residential care workers and others.

This reflection will help establish whether the support and culture of the agency are positive and strong enough to hold and support the practitioner and if the practitioner is positive and strong enough to hold and contain the family to promote the change required. This is model coherency.

3. Which lens is being utilised?

   Disability/ability
   Sex (physiological): male, female, intersex
   Gender (identity, cultural, socioeconomic): female, male, non-binary, transgender, genderqueer, gender fluid et al.
   Sexuality.
   Race or ethnicity.
   Faith.
   Role: foster carer, adopter, parent, social worker, therapist, caregiver, care-provider, educator/teacher, psychologist, mental health practitioner, health provider et al.
   Socioeconomic status.
   Political views.
   Trauma informed.
   Cognitive/emotional.
   Parent/non-parent, type of parent.
   Or as a sibling, non-sibling, etc.
   Ability to acknowledge the lens and widen it to ensure that there is no restriction caused by becoming restricted by a given and chosen lens(es). If in tune with one's own lens, then there is a greater chance there will be increased attunement to others to observe the lens(es) others use, which then may contribute to beliefs and world view. From this position, there is a chance to become a conduit for change.
   These three components are the foundation of model coherency self-awareness in Volume 1. These principles can now be seen to be the foundation of this and any child, family, or adult assessment.

4. The children's context

   It is not helpful to simply look at the child(ren's) behaviours or presentation. These must be seen within the context of their individual and sibling situations.

Table 8.3 Assessment: Siblings Context

Factor	Assessment Components: The Sibling's Context		
	Positive	Of Concern	
		Impacts Mostly on Others	Impacts Mostly on Self
Family of Origin			
Parent 'A'*			
Parent's experience: This information is gathered from parent and other sources. Look out for inconsistencies in information given. How much of these experiences still inform or impact on behaviour and relationships now. If not why not?	*Circumstances of conception:* Wished for and/or planned child, accepted.	*Circumstances of conception:* Accessory, ownership, unwanted or born of rape.	*Circumstances of conception:* Unexpected, unplanned, unprepared.
	Pregnancy: Positive, uncomplicated, and supported pregnancy.	*Pregnancy:* Stressful and/or negative pregnancy experience with complications, D/V, drug/alcohol use.	*Pregnancy:* Unaware of pregnancy, in denial, lack of support, lack of antenatal care.
	Name: The source was mutually agreed, had meaning, either personally, spiritually, generationally and/or fit the child.	*Name:* The source was negative, had a sense of ownership, entitlement, or control. May reflect negative archetypes.	*Name:* Unimportant, misspelt, suggests sentimentality or indifference. Impact of name change as a result of adoption or relocation.

(Continued)

Table 8.3 (Continued)

Factor	Assessment Components: The Sibling's Context		
	Positive	Of Concern	
Family of Origin		Impacts Mostly on Others	Impacts Mostly on Self
Parent 'A'*	**Attachment:** Secure	**Attachment:** Disorganised	**Attachment:** Insecure Avoidant or Insecure Ambivalent.
	Family Support: Positive family support Love and nurture High warmth, low criticism. Consistency Positive role models External support. Generational continuity Highly protective influences Overcomes adversity and builds resilience.	**Family Support:** Negative dangerous family. Frightening caregiver. Low warmth high criticism. Multiple ACEs. Physical abuse. Sexual abuse. Emotional abuse. Neglect. Parental mental health issues. Parental drug or alcohol use. Divorce. Incarceration. Presentation is Suspicious and/or hyper-vigilant. Love, appreciation and praise are conditional on behaviour and/or performance. The bar may be constantly raised, always being set too high and/or just out of reach, so they never achieve praise, acknowledgement or celebration. May have been controlled, belittled or bullied and any vulnerabilities they show are used against them.	**Family Support:** Ambivalent, neglectful or absent family. Frightened care giver. Low warmth high criticism. Enmeshed relationships. Co-dependency. Disability: physical, cognitive. Health issues. Anxious presentation. Resentful. Negative outlook. ACEs present. Presence of childhood psychopathology and/or unsupported neurodivergence. Parent/s were present with a positive attachment and met child's needs in early development but a sudden loss either through psychological separation (parental mental health or death) left the child emotionally and psychologically shaken and without repair. Lacked the appropriate emotional support or nourishment. The parents were misattuned or laissez-faire.

(Continued)

Table 8.3 (Continued)

Factor	Assessment Components: The Sibling's Context		
	Positive	Of Concern	
		Impacts Mostly on Others	Impacts Mostly on Self
Family of Origin			
Parent 'A'*	**IWM:** Positive Internal working model.	**IWM:** Negative Internal working model.	**IWM:** Negative Internal working model.
	Identity: Positive across domains: gender, race, sexuality, genetic gifts, ability, intellectual acumen, sporting prowess, artistic bent, emotional literacy, physical, emotional and mental health, humility and balance. Parental, familial and friendship involvement in celebrations.	**Identity:** Negative across many domains: gender, race, sexuality beliefs. Genetic gifts are pushed (greenhouse children) or belittled. Ego is inflated or deflated.	**Identity:** Conflicted identity: Negative across many domains: gender beliefs and/or gender, body dysmorphia. Intellectual, sporting, artistic and social challenges.
	Sibling experience: Treated equally but offset by chronological age, development and need. Healthy attachment relationships.	**Sibling experience:** Differential treatment; favoured or scapegoated child. Neglected or abused. Insecure, controlling, skewed, or trauma bonded.	**Sibling experience:** Differential treatment; favoured or scapegoated child. Neglected. Insecure, controlled, skewed, or trauma bonded.
	Locus of Control: Internal. Knows and understands that bad/negative things happen but that bad/negative things happen and that these things will pass – adversity is manageable. Develops resilience.	**Locus of Control:** External. Believes if people knew what they needed or wanted; they would try and stop them securing this need. Often have skewed needs that do not benefit, disadvantage and/or will hurt others i.e., sexual harm, criminal, exploit other's vulnerability, harm animals, or use others to further their own position).	**Locus of Control:** External: Believed that they will be re-harmed. That others are inherently unsafe or dangerous. Feel helpless at the mercy and vagaries of others and that it is not if but when they will be revictimised.

(Continued)

Table 8.3 (Continued)

	Assessment Components: The Sibling's Context		
Factor	Positive	Of Concern	
Family of Origin		Impacts Mostly on Others	Impacts Mostly on Self
Parent 'A'*			
Parent's presentation as a child	**Temperament:** 'Easy' child, balanced activity level, can stay on age specific task. Shows an ability to be intense. There is a regularity and consistency to their positive presentation. When this differs, the reason is understandable. Has a sensory threshold that can be challenged and developed. Can manage proximity changes with both approach and withdrawal well. Is highly adaptable. In the face of adversity shows an ability for persistence but not across all areas. Generally positive mood but can vary under understandable conditions.	**Temperament:** 'Difficult' child, High activity level, regularly distracted off task. Often hyper-driven and overfocused – age specific. Can be highly intense. There is either a regularity and consistency to their presentation (positive or negative) and when this differs the reason is often hard to see or not easily understandable. Has a sensory threshold that cannot be challenged or developed easily and maybe compromised in many areas. Can manage proximity changes with both approach and withdrawal well on their terms only. The child is highly controlling and struggles with adaptability. May be seen to dysregulate easily with a tendency to hyper-arousal causing an impact on others and themselves. In the face of adversity may show some persistence or may become highly controlling. Generally hard to read their mood or their mood is incongruent.	**Temperament:** 'Slow to warm up' child, low activity level, struggles to be motivated to undertake task. Shows little intensity. There is no regularity or consistency to their positive presentation and when this differs the reason is often hard to see or not easily understandable. The child has a severely restricted sensory threshold that cannot be challenged or developed easily. Struggles to manage both approach and withdrawal proximity changes. Has little or no adaptability. Will be seen to dysregulate easily with a tendency to hypo-arousal or hyper-arousal causing an impact on themselves. In the face of adversity shows little or compromised ability to persist. May give up or not even start. Generally low mood or their mood is incongruent.

(Continued)

Table 8.3 (Continued)

Factor	Assessment Components: The Sibling's Context		
	Positive	Of Concern	
		Impacts Mostly on Others	Impacts Mostly on Self
Family of Origin			
Parent 'A'*	**Balanced behaviour:** Can face adversity, may seek help, support or advice. Can hold their ground, be aware of their limits and boundaries.	**Externalises behaviour:** Angry, aggressive, confrontative, resistant, nnon-compliant. May use substances to enhance their sense of control. Will manipulate their surroundings for a greater sense of control.	**Internalises behaviour:** Holds everything in. The level of rage the externaliser gives out is equal to the pain the internaliser holds in. May self-harm or demonstrate self-destructive behaviour with unhealthy or dangerous lifestyles. May self-medicate or self-soothe with significant tension reducing behaviours or tics. Suicidal ideation or behaviour is possible.
	Sensory Processing/Sensorimotor: The system is integrated (sometimes referred to as accurate interpretation or effective registration). A healthy or integrated system is where the sensory systems have joined up and work together to process what is experienced. The information is received (largely) from 7 senses: **Visual** (ability to interpret what is seen),	**Sensory Processing/Sensorimotor:** May manipulate their surroundings to participate in conversations or activities in which they excel and avoid those where they struggle. May be overactive in situations requiring less energy. May present as bored. May hide their inability to develop new skills. Control individual, group and social relationships. May be rigid, OCD, process orientated/driven, concrete, comfortable with routine and procedure and struggle with nouveau, change, spontaneity, the unusual	**Sensory Processing/Sensorimotor:** May have poor attention or a decreased attention span. May discombobulate when stressed or involved in an activity which heightens others awareness of their difference. This may be seen in oppositional, defiant, antisocial, distractible or distracting behaviour. May be underactive in situations that require more energy. May seem bored or lethargic. May struggle or resist learning new skills or struggle retaining new information.

(Continued)

No Foregone Conclusions 111

Table 8.3 (Continued)

Assessment Components: The Sibling's Context

Factor	Positive	Of Concern	
		Impacts Mostly on Others	Impacts Mostly on Self
Family of Origin			
Parent 'A'*	**Auditory** (what is heard), **Gustatory** (what is tasted), **Olfactory** (what is smelled), **Tactile** (what is felt – physically), **Proprioceptive** (what is experienced by different parts of the body at the same time – e.g., muscles, bones, tendons, nerves at the same time) and **Vestibular** (balance and movement). Seen as developmentally observant, descriptive, interested, curious, dextrous, able, confident, can regulate and/or be regulated, hold attention, process, organise, decipher Can do and co coordinate their bodies, limbs, thoughts and activities, they are coordinated and can coordinate. Can take information, process, analyse, recall and respond. Are expressive, descriptive, communicative, eloquent. Are aware of and can express themselves to have their needs, desires and dreams shared, their needs met and their wants conveyed. Can play, study, emote, socialise, move and meet the world with relative ease. Will appear relatively relaxed, coordinated and dextrous and deft.	or the unexpected. May be emotionally stunted. Anxiety is hidden by control. Movement is enjoyed when it has a purpose (sport, improving skills, competitive outcomes and remaining ahead of peers). Rigidity in body when routine, expectations increases.	May struggle in, resist or avoid individual, group or social relationships. May be uncomfortable in their own skin be dyspraxic, dyslexic (all fingers and thumbs, fall over themselves, tie themselves up in knots etc). May struggle emotionally, be over or under emotional. Anxiety is debilitating. May be over or under-reactive to stimulation such as sight, sound, touch, textures, temperature, relationships. May be uncomfortable in their own skin be dyspraxic, dyslexic (all fingers and thumbs, fall over themselves, tie themselves up in knots etc). May struggle emotionally, be over or under emotional. Anxiety is debilitating. May be over or under-reactive to stimulation such as sight, sound, touch, textures, temperature, relationships. May lack muscle tone, be disinterested, emotionally or cognitively absent or be misattuned with themselves or others. Behaviour seems out of kilter, unbalanced, chaotic, distant or lack management and regulation. May lack emotional, cognitive and physiological integration, connectivity or awareness. Coordination, body awareness, play and language may be compromised.

(Continued)

Table 8.3 (Continued)

Factor	Assessment Components: The Sibling's Context		
	Positive	Of Concern	
		Impacts Mostly on Others	Impacts Mostly on Self
Family of Origin			
Parent 'A'*	**Boundaries and Limits:** Can hold the line. Is aware of their own and other's personal space. Knows when to argue their point and push and when to capitulate and acquiesce. Can seek help and support. Understands that rules are for safety and that rules can change under specific situations, bedtimes are later at weekends, or you can party harder and rest more during holidays than term-time.	**Boundaries and Limits:** Pushes boundaries and moves into others personal space. Uses people for their own ends and moves on when the person is no longer of use. Uses their power and control to enhance the chances of achieving their desired outcomes. Believes they are exempt from rules or that rules are primarily for others. May not push rules if thinking they may get caught. Can regulate to increase the chances of their desired outcomes.	**Boundaries and Limits:** Have little or no awareness of their own rights over their bodies, needs, or right to live and function in the world. Rules are impossible to understand as rules have been broken or are unaware that what has happened to them was wrong. May fear coming into proximity asking for help and support but cannot prevent others coming into proximity with them.
	Window of Tolerance: Wide and containing. Can manage stress but can ask for help when stress increases (such as: exams, health issues or bereavement).	**Window of Tolerance:** May seem wide but the individual is controlling their environment. May be vigilant, OCD and/or controlled. May lack flexibility. When they exit their WOT, they are more likely to exit into hyper-arousal and the signs may be more noticeable, extreme, aggressive, violent to others or themselves, outwardly controlling of others or themselves or dysregulated. May bounce between hypo and hyper-arousal.	**Window of Tolerance:** Narrow window of tolerance. On exiting their window, they are more likely to tend to hypo-arousal, with low affect, dissociate, 'crash,' appear catatonic with low mood, low self-worth, low energy, apathy.

(Continued)

Table 8.3 (Continued)

Factor	Assessment Components: The Sibling's Context		
	Positive	Of Concern	
Family of Origin		Impacts Mostly on Others	Impacts Mostly on Self
Parent 'A'*	**Attachment Style:** Secure **Belief System:** Core beliefs that are life enhancing and generally positive. These beliefs cover: Responsibility: I am and can be loveable, worthy, deserving, capable, attractive. I did or do the best I could, I tried, I learned. Safety: I can feel, be trusted, trust, choose, learn, be safe. Control: I'm strong, I have choices, support, I can succeed with or without support, I am capable.	**Attachment Style:** Disorganised **Belief System:** Generally negative or false ppositive beliefs. These beliefs cover: Responsibility, I am or can be bad, powerful and in control, perfect, misunderstood). I did or do something, but someone should have stopped me, it was their fault, blame others and deny. Safety: I cannot trust anyone, show emotions or trust my judgement. Control: I am safe when I'm in control and when I have neutralised vulnerability in myself and others.	**Attachment Style:** Avoidant/ ambivalent. **Belief System:** Limiting beliefs. These beliefs cover: Responsibility, I am or can be undeserving, worthless, damaged, not good enough, ugly, stupid, unlovable. I did or do nothing Safety: I cannot protect myself, show emotions, trust myself or my judgement. Control: I have no control, I'm not safe, I'm inadequate, helpless and hopeless.
	Regulation: Can self-regulate or be socially regulated when required.	**Regulation:** May appear regulated but this must not be confused with healthy regulation. Look for signs of control, hyper-vigilance, and tension. May need social regulation but will seek to avoid or draw the attention of others. May seek the attention of others, but on their terms.	**Regulation:** May struggle to self-regulate or be socially regulated. Are emotionally overwhelmed.

(Continued)

Table 8.3 (Continued)

Factor	Assessment Components: The Sibling's Context		
	Positive	Of Concern	
		Impacts Mostly on Others	Impacts Mostly on Self
Family of Origin			
Parent 'A'*	**Chronological age:** In synchrony with developmental age. Developmental stages cognitive, physiological, psychological, emotional, biological, neurological, and sexual are on track in most areas or exceeded.	**Chronological age:** Out of synchrony with developmental age. Trauma has impacted on health, genetic, birth, physical, learning, or emotional adversity. Signs of significant child psychopathology causing disruption across many or all developmental domains: cognitive, physiological, psychological, emotional, biological, neurological, and sexual.	**Chronological age:** Out of synchrony with developmental age. Signs of child psychopathology causing disruption across many developmental domains: cognitive, physiological, psychological, emotional, biological, neurological, and sexual.
	Presentation: Achieved in some or many subjects. Emotionally literate Cognitively gifted, able or coping Physically gifted, able or adaptive Behaviour and presentation adaptive to positive. Adversities have been counteracted and supported early.	**Presentation:** Confrontational. Uncooperative. Neglected. Abused. Perhaps feral. Angry/violent. Bullies others. Potentially disorganised. Cognitively gifted but undirected or unsupported. Presence of childhood psychopathology/unsupported neurodivergence, ADHD, ODD. Avoidant, dissociated, fragmented or in parts.	**Presentation:** Neglected or abused. Appearance either neglected or immaculate appearance. Masked. Compliant. Dissociative. Bullied. Insecure. Failed at many or most subjects appeared to be learning disabled or paradoxically excelled educationally but appeared emotionally absent. Cognitively challenged, learning disability. Presence of childhood psychopathology and unsupported neurodivergence: e.g., OCD, depression, anxiety.

(Continued)

Table 8.3 (Continued)

Factor	Assessment Components: The Sibling's Context		
	Positive	Of Concern	
Family of Origin	Impacts Mostly on Others	Impacts Mostly on Self	
Parent 'A'*			
	Character Strategies: Balanced: In some form of education/apprenticeship or for young adults; employed, self, employed, perhaps entrepreneurial, caring, or vocational role, artistic or creative, nature inspired or explorer. Some level of faith/belief/spirituality in nature, art, place in the world.	**Character Strategies: Self-reliant:** High powered role, entrepreneurial, sometimes political, criminal. **Charming-manipulative:** May present as entertaining, ingratiating, charming, understanding, charismatic, interested but they have an agenda and want something out of relationships, exchanges or communications, it is definitely conditional. This can be seen in entrepreneurial and political worlds as well as offending behaviour. Safety is in the lack of direct expression and a reliance of charm, misdirection, innuendo and manipulation.	**Character Strategies: Sensitive withdrawn:** Child has no trust in the world or caregivers. Internally they are fearful, highly sensitive and suspicious of the motivation of others and as a result be hyper-vigilant. May hold back or present as introverted. May present as standoffish or absent. **Sensitive emotional:** Is left desperate for help but cannot be soothed or is soothed and then requires constant reassurance. May present as clingy. **Dependent-endearing:** May present as younger than their age, particularly in adulthood where they may sound or appear childlike.

(Continued)

Table 8.3 (Continued)

Factor	Assessment Components: The Sibling's Context		
	Positive	Of Concern	
		Impacts Mostly on Others	Impacts Mostly on Self
Family of Origin			
Parent 'A'*		**Tough-Generous:** The need for mastery is a critical stage of latency, the period of around 6–12 where there is a need to achieve and become proficient in managing the environment. But because of their experiences they are overwhelmed by shame and if mirrored by peers can become overwhelmed by feelings of inferiority. This vulnerability is hidden by ego. The child presents as invulnerable, becomes pseudo-parentified and takes care of others by blunting their own feelings making them feel powerful. This can be seen as angry and controlling or benevolent but because it stems from the same drive – it becomes conditional.	**Self-reliant:** Avoids the support of others but may well support others. They may struggle to connect in relationships. Deprivation is feared and therefore seeks to meet their own needs. Others cannot be relied upon so they develop fierce independence even when they are sufficiently developed to be independent.

(Continued)

Table 8.3 (Continued)

Factor	Assessment Components: The Sibling's Context		
	Positive	Of Concern	
		Impacts Mostly on Others	Impacts Mostly on Self
Family of Origin			
Parent 'A'*		**Industrious-Overfocused:** The child never feels good enough, they seem to be committed to the project, perfectionist and perhaps denigrating of those that don't strive but internally they do not feel good enough, they do not belong and do not deserve to be at the table. They may become rigid and orcontrolling.	**Charming-Manipulative:** May be ingratiating or chameleonesque. **Burdened enduring:** Pseudo-parentified child, meets their parents needs through fear of consequences or siblings needs as they hold the belief they are responsible for their survival. Their acceptance in the world is dependent only on the condition they serve others.They may present as compliant but internally they may be irritated, become passive aggressive or resistant to change. **Industrious-Overfocused:** May work hard not to be seen, excel in maths (no emotion is required in maths) etc., may present as a perfect child (it's exhausting being perfect). **Expressive clinging:** They dramatise to keep people engaged and attentive. Can be chaotic, excitable, ambivalent, demonstrative or avoidant.

(Continued)

Table 8.3 (Continued)

Factor	Assessment Components: The Sibling's Context		
	Positive	Of Concern	
		Impacts Mostly on Others	Impacts Mostly on Self
Family of Origin			
Parent 'A'*	**Communication Content:** Coherent with the situation.	**Communication Content:** Controls the subject matter, distracts, prevaricates, dismisses, denies, fabricates, blames.	**Communication Content:** May struggle with recall, coherency and truth. Content maybe stunted, vague, guarded or confused. May steer to non-descriptive language such as 'what do you mean?' 'I don't know/remember', fine, ok, alright etc.
	Volume: Confident, appropriate to situation ability to regulate and modulate. Authoritative.	**Volume:** May over power listener, shout, raise their voice or use quiet speech to bring the listener closer in proximity to an uncomfortable degree or to create doubt or confusion. This is controlling in nature. May have a roughness to the quality of the voice.	**Volume:** May lack confidence, whisper, become mute or become fragmented in speech. May have breaks in the voice.
	Rhythm: Associated with a relaxed upbeat and generally positive outlook interspersed with periods of low affect or anxiety. Ability to experience and manage all human emotions.	**Rhythm:** May be associated with control, stress, over emphasis or fixed speech.	**Rhythm:** Stress impacts on rhythm as does anxiety. May speak faster or slower.

(Continued)

Table 8.3 (Continued)

Factor	Assessment Components: The Sibling's Context		
	Positive	Of Concern	
Family of Origin		Impacts Mostly on Others	Impacts Mostly on Self
Parent 'A'*	**Tone:** Likely to be positive and upbeat. Have energy and motivate the listener to pay attention. **Pitch:** Modulates and is within the expected range. The sound is coherent with the age and gender of the person. **Prosody:** The patterns of rhythm and sound. Able to modulate variations in duration, intensity that impact on the message being conveyed.	**Tone:** Can be controlling in its presentation or manipulative. This can be anything from charming intent to controlling at the other end of the spectrum. **Pitch:** May be much deeper or higher than expected. The older adolescent or young adult may sound like a younger child particularly in females (little girl voice). It is not confined to gender. **Prosody:** Impaired emotional prosody. May emphasise anger, disgust and negative emotion, may manipulate or control using language that may lack empathy.	**Tone:** May be flatter with less articulation. Possibility of a monotonous tone. Is likely to show a flat affect. May have a negative tone of voice. **Pitch:** May show signs of developmental delay or developmental arrest. There pitch may fail, vary or become stuck. **Prosody:** Impaired emotional prosody. An increased severity of childhood trauma is associated with reduced accuracy on the discrimination task and with slower identification of emotional prosody. Exposure to childhood trauma is associated with long-term, atypical development in the interpretation of prosodic cues in speech. The findings have implications for the intergenerational transmission of trauma. May sigh, grunt, pause and speed.

(Continued)

Table 8.3 (Continued)

Factor	Assessment Components: The Sibling's Context		Of Concern
	Positive	Impacts Mostly on Others	Impacts Mostly on Self

Family of Origin

Parent 'A'*

	Intonation: Ability to modulate affect, be authoritative, questioning, uncertain, excited, anxious within expected parameters.	**Intonation:** Angry, controlling, or forceful.	**Intonation:** Regression can be an expected outcome of trauma in children and can be a coping strategy in traumatised adults. A childlike voice is not uncommon.
	Breath: Relaxed, rhythmic, deep. **Facial expression:** Relaxed state, range of affect, can slide appropriately from one emotional range to another without inhibition.	**Breath:** Stressed, forced maybe shallow. **Facial expression:** Clenched jaw, furrowed brow or forehead, tension in tongue, throat and neck.	**Breath:** May be shallow, imperceptible, breathe from high in the chest. **Facial expression:** Maybe expressionless, dissociative, avoidant, uncertain
	Eye contact: Can hold and vary eye contact duration and depth of eye contact whilst showing a range of emotions.	**Eye contact:** Threatening or avoidant eye contact. May use eye contact to persuade or manipulate. May seem very self-assured with an edge.	**Eye contact:** Avoidant or show uncertainty in eye contact. It may show vulnerability, uncertainty or lack of self-esteem.
	Body Language: Relaxed and fluid. No or rare signs of tension reducing behaviours. May seem dextrous, organised, connected.	**Body language:** Rigid, ready for action (fight/flight symptoms), tense, arms, legs, stomach, and hands. High tension reducing behaviours.	**Body Language:** May be rigid and tense (flight mode) or flop (lack of muscle tone/given up, postural collapse, hypo-arousal, head down. May appear to be relaxed but this is defeated.

(Continued)

Table 8.3 (Continued)

Factor	Assessment Components: The Sibling's Context			
	Positive	Of Concern		
Family of Origin		Impacts Mostly on Others	Impacts Mostly on Self	
Parent 'A'*	**Self-care:** Well kempt, pride in appearance. High standard of care and/or self-care. Clean well looked after clothes. Signs of good health, exercise, interests and diet.	**Self-care:** May be immaculate, controlled, pristine and very precise (OCD) or may lack positive markers as they are focused elsewhere.	**Self-care:** May present as neglected, self-neglect, 'pinched'/sallow (poor/inadequate diet, poor health opportunities/ill-health or poorly managed health conditions). May overeat, binge or under eat/restrictive diet.	
	Common behavioural or presentation markers.	**Common behavioural or presentation markers.**	**Common behavioural or presentation markers.**	
	Honesty: Presents in an open, relaxed, forthcoming manner. Can disagree and argue a point. Is able to say that they don't know and can ask for help.	**Honesty:** Fabrication or lying to manipulate or mislead. May ask for information but this is for a pre-planned reason. Information is power.	**Honesty:** May lie, may lie about everything, may not know the truth or may not know the difference between a lie and the truth. Lying is for self-protection or a belief that they are not enough as they are.	
	Eating/Food: Copes with a balanced diet, a sufficient amount of food, range of foods, temperatures, textures, sweetness, sourness, dryness, moisture content. Is adventurous in trying new foods, mixtures of textures and types of food within their religious or dietary restrictions.	**Eating/Food:** Controls food restricts the type and quantity of food. Mealtimes are a trigger point and may become incendiary. Violence and aggression may occur. May control intake, anorexia at one extreme, may never feel sated bulimia at another extreme.	**Eating/Food:** Food may bring fear. Food may symbolise lack of care, bribery, payment, neglect etc. May respond to food with faddy or picky eating, gorging or hording food in the bedroom. may crave food but struggle to eat it. May be psychologically physiologically unable to eat or swallow and may have a gag reflex. May induce nausea, may eat very slowly or very fast. May struggle with cutlery, textures, temperatures, mixtures etc.	

(Continued)

Table 8.3 (Continued)

Factor	Assessment Components: The Sibling's Context		
	Positive	Of Concern	
		Impacts Mostly on Others	Impacts Mostly on Self
Family of Origin			
Parent 'A'*	**Transition and Change:** Has experienced few transitions and changes. Where change has been necessary this has either been well planned and prepared and the child has been carefully primed or the changes have been part of the child's culture, such as travelling families where significant parts of the child's family, extended family and friends move together. Care should be taken over assessing the impact of children in the military, the ministry or boarding school where change and/or separation may have positive or negative consequences. They may present as emotionally balanced but equally may present as pseudo-adultified or overly self-assured, traits that can be seen as positive in some parts of society.	**Transition and Change:** Running away with a parent from domestic violence is positive as it is escaping a dangerous situation, but the impact of being with a desperate and scared parent is still scary. Running away from the law (criminal activity), or Local Authority intervention (safeguarding, child protection and family proceedings) both harbour desperation and fear and therefore being with scared (maybe presenting as angry) parent/s has a similar impact. Each change may have an impact on loss, the loss of family, friends, schools, teachers, peers, learning, geography, culture, consistency, familiarity and a host of other knowns. May present as emotionally stunted or emotionally illiterate cold, rigid, extrovert (but this may lack coherency).	**Transition and Change:** Change has been ill-prepared, not considered and may be experienced as a lack of care or importance such as neglect. The impact of change has been frightening for the child, they may dissociate become over-emotional, clingy, ambivalent or avoidant. They may become insular, introverted, shy and lack the tools and social literacy to engage, respond or communicate with others.

(Continued)

No Foregone Conclusions   123

Table 8.3 (Continued)

Factor	Assessment Components: The Sibling's Context		
	Positive	Of Concern	
Family of Origin		Impacts Mostly on Others	Impacts Mostly on Self
Parent 'A'*			
	Night-time:Dreams: Has dreams that they can process by talking to a parent, drawing or playing through. May experience some nightmares but response to parental support and reassurance.	**Night-time:Night Terrors:** Child is distraught when wakes. May wet or soil the bed, be sweaty, disorientated and scream or shout out. In very severe cases the child may appear awake with all the above symptoms but be unresponsive. They do not respond to reassurance – It feels they are reliving something.	**Night-time:Nightmares:** Child may wet the bed, be distraught on waking or even hide their fear but their terror may be visible. They may be sweaty and/or disorientated and may or may not respond to reassurance.
	Night-time Routine: Manages routines, hygiene (bath/shower, teeth cleaning, face wash etc) with or without support, reduction in screen time before bed, snack, drink, toileting, bedtime story, lights out etc. Can manage the differences between weekends, holidays and weekday routines.	**Night-time Routine:** Is oppositional, defiant, aggressive. Pushes boundaries, ignores limits and controls. May manage hygiene may push back nurture or displays of care and nurture. May go slow, demand attention or push it away or both.	**Night-time Routine:** May be fearful, may need or reject proximity and care. May refuse food or horde food. May struggle with hygiene, be fearful of being left alone or in relationship. May struggle with story time. Maybe fearful of the dark or what the dark brings.
	Toileting: No difficulty in recognising need and supporting self. Manages or can seek support. Actively manages hygiene routines or seeks help to do this.	**Toileting:** May use the toilet as control. Scatological behaviours. Smears on walls, towels, door handles. Hides faeces in clothing, draws, cupboards etc. Urinates on carpets, walls, in containers etc. May not feel the signs of need of motion or bladder.	**Toileting:** Toileting is beyond child's control. Nocturnal enuresis Nocturnal encopresis. Diurnal enuresis Diurnal encopresis Doubly or singularly incontinent. Stomach problems such as irritable bowel syndrome (IBS). Diarrhoea or constipation. May not feel the signs of need of motion or bladder.

(Continued)

Table 8.3 (Continued)

Factor	Assessment Components: The Sibling's Context		
	Positive	Of Concern	
		Impacts Mostly on Others	Impacts Mostly on Self
Family of Origin			
Parent 'A'*	**Denial:** Absence of, takes responsibility, manages guilt (does not go to shame), learns from the experience, is open about their mistakes, misdemeanours, and errors, gets things wrong but rarely repeats mistakes. Names what they did. Can describe outcomes for their behaviour (when I do…this puts me and others at risk of …). I can prevent this happening again by…	**Denial:** Denial of understanding (I don't know what you are talking about). Straightforward denial (I didn't do it).	**Denial:** Justification (I did it but…). Dissociation or avoidance or both (I can't remember, but I accept I did…). Acceptance without analysis (I did…).

(Continued)

Table 8.3 (Continued)

Factor	Assessment Components: The Sibling's Context		
	Positive	Of Concern	
Family of Origin		Impacts Mostly on Others	Impacts Mostly on Self
Parent 'A'*	**Play:** Child's ability is developmentally on track. They can play freely, by themselves and with others (where developmentally expected). They show 8 'C's and 5 'P's. They are relaxed. They can play symbolically and in the metaphor. Play is enjoyable in isolation or in connection with others. Play relieves anxiety. Play is spontaneous. They can play through the different developmental stages of play: sensory, sensorimotor, embodiment, projective and role play. They can manage structured play, free and/or non-directive play, outdoor, indoor, competitive, construction, artistic, musical, sport based, dance, movement, rhythmic, risky, sensory, self and other directed as well as collaborative.	**Play:** The child may not play or may not be able to play. Where the child can play they may present as controlling. They may identify as the aggressor. The play may feel real and therefore is not play. Play may promote anxiety. Play may be acceptable if it is competitive. In competitive play, participating but losing does not bring joy. Winning may not bring joy. Winning and mocking the loser may bring joy. The play may revolve around changing rules to ensure they cannot lose. Violence and aggression may be constant themes. There are seldom happy or positive endings. There is a lack of symbolic distancing. Play tends to be concrete. The child may present as stuck. They may be stuck at a specific developmental stage of play if they can play at all.	**Play:** Child is too scared to play, and/or they may not know how to play. The repetition of play provides no relief from the anxiety they experience and yet may continue to replay compulsively. The link between play and reality may remain unconscious and unmetabolised. Play does not relieve anxiety. Play may contain constant themes of hopelessness, helplessness and certain future disaster, re-trauma or further harm. There are seldom happy or positive endings. There is a lack of symbolic distancing. The child may present as stuck. They may be stuck at a specific developmental stage of play if they can play at all.

(Continued)

Table 8.3 (Continued)

Factor	Assessment Components: The Sibling's Context		
	Positive	Impacts Mostly on Others	Impacts Mostly on Self
		Of Concern	
Family of Origin			
Parent 'A'*	8 + 3 'C's: Evidence of: Compassion, Creativity, Connectedness, Clarity, Confidence, Courage, Curiosity and Calm. Also able to show Commitment, Consistency and Contentment.	8 + 'C's: Significantly lacking or compromised in many of the domains: Compassion, Creativity, Connectedness, Clarity, Confidence, Courage, Curiosity and Calm.	8 + 3 'C's: Significantly compromised in one or two or lacking in some of the domains: Compassion, Creativity, Connectedness, Clarity, Confidence, Courage, Curiosity and Calm.
	5 'P's: Presence of: Presence, Patience, Perspective, Persistence, Playfulness.	5 'P's: Significantly lacking or compromised in many of the domains:: Presence, Patience, Perspective, Persistence, Playfulness.	5 'P's: Significantly compromised in one or two or lacking in some of the domain:. Presence, Patience, Perspective, Persistence, Playfulness.
	Levels of Stress or Trauma: Manageable stress and/or responded to the treatment or Type 1 trauma.	**Levels of Stress or Trauma:** High stress, Toxic stress, evidence of Type 1, 2, 3 and/or 4 trauma	**Levels of Stress or Trauma:** High stress, Toxic stress, evidence of Type 1, 2, 3 and or 4 trauma.
	Shame: Little or no evidence of shame as the child can manage feelings of guilt.	**Shame:** Hard to see but the child is working hard to keep feelings of toxic shame hidden through control or rage.	**Shame:** Child is severely compromised by feelings of toxic shame.

(Continued)

Table 8.3 (Continued)

Factor	Assessment Components: The Sibling's Context		
	Positive	Impacts Mostly on Others	Of Concern — Impacts Mostly on Self
Family of Origin			
Parent 'A'*	**Parts:** Presents as balanced with all parts in synchrony. Has some levels of difference, e.g., being on their own, with family, at school or in other social situations there are subtle differences that may enhance comfort over performance for example. In this state the 8 (11) 'C's and 5 'P's will be present.	**Parts: Managers** are to the fore. They are the day-to-day protectors that help deal with difficult situations. However, when they become burdened by having to manage too much adversity they see the emotional reaction as the problem and exile parts of ourselves that they see as vulnerable and unhelpful.	**Parts: Exiles.** These are the parts that are seen to be weak or vulnerable that have been exiled. They tend to be the young parts that have experienced high stress, enduring stress and trauma in their development. They hold the pain, fear and shame. In reality they are shut away for either their protection or a skewed belief that they are also responsible for the harm the system has been experienced. As a result they harbour dependency, rage, terror, isolation, harm, loneliness, the burden and grief to name a few.

(Continued)

Table 8.3 (Continued)

Factor	Assessment Components: The Sibling's Context		
	Positive	Of Concern	
		Impacts Mostly on Others	Impacts Mostly on Self
Family of Origin			
Parent 'A'*		**Firefighters** come to the fore when Managers are overwhelmed or the strategy stops working. Firefighters are essentially protectors who step in when the individual perceives threat to their system or integrity. This threat or danger is either real or perceived (the outcome is the same as it feels real). Firefighters' strength is that is allows people to carry on without worrying about survival, but the downside is that they are personally draining. These protectors may lead to substance use/abuse, binge eating or dietary restrictions, self-harming or hurting behaviour, harmful sex in either HSB, CSE and/or sexual exploitation as an adult (either being coerced or coercing others) being trapped in the sex industry but believing it is a lifestyle or professional choice. These protectors numb. Soothe or distract the individual.	

(Continued)

Table 8.3 (Continued)

	Assessment Components: The Sibling's Context			
	Positive	Of Concern		
Factor		Impacts Mostly on Others	Impacts Mostly on Self	
Family of Origin				
Parent 'A'*				
Parent's relationship with grandparent 1?	Attachment: secure	Attachment: insecure ambivalent or avoidant	Attachment: Insecure Ambivalent AND Avoidant, disorganised	
Parent's relationship with grandparent 2?	Repeat/as above	Repeat/as above	Repeat/as above	
Parents relationship with grand stepparent(s)? repeat as necessary	Repeat/as above	Repeat/as above	Repeat/as above	
Parent relationship with great grandparent(s) repeat as necessary	Repeat/as above	Repeat/as above	Repeat/as above	
Parent relationship with great grand stepparent(s)repeat as necessary	Repeat/as above	Repeat/as above	Repeat/as above	
Parent relationship with foster carer (s–) repeat(s) as necessary	Repeat/as above	Repeat/as above	Repeat/as above	

(Continued)

130 A Trauma Model for Assessing Siblings

Table 8.3 (Continued)

Factor	Assessment Components: The Sibling's Context		
	Positive	Of Concern	
Family of Origin Parent 'A'*		Impacts Mostly on Others	Impacts Mostly on Self
Parent relationship with adoptive parent(s) repeat as necessary	Repeat/as above	Repeat/as above	Repeat/as above
Parent presentation as an adult	**Character Strategies: Balanced:** See previous list	**Character Strategies: Self-reliant** See previous list **Charming-manipulative.** See previous list **Tough – Generous** See previous list **Industrious-Overfocused** See previous list	**Character Strategies: Sensitive withdrawn:** See previous list **Sensitive emotional:** See previous list **Dependent-endearing:** See previous list **Self-reliant:** Sometimes **Charming-Manipulative** Ingratiating **Burdened enduring.** See previous list **Overfocused** or fixated. **Expressive clinging:** Chaotic, ambivalent, avoidant Laissez faire
Geographic safety	Unpolluted Fresh air Access to nature Clean water Active community Community participation Community safety Good travel links High employment rate	High pollution Overcrowded Lack of basic human needs Gang culture and postcode wars. Territorial High deprivation High unemployment Aggressive/violent High crime; including drugs, county lines, exploitation, and sexual exploitation of both children and adults.	Geographically isolated Insular Lack of community, neighbourhood links or support. Closed or rigid outlooks or views. Territorial Oppressed. Low positive role models

(Continued)

No Foregone Conclusions 131

Table 8.3 (Continued)

Factor	Assessment Components: The Sibling's Context			
	Positive	Impacts Mostly on Others	Of Concern	Impacts Mostly on Self
Family of Origin				
Parent 'A'*				
School/ education Nursery	Well-funded Thriving Positive culture Parental participation Achieved primary. Achieved secondary/high. Achieved college/ further education. Mixed gender options Diverse and inclusive Public school education (UK private system) or other 3rd sector education impact: privileged but balanced. Positive peer groups	Toxic Paternalistic, Autocratic Single gender Rundown inner city or limited choice. Success at others expense. Public school education (UK private system) or other 3rd sector education impact: elitist or entitled. Influential peer groups/in-crowd	Rundown Isolated ideology Lack of choice Lack of representation Lack of open/multifaith celebration, recognition Public school education (UK private system) or other 3rd sector education impact: isolated, rejected, abandoned, sometimes referred to as 'rich man's care.'Marginalised	
School/ education Primary	Repeat/as above	Repeat/as above	Repeat/as above	
School/ education Secondary/ High	Repeat/as above	Repeat/as above	Repeat/as above	
School/ education College/ further education/ apprenticeship	Repeat/as above	Repeat/as above	Repeat/as above	
School/ education University	Repeat/as above	Repeat/as above	Repeat/as above	

(Continued)

Table 8.3 (Continued)

Factor	Assessment Components: The Sibling's Context			
	Positive		Of Concern	
		Impacts Mostly on Others		Impacts Mostly on Self
Family of Origin				
Parent 'A'*				
Sibling relationship with sibling B and sibling B's views if different	Repeat/as above	Repeat/as above	Repeat/as above	Repeat/as above
Sibling relationship with sibling C and sibling C's views if different	Repeat/as above	Repeat/as above	Repeat/as above	Repeat/as above
Sibling B's relationship with sibling C and sibling Cs views if different	Repeat/as above	Repeat/as above	Repeat/as above	Repeat/as above
Sibling A, B, and C's relationship as a sibling group	Repeat/as above	Repeat/as above	Repeat/as above	Repeat/as above

Table 8.4 The Child

Assessment Components: The Child/ren

Factor	Positive		Of Concern	
Child 'A' (name)				
Child's experience	**Circumstances of conception:** Wished for and/or planned child, accepted.	**Circumstances of conception:**	**Circumstances of conception:** Accessory, ownership, unwanted or born of rape.	**Circumstances of conception:** Unexpected, unplanned, unprepared.
	Pregnancy: Positive, uncomplicated, and supported pregnancy		**Pregnancy:** Stressful and/or negative pregnancy experience with complications, D/V, drug/alcohol use.	**Pregnancy:** Unaware of pregnancy, in denial, Maternal mental health issues, lack of support, lack of antenatal care.
	Name: The source was mutually agreed, had meaning, either personally, spiritually, generationally and/or fit the child.		**Name:** The source was negative, had a sense of ownership, entitlement, or control. May reflect negative archetypes.	**Name:** Unimportant, misspelt, suggested sentimentality or indifference. Impact of name change as a result of adoption or relocation.
	Attachment: Secure		**Attachment:** Disorganised	**Attachment:** Insecure Avoidant or Insecure Ambivalent.

(Continued)

134 A Trauma Model for Assessing Siblings

Table 8.4 (Continued)

Assessment Components: The Child/ren

Factor	Positive	Of Concern
Child 'A' (name)	**Family Support:** Positive family support Love and nurture High warmth, low criticism. Consistency Positive role models External support. Generational continuity Highly protective influences Overcoming adversity and builds resilience	**Family Support:** Negative dangerous family. Frightening caregiver. Low warmth high criticism. Multiple ACEs Physical abuse Sexual abuse Emotional abuse Neglect Parental mental health issues Parental drug or alcohol use Divorce incarceration presentation as suspicious, hyper-vigilant. Love, appreciation and praise is conditional on behaviour and/or performance. The bar may be constantly raised, always being set too high and/or just out of reach, so they never achieve praise, acknowledgement or celebration. They may have been controlled, belittled or bullied and any vulnerabilities they show are used against them. Differential treatment: favoured
	IWM: Positive Internal working model.	**IWM:** Negative Internal working model.
		Family Support: Ambivalent, neglectful or absent family. Frightened care giver Low warmth high criticism. Enmeshed relationships Co-dependency Disability: physical, cognitive Health issues Anxious presentation Resentful Negative outlook ACEs present Presence of childhood psychopathology/ unsupported neurodivergence. Parent/s were present with a positive attachment and met child's needs in early development but a sudden loss either through psychological separation (parental mental health or death) left the child emotionally and psychologically shaken. Lacked the appropriate emotional support or nourishment. The parents were misattuned or laissez-faire. Differential treatment: scapegoated
		IWM: Negative Internal working model.

(Continued)

Table 8.4 (Continued)

Assessment Components: The Child/ren

Factor	Positive	Of Concern
Child 'A' (name)	**Identity:** Positive. Across domains: gender, race, sexuality, genetic gifts, ability, intellectual acumen, sporting prowess, artistic bent, emotional literacy, physical, emotional and mental health, humility and balance. Parental, familial and friendship involvement in celebrations. **Sibling experience:** Treated equally but offset by chronological age, development and need. Healthy attachment relationships	**Identity:** Negative Across many domains: gender, race, sexuality beliefs. Genetic gifts are pushed (greenhouse children) or belittled. Ego is inflated or deflated. **Sibling experience:** Differential treatment; favoured or scapegoated child. Neglected or abused. Insecure, controlling, skewed or trauma bonded.	**Identity:** Conflicted identity: Negative. Across many domains: gender beliefs and/or gender, body dysmorphia. Intellectual, sporting, artistic and social challenges. **Sibling experience:** Differential treatment; favoured or scapegoated child. Neglected. Insecure, controlled, skewed or Trauma bonded.
Child's relationship with parent 1	Repeat/as above	Repeat/as above	Repeat/as above
Child's relationship with parent 2	Repeat/as above	Repeat/as above	Repeat/as above
Child's relationship with parent			

(Continued)

Table 8.4 (Continued)

Assessment Components: The Child/ren

Factor	Positive	Of Concern
Child 'A' (name)		
This quality of relationship must be repeated with each grandparent, step-grandparent et al. Where families have been broken it is not unusual for a child other people who were 'parental relatives.		
Child's Presentation at home and also in each 'home placement' e.g. grandparents, foster, adoptive.	**Locus of Control:** Internal. Knows and understands that bad/negative things happen but that bad/negative things happen and that these things will pass – adversity (manageable) develops resilience.	**Locus of Control:** External. Believe if people knew what they wanted, they would try and stop them securing this need (often skewed needs that don't benefit, disadvantage or hurt others i.e. sexual harm, criminal, exploit others vulnerability, harm animals, or use others to further their own position)
		Locus of Control: External: believes that they will be re-harmed that others are inherently unsafe or dangerous. They feel helpless at the vagaries of others and that it is not if but when they will be revictimised.

(Continued)

Table 8.4 (Continued)

Assessment Components: The Child/ren

Factor	Positive	Of Concern
Child 'A' (name)	**Temperament:** 'Easy child,' balanced activity level, can stay on task – age specific, shows an ability to be intense. There is a regularity and consistency to their positive presentation and when this differs the reason is understandable. The child has a sensory threshold that can be challenged and developed. Can manage proximity changes with both approach and withdrawal well. The child is highly adaptable. In the face of adversity shows an ability to persistence but not across all areas. Generally positive mood but can vary under understandable conditions.	**Temperament:** 'Difficult child,' High activity level, regularly distracted off task often or hyper-driven and overfocused – age specific. Can be highly intense. There is either a regularity and consistency to their presentation (positive or negative) and when this differs the reason is often hard to see or not easily understandable. The child has a sensory threshold that cannot be challenged or developed easily and maybe compromised in many areas. Can manage proximity changes with both approach and withdrawal well on their terms only. The child is highly controlling and struggles with adaptability. May be seen to dysregulate easily with a tendency to hyper-arousal causing an impact on those around them and themselves. In the face of adversity may show an ability to persistence or may become highly controlling. Generally hard to read their mood or their mood is incongruent.	**Temperament:** 'Slow to warm up child,' low activity level, struggles to be motivated to undertake task. Shows little intensity. There is no regularity or consistency to their positive presentation and when this differs the reason is often hard to see or not easily understandable. The child has a severely restricted sensory threshold that cannot be challenged or developed easily. Struggles to manage proximity changes with both approach and withdrawal. The child has little or no adaptability and will be seen to dysregulate easily with a tendency to hypo-arousal or hyper-arousal causing an impact on themselves. In the face of adversity shows little or compromised ability to persistence and may give up or not even start. Generally low mood or their mood is incongruent.

(Continued)

No Foregone Conclusions 137

Table 8.4 (Continued)

Assessment Components: The Child/ren

Factor	Positive	Of Concern	
Child 'A' (name)			
	Balanced behaviour: Can face adversity, may seek help, support or advice. They can hold their ground, be aware of their limits and boundaries.	**Externalises behaviour:** Angry, aggressive, confrontative, resistant, non-compliant. May use substances to enhance their sense of control, will manipulate their surroundings for a greater sense of control.	**Internalises behaviour:** Holds everything in. The level of rage the externaliser shows is equal to that of the pain the internaliser holds in. They may self-harm or demonstrate self-destructive behaviour with unhealthy or dangerous lifestyles. They may self-medicate, or self-soothe with significant tension reducing behaviours or tics.

(Continued)

No Foregone Conclusions 139

Table 8.4 (Continued)

Assessment Components: The Child/ren

Factor	Positive	Of Concern
Child 'A' (name)	**Sensory Processing/ Sensorimotor:** The system is integrated (sometimes referred to as accurate interpretation or effective registration). The signs of a healthy or integrated system are where the sensory systems have joined up and work together to process what is experienced. The information is received (largely) from 7 senses: **Visual** (ability to interpret what is seen), **Auditory** (what is heard), **Gustatory** (what is tasted), **Olfactory** (what is smelt), **Tactile** (what is felt – physiologically), **Proprioceptive** (what is experienced by different parts of the body – e.g., muscles, bones, tendons, nerves at the same time) and **Vestibular** (balance and movement). Children will be seen as developmentally observant, descriptive, interested and curious, dextrous and able, confident, able to regulate and/	**Sensory Processing/ Sensorimotor:** May manipulate their surroundings to participate in communication or activities in which they excel and avoid those where they struggle. They may be overactive in situations that require less energy. They may present as bored. They may hide their inability to develop new skills. They control individual, group and social relationships. They may be rigid, OCD, process orientated/driven, concrete, comfortable with routine and procedure and struggle with nouveau, change, spontaneity, the unusual or the unexpected. Their anxiety is emotionally stunted. May be hidden by control. Movement is enjoyed when it has a purpose	**Sensory Processing/ Sensorimotor:** They may have poor attention or a decreased attention span. They may discombobulate when stressed or undertaking an activity that heightens others awareness of their difference (this may be seen in opposition or defiant behaviour, antisocial or distractible or distracting behaviour). They may be underactive in situations that require more energy. They may seem bored or lethargic. They may struggle or resist learning new skills or struggle retaining new information. They may struggle in, resist or avoid individual, group or social relationships. They may be uncomfortable in their own skin be dyspraxic, dyslexic

(Continued)

Table 8.4 (Continued)

Assessment Components: The Child/ren

Factor	Positive	Of Concern
Child 'A' (name)	or be regulated, hold attention, process, organise, decipher, coordinate their bodies, limbs, thoughts and activities, they are coordinated and can coordinate. They can take information, process, analyse, recall and respond. They are expressive, descriptive, communicative, eloquent. They are aware of and can express themselves to have their needs, desires and dreams shared, their needs met and their wants conveyed. They can play, study, emote, socialise, move and meet the world with relative ease. They will appear relatively relaxed, coordinated and dextrous and deft.	(sport, improving skills, competitive outcomes and remaining ahead of peers). Rigidity in body, routine, expectations etc will increase. (all fingers and thumbs, fall over themselves, tie themselves up in knots etc). They may struggle emotionally, be over or under emotional. Their anxiety is debilitating. They may be over or under-reactive to stimulation such as sight, sound, touch, textures, temperature, relationships. They may me under-toned floppy, disinterested, emotionally or cognitively absent or be misattuned with themselves or others. Their behaviour may seem out of kilter, unbalanced, chaotic, distant or lack management and regulation. They may lack emotional, cognitive and physiological integration, connectivity or awareness. Their coordination, body awareness, play and language may be compromised.

(Continued)

Table 8.4 (Continued)

Assessment Components: The Child/ren

Factor	Positive	Of Concern	
Child 'A' (name)			
	Boundaries and Limits: Can hold the line. Is aware of their and others personal space. Knows when to argue their point and push and when to capitulate and acquiesce. They can seek help and support and understands that rules are for safety and that rules can change under specific situations (i.e. bedtimes are later at weekends, or you can party harder and rest more during holidays than term-time.	**Boundaries and Limits:** Pushes boundaries and moves into others personal space. Uses people for their own ends and moves on when the person is no longer of use. Uses their power and control to enhance their chances of achieving their desired outcomes. Believes they are exempt from rules or that rules are primarily for others. May not push rules if they think they may get caught, they can regulate to increase their chances of the desired outcomes.	**Boundaries and Limits:** Have little or no awareness of their own rights over their bodies, needs or right to live and function in the world. They may not understand rules as rules have been broken or they were not aware that what happened to them was wrong. They may fear coming into proximity asking for help and support but can't prevent others coming into proximity with them.
	Window of Tolerance: Wide and containing. They can manage stress but can ask for help when stress increases (such as: exams, health issues or bereavement).	**Window of Tolerance:** May seem wide but the individual is controlling their environment. They may be vigilant, OCD and/or controlled. They may lack flexibility. When they exit their WOT, they are more likely to exit into hyper-arousal and the signs may be more noticeable or extreme, aggressive, violent to others or themselves, outwardly controlling of others or themselves or dysregulated. They may bounce between hypo and hyper-arousal.	**Window of Tolerance:** Small window of tolerance. When they exit their window they are more likely to tend to hypo-arousal, with low affect, dissociate, 'crash', appear catatonic, low mood, low self-worth, low energy, apathy

(Continued)

Table 8.4 (Continued)

Assessment Components: The Child/ren

Factor	Positive	Of Concern
Child 'A' (name)	**Attachment:** Secure **Belief System:** The child develops core beliefs that are life enhancing and generally positive. These beliefs cover: Responsibility, I am/can (I am loveable, worthy, deserving, capable, attractive etc). Responsibility, I did/do(the best I could, I tried, I learned etc). Safety, I can (feel, be trusted, trust, choose, learn, be safe etc). Control: (I'm strong, I have choices, support, I am capable etc). **Regulation:** Can self-regulate or be socially regulated when required.	**Attachment:** Disorganised **Belief System:** The child develops generally negative or false positive beliefs. These beliefs cover: Responsibility, I am/can (bad, powerful and in control, perfect, misunderstood). Responsibility, I did/do (but someone should have stopped me, it was their fault, blame and denial). Safety, I can (I cannot trust anyone, I cannot show emotions, trust my judgement). Control: (I am safe when I'm in control and when I have neutralised vulnerability in myself and others). **Regulation:** May appear regulated but this must not be confused with healthy regulation. Look for signs of control, hyper-vigilance, and tension. They may need social regulation but will seek to avoid the attentions of others coming to them – they seek the attention of others on their terms.	**Attachment:** Avoidant/ambivalent. **Belief System:** The child develops limiting beliefs. These beliefs cover: Responsibility, I am/can (undeserving, worthless, damaged, not good enough, ugly, stupid, unlovable etc) Responsibility, I did/ do Safety, I can (Cannot protect myself, show emotions, trust myself or my judgement). Control: (I have no control, I'm not safe, I'm inadequate, helpless and hopeless). **Regulation:** May struggle to self-regulate or be socially regulated. They are overwhelmed.

(Continued)

Table 8.4 (Continued)

Assessment Components: The Child/ren

Child 'A' (name)

Factor	Positive	Of Concern
Chronological age:	In synchrony with developmental age. Child developmental stages are on track in most areas or exceeded: cognitive, physiological, psychological, emotional, biological, neurological, and sexual.	**Chronological age:** Out of synchrony with developmental age. Impacted by trauma, health, genetic, birth and/or physical, learning, or emotional adversity. Signs of significant child psychopathology causing disruption across many or all developmental domains: cognitive, physiological, psychological, emotional, biological, neurological, and sexual. **Chronological age:** Out of synchrony with developmental age. Signs of child psychopathology causing disruption across some developmental domains: cognitive, physiological, psychological, emotional, biological, neurological, and sexual.
Presentation:	Achieved in some or many subjects. Emotionally literate Cognitively gifted, able or coping Physically gifted, able or adaptive Behaviour and presentation adaptive to positive. Adversities counteracted and supported early.	**Presentation:** Confrontational Uncooperative. Neglected Abused. Perhaps feral. Angry/violent Bullied others Potentially disorganised Cognitively gifted but undirected or unsupported Presence of childhood psychopathology/ unsupported neurodivergence: e.g. ADHD, ODD etc. Avoidant, dissociated, fragmented or in parts. **Presentation:** Neglected or abused. From neglected appearance to immaculate appearance. Masked Compliant Dissociative Bullied Insecure Failed at many or most subjects or excelled educationally but appeared emotionally absent. Cognitively challenged, learning disability. Presence of childhood psychopathology/ unsupported neurodivergence: e.g. OCD, depression, anxiety

(Continued)

Table 8.4 (Continued)

Assessment Components: The Child/ren

Factor	Positive	Of Concern
Child 'A' (name)	**Character Strategies: Balanced:** In some form of education/ apprenticeship or for young adults; employed, self, employed, perhaps entrepreneurial, caring, or vocational role, artistic or creative, nature inspired or explorer. Some level of faith/belief/ spirituality (nature, art, place in the world)	**Character Strategies: Self-reliant:** High powered role, entrepreneurial, sometimes political, sometimes criminal. **Charming-manipulative:** They may present as entertaining, ingratiating, charming, understanding, charismatic, interested but they have an agenda and want something out of the relationship, exchange or communication – it is definitely conditional. This can be seen in entrepreneurial and political worlds as well as offending behaviour. Safety is in the lack of direct expression and a reliance of misdirection, charm, innuendo and manipulation. **Tough-Generous:**	**Character Strategies: Sensitive withdrawn:** Child has no trust in the world or caregivers. Internally they are fearful, highly sensitive and suspicious of the motivation of others and as a result be hyper-vigilant. They may hold back or present as introverted. May present as standoffish or absent. **Sensitive emotional:** The child is left desperate for help but cannot be soothed or is soothed and then requires constant reassurance. May present as clingy. **Dependent-endearing:** May present as younger than their age, particularly in adulthood where they may sound or appear childlike. **Self-reliant:** Avoids the support of others but may well support others. They may struggle to connect in relationships. Deprivation is feared and therefore seeks to meet their own needs.

(Continued)

Table 8.4 (Continued)

Assessment Components: The Child/ren

Factor	Positive	Of Concern
Child 'A' (name)	The need for mastery is a critical stage of latency, the period of around 6–12 where they need to achieve and become proficient in managing their environment. But because of their experiences they are overwhelmed by shame and if mirrored by peers can become overwhelmed by feelings of inferiority. Thus, the vulnerability is hidden by ego and the child presents as invulnerable, becomes pseudo-parentified and takes care of others by blunting their own feelings making them feel powerful. They can be seen as angry and controlling or benevolent but because it stems from the same drive – it becomes conditional. **Industrious-Overfocused:** The child never feels good enough, they seem to be committed to the project, perfectionist and perhaps denigrating of those that don't strive enough, they don't belong and don't deserve to be at the table. They may become rigid and/or Controlling.	Others cannot be relied upon so they develop fierce independence even when they are sufficiently developed to be independent. **Charming-Manipulative:** May be ingratiating or chameleonesque. **Burdened enduring:** Pseudo-parentified child, meets their parents' needs through fear of consequences or siblings needs as they hold the belief they are responsible for their survival. Their acceptance in the world is dependent only on the condition they serve others. They may present as compliant but internally they may be irritated, become passive aggressive or resistant to change. **Industrious-Overfocused:** May work hard not to be seen, excel in maths (no emotion is required in maths) etc, may present as a perfect child (it's exhausting being perfect). **Expressive clinging:** They dramatise to keep people engaged and attentive. Can be chaotic, may be excitable, ambivalent, demonstrative or avoidant.

(Continued)

146   A Trauma Model for Assessing Siblings

Table 8.4 (Continued)

Assessment Components: The Child/ren

Factor	Positive	Of Concern
Child 'A' (name)	**Communication Content:** Coherent with the situation.	**Communication Content:** May struggle with recall, coherency and truth. Content maybe stunted, vague, guarded or confused. May steer to non-descriptive language such as 'what do you mean?', 'I don't know/remember,' fine, ok, alright etc.
	Communication Content: Controls the subject matter, distracts, prevaricates, dismisses, denies, fabricates, blames.	
	Volume: Confident, appropriate to situation ability to regulate and modulate. Authoritative.	**Volume:** May lack confidence, whisper, become mute or whisper or become fragmented in speech. May have breaks in the voice.
	Volume: May over power listener, shout, raise their voice or use quiet speech to bring the listener closer in proximity to an uncomfortable degree or to create doubt or confusion. This is controlling in nature. May have a roughness to the quality of the voice.	
	Rhythm: Associated with a relaxed upbeat and generally positive outlook interspersed with periods of low affect or anxiety in an ability to experience and manage all human emotions.	**Rhythm:** Stress impacts on rhythm as does anxiety. May speak faster or slower.
	Rhythm: May be associated with control, stress, over emphasis or fixed speech.	
	Tone: Is likely to be positive and upbeat. Have energy and motivate the listener to pay attention.	**Tone:** May be flatter with less articulation. Possibility of a monotonous tone. Is likely to show a flat affect. May have a negative tone of voice.
	Tone: Can be controlling in its presentation or manipulative. This can be anything from charming intent to controlling at the other end of the spectrum.	

(Continued)

Table 8.4 (Continued)

Assessment Components: The Child/ren			
Factor	*Positive*	*Of Concern*	
Child 'A' (name)			
	Pitch: Modulates and is within the expected range. The sound is coherent with the age and gender of the person.	**Pitch:** May be much deeper or higher than expected. The older adolescent or young adult may sound like a younger child particularly in females (little girl voice), but is not confined to gender.	**Pitch:** May show signs of developmental delay or developmental arrest. There pitch may fail, vary or become stuck.
	Prosody: The patterns of rhythm and sound. Able to modulate variations in duration, intensity which impacts on the message being conveyed.	**Prosody:** Impaired emotional prosody. May emphasise anger, disgust and negative emotion, may manipulate or control using language that may lack empathy.	**Prosody:** Impaired emotional prosody. An increased severity of childhood trauma is associated with reduced accuracy on the discrimination task and with slower identification of emotional prosody. Exposure to childhood trauma is associated with long-term, atypical development in the interpretation of prosodic cues in speech. The findings have implications for the intergenerational transmission of trauma. May sigh, grunt, pause and speed.
	Intonation: Ability to modulate affect, be authoritative, questioning, uncertain, excited, anxious all within expected parameters.	**Intonation:** Angry, controlling, or forceful.	**Intonation:** Regression can be an expected outcome of trauma in children and can be a coping strategy in traumatised adults. A childlike voice is not uncommon.

(Continued)

Table 8.4 (Continued)

Assessment Components: The Child/ren

Factor	Positive		Of Concern
Child 'A' (name)			
	Breath: Relaxed, rhythmic, deep.	**Breath:** Stressed, forced maybe shallow.	**Breath:** May be shallow, imperceptible, breathe from high in the chest.
	Facial expression: Relaxed state, range of affect, can slide appropriately from one emotional range to another without inhibition.	**Facial expression:** Clenched jaw, furrowed brow or forehead, tension in tongue, throat and neck.	**Facial expression:** Maybe expressionless, dissociative, avoidant, uncertain.
	Eye contact: Can hold and vary eye contact duration and depth whilst showing a range of emotions.	**Eye contact:** Threatening or avoidant eye contact. May use eye contact to persuade or manipulate. May seem very self-assured with an edge.	**Eye contact:** Avoidant or show uncertainty in eye contact. It may show vulnerability, uncertainty or lack of self-esteem.
	Body Language: Relaxed and fluid. No or rare signs of tension reducing behaviours. Dextrous, organised, connected.	**Body language:** Rigid, ready for action (fight/flight symptoms), tense, arms, legs, stomach, and hands. High tension reducing behaviours.	**Body Language:** May be rigid and tense (flight mode) or flop (lack of muscle tone/given up, postural collapse, hypo-arousal, head down. May appear to be relaxed but this is defeated.
	Self-care: Well kempt, pride in appearance. High standard of care and/or self-care. Clean well looked after clothes. Signs of good health, exercise, interests and diet.	**Self-care:** May be immaculate, controlled, pristine and very precise (OCD) or may lack positive markers as they are focused elsewhere.	**Self-care:** May present as neglected, self-neglect, 'pinched'/sallow (poor/inadequate diet, poor health opportunities/ill-health or poorly managed health conditions). May overeat, binge or under eat/restrictive diet.

(Continued)

Table 8.4 (Continued)

Assessment Components: The Child/ren

Factor	Positive	Of Concern	
Child 'A' (name)	**Common behavioural or presentation markers. Honesty:** Presents in an open, relaxed, forthcoming manner. Can disagree and argue a point. Is able to say that they don't know and can ask for help.	**Common behavioural or presentation markers. Honesty:** Fabrication/ lying to manipulate or mislead. May ask for information but this is for a pre-planned reason (information is power).	**Common behavioural or presentation markers. Honesty:** May lie, may lie about everything, may not know the truth or may not know the difference between a lie and the truth. Lying is for self-protection or a belief that they are not enough as they are.
	Eating/Food: Copes with a balanced diet, a sufficient amount of food, range of food, temperatures, textures, sweetness, sourness, dryness, moisture content. Is adventurous in trying new foods, mixtures of textures and types of food within their religious or dietary restrictions.	**Eating/Food:** Controls food restricts the type and quantity of food. Mealtimes are a trigger point and may become incendiary, violence and aggression may occur. May control intake (anorexia at extreme) may never feel sated (bulimia at extreme).	**Eating/Food:** Food may bring fear. Food may symbolise lack of care, bribery, payment, neglect etc. May respond to food with faddy or picky eating, gorging or hording food in the bedroom. May crave food but struggle to eat it. May be psychologically physiologically unable to eat or swallow and may have a gag reflex. May induce nausea, may eat very slowly or very fast. May struggle with cutlery, textures, temperatures, mixtures etc.

(Continued)

Table 8.4 (Continued)

Assessment Components: The Child/ren

Factor	Positive	Of Concern
Child 'A' (name)	**Transition and Change:** Has experienced few transitions and changes. Where change has been necessary this has either been well planned, prepared and the child has been carefully primed. Or the changes have been part of the child's culture, such as travelling families where significant parts of the child's family, extended family and friends move together. Additional care is needed when assessing the impact on children in the military, the ministry or boarding school where change and/or separation may have positive or negative consequences. These children may present as emotionally balanced but equally may present as pseudo-adultified or overly self-assured, traits that can be seen as positive in some parts of society.	**Transition and Change:** Running away with a parent from domestic violence is positive as it is escaping a dangerous situation, but the impact of being with a desperate and scared parent is still scary. Running away from the law (criminal activity), or Local Authority intervention (safeguarding, child protection and family proceedings) both harbour desperation and fear and therefore being with scared (maybe presenting as angry) parent/s has a similar impact. Each change may have an impact on loss, the loss of family, friends, schools, teachers, peers, learning, geography, culture, consistency, familiarity and a host of other knowns. May present as emotionally stunted or emotionally illiterate cold, rigid, extrovert (but this may lack coherency).	**Transition and Change:** Change has been ill-prepared, not considered and may be experienced as a lack of care or importance such as neglect. The impact of change has been frightening for the child, they may dissociate become over-emotional, clingy, ambivalent or avoidant. They may become insular, introverted, shy and lack the tools and social literacy to engage, respond or communicate with others.

(Continued)

Table 8.4 (Continued)

Assessment Components: The Child/ren

Factor	Positive	Of Concern
Child 'A' (name)		
	Night-time: Dreams: Has dreams that they can process by talking to a parent, drawing or playing through. May experience some nightmares but had access to parental support and reassurance.	**Night-time: Night Terrors:** Child is distraught when wakes. May wet or soil the bed, be sweaty, disorientated and scream or shout out. In very severe cases the child may appear awake with all the above symptoms but be unresponsive. They do not respond to reassurance – It feels they are reliving something.
		Night-time: Nightmares: Child may wet the bed, be distraught on waking or even hide their fear but their terror may be visible. They may be sweaty and/or disorientated and may or may not respond to reassurance.
	Night-time Routine: Manages routines, hygiene (bath/shower, teeth cleaning, face wash etc) with or without support. Before bed reduction in screen time, snack, drink, toileting, bedtime story, lights out etc. Can manage the difference between weekends, holidays and weekday routines.	**Night-time Routine:** Is oppositional, defiant, aggressive. Pushes boundaries, ignores limits and controls. May manage hygiene may push back nurture or displays of care and nurture. May go slow, demand attention or push it away or both.
		Night-time Routine: May be fearful, may need or reject proximity and care. May refuse food or horde food. May struggle with hygiene, be fearful of being left alone or in relationship. May struggle with story time. Maybe fearful of the dark or what the dark brings.

(Continued)

No Foregone Conclusions 151

Table 8.4 (Continued)

Assessment Components: The Child/ren

Factor	Positive	Of Concern
Child 'A' (name)		
Toileting:	No difficulty in recognising need and supporting self. Manages or can seek support. Actively manages toileting-hygiene routines or seeks help to do this.	May use the toilet as control. Scatological behaviours. Smears on walls, towels, door handles. Hides faeces in clothing, draws, cupboards etc. Urinates on carpets, walls, in containers etc. May not feel the signs of need of motion or bladder.
Denial:	Absence of, takes responsibility, manages guilt without shame, learns from the experience, is open about their mistakes, misdemeanours, and errors. Gets things wrong but rarely repeats mistakes. Names what they did. can describe outcomes for their behaviour (when I do…this puts me and others at risk of …). I can prevent this happening again by…	Denial of understanding (I don't know what you are talking about). straightforward Denial (I didn't do it).
Toileting:		Toileting is beyond child's control. Nocturnal enuresis Nocturnal encopresis. Diurnal enuresis Diurnal encopresis Doubly or singularly incontinent. Stomach problems such as IBS. Diarrhoea or constipation. May not feel the signs of need of motion or bladder.
Denial:		Justification (I did it but…). Dissociation or avoidance or both (I can't remember, but I accept I did…). acceptance without analysis (I did…).

(Continued)

Table 8.4 (Continued)

Assessment Components: The Child/ren

Factor	Positive	Of Concern
Child 'A' (name)		
	Play: Play is on track through the different developmental stages of play: sensory, sensorimotor, embodiment, projective and role play. They can manage structured play, free and/or non-directive play, outdoor, indoor, competitive, construction, artistic, musical, sport based, dance, movement, rhythmic, risky, sensory, self and other directed. Show 8 (11) 'C's and 5 'P's. Are relaxed. Can play symbolically and in the metaphor. Can play freely, in isolation or in connection with others. Play relieves anxiety, is spontaneous.	**Play:** The child may not play or may not be able to play. Where the child can play, they may present as controlling. They may identify as the aggressor. The play may feel real and therefore is not play. Play may promote anxiety. Play may be acceptable if it is competitive. In competitive play, participating but losing does not bring joy. Winning may not bring joy. Winning and mocking the loser may bring joy. The play may revolve around changing rules to ensure they cannot lose. Violence and aggression may be constant themes. There are seldom happy or positive endings. There is a lack of symbolic distancing. Play tends to be concrete. The child may present as stuck. They may be stuck at a specific developmental stage of play if they can play at all.	**Play:** Child is too scared to play, and/or they may not know how to play. The repetition of play provides no relief from the anxiety they experience and yet may continue to replay compulsively. The link between play and reality may remain unconscious and unmetabolised. Play does not relieve anxiety. Play may contain constant themes of hopelessness, helplessness and certain future disaster, re-trauma or further harm. There are seldom happy or positive endings. There is a lack of symbolic distancing. The child may present as stuck. They may be stuck at a specific developmental stage of play if they can play at all.

(Continued)

Table 8.4 (Continued)

Assessment Components: The Child/ren

Factor	Positive		Of Concern
Child 'A' (name)	**8 (11) 'C's:** Compassion, Creativity, Connectedness, Clarity, Confidence, Courage, Curiosity and Calm. Also able to show Commitment, Consistency and Contentment.	**8 (11) 'C's:** Significantly lacking or compromised in many of the domains. Compassion, Creativity, Connectedness, Clarity, Confidence, Courage, Curiosity and Calm.	**8 (11) 'C's:** Significantly compromised in one or two or lacking in some of the domains. Compassion, Creativity, Connectedness, Clarity, Confidence, Courage, Curiosity and Calm.
	5 'P's; Presence, Patience, Perspective, Persistence, Playfulness.	**5 'P's:** Significantly lacking or compromised in many of the domains. Presence, Patience, Perspective, Persistence, Playfulness.	**5 'P's:** Significantly compromised in one or two or lacking in some of the domains. Presence, Patience, Perspective, Persistence, Playfulness.
	Levels of Stress or Trauma: Manageable stress and/or responded to the treatment of Type 1 trauma. **Shame:** Little or no evidence of shame. Can manage feelings of guilt.	**Levels of Stress or Trauma:** High stress, Toxic stress, evidence of Type 1, 2, 3 and/or 4/ trauma. **Shame:** Hard to see but the child is working hard to keep feelings of toxic shame hidden through control or rage.	**Levels of Stress or Trauma:** High stress, Toxic stress, evidence of Type 1, 2, 3 and/or 4 trauma. **Shame:** Child is severely compromised by feelings of toxic shame.

(Continued)

Table 8.4 (Continued)

Assessment Components: The Child/ren

Factor	Positive	Of Concern
Child 'A' (name)		
	Parts: Presents as balanced with all parts in synchrony. Has some levels of difference, e.g. being on their own, with family, at school or in other social situations where there are subtle differences which may enhance comfort over performance for example. In this state the 8 'C's and 5 'P's will be present.	**Parts: Managers** are the day-to-day protectors that help deal with difficult situations. However, when they become burdened by have to manage too much adversity they see the emotional reaction as the problem and exile parts of ourselves that they see as vulnerable and unhelpful. **Parts: Exiles.** These are the parts that are seen to be weak or vulnerable that have been exiled. They tend to be the young parts that have experienced high stress, enduring stress and trauma in their development. They hold the pain, fear and shame. In reality they are shut away for either their protection or a skewed belief that they are also responsible for the harm the system has been experienced. As a result the harbour dependency, rage, terror, isolation, harm, loneliness, the burden and grief to name a few.

(Continued)

Table 8.4 (Continued)

Assessment Components: The Child/ren

Factor	Positive	Of Concern
Child 'A' (name)		**Firefighters** are essentially protectors who step in when the individual perceives threat to their system or integrity. This threat or danger is either real or perceived (the outcome is the same as it feels real). Firefighters' strength is that is allows people to carry on without worrying about survival, but the downside is that they are personally draining. These protectors may lead to substance use/abuse, binge eating or dietary restrictions, self-harming or hurting behaviour, harmful sex in either HSB, CSE and/or sexual exploitation as an adult (either being coerced or coercing others) being trapped in the sex industry but believing it is a lifestyle or professional choice. These protectors numb. Soothe or distract the individual.

(Continued)

Table 8.4 (Continued)

Assessment Components: The Child/ren

Factor	Positive	Of Concern
Child 'A' (name)		
Child's Presentation in Nursery	Balanced. Achieved in some or many subjects. Emotionally literate Cognitively gifted, able or coping Physically gifted, able or adaptive Behaviour and presentation adaptive to positive. Adversities counteracted and supported early	Externalises Confrontational Uncooperative. Neglected Abused. Perhaps feral. Angry/violent Bullied others Potentially disorganised Cognitively gifted but undirected or unsupported Presence of childhood psychopathology/ unsupported neurodivergence: e.g. ADHD, ODD etc. / Internalises Avoidant/ambivalent Neglected or abused. From neglected appearance to immaculate appearance. Masked Compliant Dissociative Bullied Insecure Failed at many or most subjects or excelled educationally but appeared emotionally absent. Cognitively challenged, learning disability. Presence of childhood psychopathology/ unsupported neurodivergence: e.g. OCD, depression, anxiety
Child's Presentation in Primary school	Repeat/as above	Repeat/as above
Child's Presentation in Secondary/high school	Repeat/as above	Repeat/as above
Child's Presentation in College/ Further education/	Repeat/as above	Repeat/as above

(Continued)

Table 8.4 (Continued)

Assessment Components: The Child/ren

Factor	Positive	Of Concern
Child 'A' (name)		
Geographic safety	Unpolluted Fresh air Access to nature Clean water Active community Community participation Community safety Good travel links High employment rate	High pollution Overcrowded Lack of basic human needs Gang culture and postcode wars. Territorial High deprivation High unemployment Aggressive/violent High crime, including drugs, county lines, exploitation and sexual exploitation of both children and adults.	Geographically isolated Insular Lack of community, neighbourhood links or support. Closed or rigid outlooks or views. Territorial Oppressed. Low positive role models
School/education	Well-funded Thriving Positive culture Parental participation Achieved primary. Achieved secondary/high. Achieved college/further education. Mixed gender options Diverse and inclusive Public school education (UK private system) or other 3rd sector education impact: privileged but balanced. Positive peer groups	Toxic Paternalistic, Autocratic Single gender Rundown inner city or limited choice. Success at others expense. Public school education (UK private system) or other 3rd sector education impact: elitist or entitled. Influential peer groups/in-crowd	Rundown Isolated ideology Lack of choice Lack of representation Lack of open/multifaith celebration, recognition Public school education (UK private system) or other 3rd sector education impact: isolated, rejected, abandoned, 'rich man's care.' Marginalised

(Continued)

Table 8.4 (Continued)

Assessment Components: The Child/ren

Child 'A' (name)

Factor	Positive	Of Concern	Of Concern
Sibling relationships			
Sibling relationship (child A) with child B and child B's views if different	**Age:** Children with a significant age gap are able to provide or seek an extra layer of advice or support. Children close in age have a confidante. More siblings may equate to greater levels of support or back up in social or education situations. Their connection may surpass age differences.	**Age:** Older children may leave the family home and abandon their sibling relationships. Older siblings may expose their younger siblings to material or experiences that the younger sibling is not yet developmentally ready to process such as older rated films, games, news or imagery. Viewing pornography can cause as much damage as direct sexual abuse. A classic mistake can be the sharing of life story work with an older child who will share with a younger sibling information they are not ready to handle, or not sharing information with an older child something they need to know because they may share it with a younger sibling.	**Age:** Younger children may feel abandoned by their older siblings and may feel alienated as a result. Younger siblings may be exposed to information, material or experiences that they are not yet developmentally ready to process such as older rated films, games, news or imagery. Viewing pornography can cause as much damage as direct sexual abuse. A classic mistake can be the sharing of life story work with an older child who will share with a younger sibling information they are not ready to handle, or not sharing information with an older child something they need to know because they may share it with a younger sibling.

(Continued)

Table 8.4 (Continued)

Assessment Components: The Child/ren

Factor	Positive	Of Concern
Child 'A' (name)	**Parentage:** Due to high levels of family support, love and nurture, with positive, non-judgemental communication the child is secure in family makeup regardless of its type. Meets siblings with openness and equality regardless of sibling status.	**Parentage:** Uses difference to leverage status. I.e. uses birth parent as a higher status, or a stepchild division. The siblings here use control and manipulation in a more overt manner.	**Parentage:** The children here tend to be more confused, unclear or uncertain. They may find it difficult to differentiate between relationships but are more likely to exit their WOT over anything and thus harder to see if these different parent relationships are the trigger or not or a blend of triggers.
	Gender: Sees themselves as secure and can meet others on an equal playing field. They are aware of the differences of male and female but also aware of and accepting of the many forms of gender people may identify as. They will be a source of support to a sibling making sense of their gender as much as their sexuality.	**Gender:** Dismissive and rigid about gender. May see hierarchy or patriarchy as a response. They are more likely to use the information to demean, belittle or control than provide comfort or support.	**Gender:** May see gender roles or assign fear, strength or weakness to gender. Gender here may be stereotyped but often it is a concept lost on a sea of confusing issues.
	Parental stress: Less stress in parents translates as less stress in children and thus less stress in sibling relationships. High stress in families that is unusual and out experience can be scary but can be managed.	**Parental stress:** High parental work stress can lead to high achievers with low emotional expectations. High family stress with domestic harm or abuse can see similar controlling behaviours in some children. Financial stress can lead to loan sharks and other additional stressors that may lead to higher anger stress responses that may be played out between siblings.	**Parental stress:** Where high stress leads to neglect, children may feel worthless and if they feel worthless may see no worth in their siblings or conversely become pseudo-parentified.

(Continued)

Table 8.4 (Continued)

Assessment Components: The Child/ren

Factor	Positive	Of Concern
Child 'A' (name)	**Faith:** Understands faith regardless of their own beliefs. They acknowledge their parents' beliefs where the child has none and can celebrate their parents' beliefs where they have none or is different. Because faith is open in such a way the siblings can support each other regardless of difference.	**Faith:** Either rejecting of faith or devout. This child is more likely to manage at the extremes or the polar opposite. Their belief defines them as does their agnosticism. They have no time for sibling's view but will tend towards criticism and control. Risk of radicalisation or denunciation of faith – this is the grounds for polar opposites.
	Ability/disability: The children grow up delighting in their genetic makeup and gifts. Support is found to offset the challenges of diversity and difference and the siblings are able to communicate with each other their need for help or able to provide help and assistance without being requested to do so. There is no sense of parental responsibility or ownership of the role of sibling support.	**Ability/disability:** Ability has been seen as the favoured parental response and inability/disability scapegoated. Where the parent sees the child as special this promotes the sense of favouritism. All outcomes lead to more challenging sibling relationships.

| | | **Faith:** The child doesn't know who they are let alone who they or their siblings believe in. Faith may be a source of fear. Faith represents a ritual or routine in the lives of children who may have no routine. |
| | | **Ability/disability:** Are often unaware of their needs and thus are unaware of their siblings needs. Shame may be present. The diversity and difference of this child is not offset and the disabled child becomes at increased risk of vulnerability by others. Their siblings may be unaware of this vulnerability as they are vulnerable themselves. |

(Continued)

Table 8.4 (Continued)

Assessment Components: The Child/ren

Factor	Positive	Of Concern
Child 'A' (name)	**Health:** Good emotional and physical health are supported. Where the child has a health condition this is taken into consideration and offset as much as possible. The promotion of empathy appears in so many aspects of children's development – it requires nurturing. There is a difference between a parents seeing their child with a health issue or disability as special is unhelpful an potentially sentimental in nature and can cause ruptures in sibling relationships. The ability to see their child as requiring extra support is different and this reflects in siblings' ability to have empathy and not parent their sibling but want to support them.	**Health:** Health is overfocused. Perhaps the ill child as mentioned previously is seen as special has outcomes akin to favouritism. Conversely any perceived weakness may be seen as needy, high maintenance and resented and they may subsequently be scapegoated. Both these outcomes lead to disruptions within the sibling group. Where fitness and diet become the focus, the dangers may include eating issues or OCD in fitness regimes or both.	**Health:** Financial restrictions, geographical locations, poverty, dangerous communities familial neglect by omission or commission can all lead to reduced health and life expectancy. Where this is normalised in families so too may it be normalised in sibling groups. Helplessness and hopelessness may be a feature.

(Continued)

No Foregone Conclusions 163

Table 8.4 (Continued)

Assessment Components: The Child/ren

Factor	Positive	Of Concern
Child 'A' (name)	**Education experience:** Experienced a caring school environment that was encouraging, nurturing and boundaried the child was able to learn and because they were able to learn they were able to support their siblings' transitions or allow siblings to support their own transitions. They can excel, face challenges and socialise well. Peer support helps sibling support and vice versa.	**Education experience:** Strict, cold, authoritarian or hot house high pressure, cognitive heavy focus can lead to unbalanced children who cut off or under develop their holistic selves. The high achieving child may find competition from a sibling hard to bear or may see their own advancement as the only important factor. They may push their siblings back or use them for leverage. They are getting ready for a cutthroat competitive world, and this may be acted out in sibling relationships. Bullying behaviour may be seen as authoritative alpha behaviour where in fact it is just bullying.	**Education experience:** Laissez-faire, neglectful or under resourced and stressed schools incubate children in a similar fashion. The children may seep hopelessness and helplessness and struggle to define or envisage a sense of future. Failure may be expected or painfully and pitifully low expectations develop a similar outlook between siblings – they hold each other back. The children may bully or be bullied. There is little support in school or home to see or manage this and the children act out the same.

(Continued)

Table 8.4 (Continued)

Assessment Components: The Child/ren

Factor	Positive	Of Concern
Child 'A' (name)		
	Sexuality: Healthy sexuality is encouraged and celebrated as part of who the child or young person is – it doesn't define them. They are supportive of siblings whose sexuality differs from their own as well as similar.	**Sexuality:** Shamed, demeaned, not accepted or rejected. Negative belief about self leads to overcompensation and a negative belief of others, which may include their siblings. Sexuality may become the definition of who the child is as opposed to part of their gift set.
		Sexuality: Confused and abandoned to negotiate this developmental minefield as the child struggles with identity issues across the developmental spectrum. They have no support so can't support others. they may be ambivalent seek to support and then mock or vice versa. They may avoid or become hopeless and helpless in their aloneness. They may hate their bodies, and you would never know. Shut down, dissociation, disconnection and low affect can often be seen here, and siblings struggle to support or see their brothers and sisters struggles.

(Continued)

Table 8.4 (Continued)

Assessment Components: The Child/ren

Factor	Positive	Of Concern
Child 'A' (name)		
	Sexual/body curiosity and exploration: Taking into account age and development (consider the work of Johnson and Gil) for further in-depth understanding of healthy sexuality vs sexually concerning behaviour. Similar age siblings show curiosity about each other's bodies. They are comfortable with a level of nakedness (age dependent), exploration of younger siblings in role play is light-hearted, fun, intermittent and easily redirected without evoking shame. The children are relaxed and playful.	**Sexual Harmful Behaviour:** Age and developmental differences. Involves levels of secrecy, lies, threats, bribes. Is generally concealed, there is no levity, openness, playfulness or exploration. There are tones of exploitation, advantage, control, manipulation and fear. Neither child is open about the content of the events, high levels of stress or incongruence. There may have been a long history of 'low level' concerns or 'out of the blue' behaviour (neither of which are as described on assessment). **Sexual Reactivity:** Children are sexualised as a result of their environment, experiences and premature sexualisation. The children may not see 'wrong' in their behaviour, they may expect adults to join in or their behaviour may not be seen. The younger the children the more likely the adults/professionals will try to find more palatable explanations for the children's behaviour. This is not HSB because there is no intent – they are reacting to their bodies experience, a powerful reminder of a skewed but powerful connection.

(Continued)

Table 8.4 (Continued)

Assessment Components: The Child/ren

Factor	Positive	Of Concern
Child 'A' (name)	**Parental financial circumstances.** Financial security brings levels of empowerment where the parents' choices are for the benefit of the family and community. They do not have to be wealthy or even well-off. Where the home living conditions are anywhere from manageable (maintained, clean, loved) to more affluent. Finances are budgeted for welling being, diet, health, warmth, clothing and presentation, family celebrations, family holidays or outings, travel and possibly savings. The children learn the importance or prioritisation and living out of the clutches of debt. If parents prioritise well-being, then this too will be more frequently seen reflected in sibling behaviour.	**Parental financial hardship.** Parents meet this by prioritising their own needs or by manipulating others. Power, control are present. The children may be neglected, targeted or used to support parental gain. The child in this situation again may appear controlling of siblings as survival is about strength but this is skewed. The child learns that weakness and vulnerability are not an option and thus everyone around you is a commodity for your benefit.	**Parental financial hardship.** Financial hardship leads to desperate measures. Multiple low paid jobs may mean less parent support. Hard working well-meaning but overwhelmed parents may reduce their availability to their children. Spiralling debt may lead to loan sharks inducing and greater chance of violence. Desperation is chaos inducing and greater chance of spiralling finances. Parental health may influence their capacity to work or manage financially. Mental health, reliance on alcohol, gambling, drugs or other addictions may become the parental primary focus. Desperate people do desperate things and the sex, or drugs industries may appear to be the only apparent way out of a hopeless situation – that compounds the issues. Crime may be an outcome. The sibling group will be affected by the stress and chaos and their responses to this are adaptive in a maladaptive situation (but maladaptive in an adaptive situation).

(Continued)

Table 8.4 (Continued)

Assessment Components: The Child/ren

Factor	Positive	Of Concern
Child 'A' (name)	**Geographical:** Inner city, rural, suburbs or remote. The surroundings may be extreme but are generally safe, free from war, terror, adverse climate conditions (drought, landslides, Tsunami, volcanic activity, water, land or air pollution etc). The area is relatively free of or managed in relations to drugs, street crime, antisocial behaviour, trafficking and exploitation. The absence of these major stressors are the foundations for safer communities, safer families and safer sibling relationships in a model coherent world.	**Geographical:** Inner city life may be a challenge that leads to machismo and alpha type behaviour. The joining of gangs for identity may be a proactive 'choice.' Street crime, county lines and the lure of quick 'easy' money may be a temptation too hard to resist. Peer pressure or more accurately peer normalisation may lead to similar behaviour within the sibling group or see polarisation in the sibling group. Rural and other areas will have similar but different issues.	**Geographical:** The children here are at the vagaries of the outside world. They have an external locus of control and are more likely to be targeted as a result of their vulnerabilities and coerced into gangs exploited and/or used in county lines. They may not see danger or when they do cannot find the supports to avoid it. This is played out in the sibling's group where the chaos in the outside world is presented in the sibling group.

(Continued)

Table 8.4 (Continued)

Assessment Components: The Child/ren

Factor	Positive	Of Concern
Child 'A' (name)	**Stress/trauma/ACEs** Minimal impact of stress, ACEs and trauma means that the child is likely to be more stable. Where a sibling has had trauma, they may be able to support their sibling. Where the sibling alleges abuse by the child's parent/parents they may not be able to support their sibling even when it is true.	**Stress/trauma/ACEs** High impact of stress, ACEs and trauma means that the child is likely to be more challenged. These children may be stuck, *appear therapy resistant*, be controlling, aggressive, self-assured, defiant, oppositional but may appear to be functioning well within a rigid manner. They tend towards hyper-vigilance; therefore, they are likely to be this way with their siblings. Two eloquent, educationally succeeding children does not make them secure or a good placement match – the question 'what are they working so hard to avoid?' must be asked. Siblings' disclosures are shut down.	**Stress/trauma/ACEs** High impact of stress, ACEs and trauma means that the child is likely to be more unstable, inconsistent, dissociative, dysregulated, penduluming and avoidant. They are in a state of constant movement or freeze. The chaos you see in the individual is highly likely in the sibling group. Two children in freeze is not positive. A sibling disclosure leads to blame, denial disbelief, siding with the perpetrator even when it has happened to the child too.
	Emotional connection: Presence of sibling warmth, including healthy presence and proximity or managed separation (i.e., university), levels of affection, brother/sister/ otherhood (companionship), closeness and support.	**Emotional connection:** Cold, distant, bullying, pseudo parentified, overly involved, overly protective, controlling, excessive fighting, arguing, negativity, aggression, and hostility.	**Emotional connection:** Sibling rivalry quickly breaks down into sibling chaos. there is evidence of words of connection but this is generally sentimentality or closing of ranks.

(Continued)

No Foregone Conclusions 169

Table 8.4 (Continued)

Assessment Components: The Child/ren

Factor	Positive		Of Concern	
Child 'A' (name)				

Coherence of connection (roles and responsibilities): Relationships between siblings are positive and healthy within the context of age differences, parental expectations etc. Where siblings are close in age there is a relative closeness although this can wax and wane across the lifespan, more often than not they find their way back to each other. **Achievements:** Birthdays and other celebrations are rejoiced. **Sharing:** Is mutual, easy and commonplace. They can also share in boisterous play (rough and tumble), imaginative experiences (role play), Rituals (routines such as bedtime, mealtime, etc.), Jokes, banter and fun, secrets (innocent and devoid of harm, intent or power and control). There is a sense of unity.	**Coherence of connection (roles and responsibilities):** Relationships between siblings are negative with signs of dysfunction. Controlling, manipulative and coercive of sibling. Relationships between siblings are toxic, highly stressed, trauma bonded. **Achievements:** Birthdays and other celebrations are a threat, ignored or demeaned. **Sharing:** Is replaced with withholding or taking. Boisterous play can be utilised to breakdown boundaries, imaginative play for a purpose, rituals to fit in, jokes etc are to demean and belittle and lack equality. Similarly the receiving of such leads to anger or rage and secrets feel dangerous and unsafe. There is a sense of hierarchy.	**Coherence of connection (roles and responsibilities):** Relationships between siblings are ambivalent or avoidant with signs of dysfunction. Dismissive vs dismissed. Lack of affect or swing in mood in relation to one another. Affect is low in mood, emotional vs flat, **Achievements:** Birthdays and other celebrations are not expected. **Sharing:** Is either at the detriment of the sharer (pseudo-parentified) or hoarding. Boisterous play leads to exiting WOT. Imaginative play is limited, rituals may be confusing, induce fear or uncertainty being out of their experience or associated with danger. Jokes and banter are hard to relate to and can lead to confusion or rage or dysregulation. Secrets are scary. There is a sense of chaos, disunity or fragmentation.

(Continued)

Table 8.4 (Continued)

Assessment Components: The Child/ren

Factor	Positive	Of Concern
Child 'A' (name)		
	Banter: They can tease and annoy with affection and stop and apologise when it goes too far. They can regulate or be regulated by their sibling. There is a sense of playfulness.	**Banter:** They are more likely to belittle, demean, crush and usually mean what they say. If their sibling gets upset or angry it doesn't bring about guilt or empathy – it may provoke further torment. This is too real to be play.	**Banter:** They may see each other as a threat. The notion of banter requires feeling secure in a relationship but where relationships are insecure there is no playfulness and therefore banter is less likely. They are too scared to play.
	Resolution and repair: Can argue and debate but can know the difference between their ability and their sibling's ability dependent on chronological and developmental ages. Even when right, they can separate out the cognitive facts and the emotional impact. They can make repairs and seek resolution.	**Resolution and repair:** Can argue but rarely debates. Winning is the intended outcome, and the means always justifies that it their mind. Chronological or developmental ability is of little or no consequence.	**Resolution and repair:** They do not have the cognitive – emotional stability for this. they may be inconsistent; their thoughts may be undermined by emotional response. They may become disorganised, hyper-emotional, dissociate or become hypo-aroused. They may acquiesce if pseudo-parentified.
	Responsibility: Can accept responsibility when wrong, or when they had made an error of judgment. They can feel guilt and remorse and actively want to make amends and make a repair.	**Responsibility:** They do not accept fault, will blame others and will argue and manipulate their way out. The feelings of shame are not seen but underlie this presentation.	**Responsibility:** May not know the difference between right and wrong. May know the difference dependent on how triggered they are and that this may not make sense. They may lie, become disorganised, plead and/ or protest. Have little ability for cogent thought or emotional consequences.

(Continued)

Table 8.4 (Continued)

Assessment Components: The Child/ren

Factor	Positive	Of Concern
Child 'A' (name)	**Equality:** They know they are equally loved by their parents because they are treated equally.	**Favoured child:** They have an expectation their needs will be met first. Privileged, idolised or feared.	**Scapegoated child:** They don't really know what love is. It may be conditional/an exchange/bartered. They may be favoured at times, but this is inconsistent.
	Affect: Is positive. Sibling responses cover the whole spectrum but are mainly positive or return to positive. Where sibling rivalry occurs, it is within the realms of healthy competition, and no one gets hurt. Their bragging/celebration may be based on comparison where individual gifts such as academic or sporting prowess, personal features such as attractiveness, fitness are themes and peer relationships may bring balance back into the frame.	**Affect:** Is negative. Sibling responses are angry, volatile, shaming, dismissive, patronising. This goes beyond sibling rivalry as maintaining the position in the family is the key factor.	**Affect:** Is blank, dissociative, low mood/no mood, pendulums. There is no sibling rivalry as there is no expectation of anything good happening so a sense of helplessness and hopelessness are often a feature.

(Continued)

172 A Trauma Model for Assessing Siblings

Table 8.4 (Continued)

Assessment Components: The Child/ren

Factor	Positive	Of Concern
Child 'A' (name)	**Roles that are adopted:** Eldest male child knows this to be a fact rather than a privilege. They do not use this to their advantage. They do not take on a sense of responsibility but grow to want to be a protective and supportive factor in their sibling's life. understands that everyone has gifts, and their interests and hobbies are examples of such. They know that all siblings' activities will be encouraged and supported, and they will too. Their personality is unique, and they manage to buffer along with their siblings Defends and protects sibling in a balanced manner. The key is the balance between loyalty and coherence. Has empathy and can identify and respond to different states of affect. The child can receive support and comfort from their sibling as a source and not a means. Is a source of comfort not the means of comfort. Can initiate play with siblings and can respond to sibling's desire to play. Play is balanced and tends towards the age of the child they are playing with. Can be competitive, but can celebrate winning and the winner in equal measure and can manage losing as participation is key. Wants to/and can support/help and can accept help in relation to siblings.	**Roles that are adopted:** Eldest child is a boy. They may experience their father's masculinity as dangerous and thus it is safer to become dangerous than be in danger. They only have time for their own activities and hobbies and are likely to be disinterested or dismissive about their siblings' interests. Their personality may be charismatic, egocentric, rigid, or vigilant. Will defend a sibling if the act secures their position. At other times their sibling is a tool/a means to an end. They have a sense of entitlement and privilege and feel superior in some aspects. Empathy is seldom seen here. The words may be spoken but it feels incoherent as there is no emotional congruence. Does not desire connection let alone comfort. Will not give or receive unless there is a hidden motive. Has no interest in play	**Roles that are adopted:** Eldest child is a boy and may feel their masculinity is dangerous as their father was dangerous. Can't defend a sibling because they can't defend themselves. Can defend a sibling out of a sense of duty (pseudo-parentified). Their personality may be undefined, rigid or lost in chaos. they may sense that everything is a potential danger. Will defend out of sentimentality, will fail to defend out of survival or may be inconsistent. Sentimentality rather than empathy. If you can't have empathy for yourself. It's difficult to have it for others. Is too exhausted to give or receive. May keep on keeping on if burdened enduring and pseudo- parentified. Can't play. Is too scared or tired to play. Hasn't learned how to

(Continued)

Table 8.4 (Continued)

Assessment Components: The Child/ren

Factor	Positive	Of Concern
Child 'A' (name)		
	unless it is conditional, a bargaining tool. Maybe can't play, where play is seen it is either competitive (responses to winning and losing are important here: losing is shameful, winning is ok, winning whilst shaming the loser is most satisfying). Helps or teaches when there is an ulterior motive. Is generally not wanting or willing to support.	play. Has significant developmental ruptures in play, may play younger than their chronological years. May help if they are able, may have a sense of duty/responsibility (pseudo-parentified)
	Sibling absence: Will miss the sibling when away. Will celebrate moving to university with the simultaneous expression of loss that they will miss them. Boarding school may be mixed, dependent on the other children's school and circumstances. Where the sibling is in hospital there will be concern, fear and anger. They will be able to articulate these emotions and feelings. On holiday they will hold their sibling in mind or be held in mind. The siblings will miss each other but tempered with enjoyment or celebration of the event.	**Sibling absence:** The child seldom if ever mentions their sibling. Where they do, there is a mismatch between what the child says and their emotional connection to those words. They may be patronising, feel entitled or jealous. Where a change of placement, they may worry what their sibling may say out of proximity. **Sibling absence:** Expects loss. Their low mood may make it hard to know what they are feeling or what caused the low mood. Where it is a change of placement they may cling to their sibling or be relieved or both.

(Continued)

Table 8.4 (Continued)

Assessment Components: The Child/ren

Factor	Positive	Of Concern
Child 'A' (name)	**Intimacy:** Reciprocity is key, proud of self and siblings, can give prise and constructive criticism. Knows the boundaries of intimacy. Is not scared to give or receive advice, concern, thoughts, hopes, fears, dreams etc.	**Intimacy:** There is no reciprocity although it may look that way. They will take praise and not give it unless in giving it raises their standing. They cannot bear criticism and constructive criticism is still hard. Knows the boundaries of intimacy and crosses them anyway. They will question and listen as information is power. They are likely to talk as this is an opportunity to redirect, confuse, create doubt or a smoke screen.
		Intimacy: These children are too disorganised for reciprocity, chaos is more likely. There may be moments, but this is inconsistent. Has little understanding of intimacy and boundaries, may exceed taboos as these are normal and therefore not shameful. They may see others' views on intimacy as confusing.
	Attachment The siblings' attachments are in line with the secure attachments of the birth parents or are responding to the new attachment relationship (kinship, step, half, foster, adoptive, etc.).	**Attachment** Ambivalent or avoidant in nature.
		Attachment Ambivalent AND avoidant or disorganised
	Locus of Control Internalised. Balanced in relationship.	**Locus of Control** Internalised (control) Externalised when out of WOT.
		Locus of Control Externalised (not in control of external events. Cannot see that bad things happen to everyone only that they are at the mercy of the world.

(Continued)

Table 8.4 (Continued)

Assessment Components: The Child/ren

Factor	Positive	Of Concern
Child 'A' (name)	**Temperament** 'Easy child,' balanced activity level, can stay on task – age specific, shows an ability to be intense. There is a regularity and consistency to their positive presentation and when this differs the reason is understandable. The child has a sensory threshold that can be challenged and developed. Can manage proximity changes with both approach and withdrawal well. The child is highly adaptable. In the face of adversity shows an ability to persistence but not across all areas. Generally positive mood but can vary under understandable conditions.	**Temperament** 'Difficult child,' High activity level, regularly distracted off task often or hyper-driven and overfocused – age specific. Can be highly intense. There is either a regularity and consistency to their presentation (positive or negative) and when this differs the reason is often hard to see or not easily understandable. The child has a sensory threshold that cannot be challenged or developed easily and maybe compromised in many areas. Can manage proximity changes with both approach and withdrawal well on their terms only. The child is highly controlling and struggles with adaptability. May be seen to dysregulate easily with a tendency to hyper-arousal causing an impact on those around them and themselves. In the face of adversity may show an ability to persistence or may become highly controlling. Generally hard to read their mood or their mood is incongruent.	**Temperament** 'Slow to warm up child,' low activity level, struggles to be motivated to undertake task. Shows little intensity. There is no regularity or consistency to their positive presentation and when this differs the reason is often hard to see or not easily understandable. The child has a severely restricted sensory threshold that cannot be challenged or developed easily. Struggles to manage proximity changes with both approach and withdrawal. The child has little or no adaptability and will be seen to dysregulate easily with a tendency to hypo-arousal or hyper-arousal causing an impact on themselves. In the face of adversity shows little or compromised ability to persistence and may give up or not even start. Generally low mood or their mood is incongruent.

(Continued)

Table 8.4 (Continued)

Assessment Components: The Child/ren

Factor	Positive	Of Concern
Child 'A' (name)	**Behaviour:** They are in a state of homeostasis. They can self-regulate or be self-regulated. They can have varying degrees of affect. Can become highly excited, nervous, angry etc but come back to balance. When out of kilter they can still regulate to meet the needs of a sibling who requires their help, support or attention. **Boundaries:** Is aware of own and sibling's personal space. Can know and read when too close and not close enough. Is aware that rules can change dependent on circumstances and need. Very aware of own and others boundaries. **Power imbalance** Balanced, creates opportunities to level the playing field. Wants to be a positive influence on their siblings, wants to enjoy and celebrate their achievements.	**Behaviour:** They are in a state of control or out of control. They can regulate to meet their needs. they will do things for others when it meets their needs primarily. They are often seen as being in their WOT – but this takes a lot of energy. **Boundaries:** Is aware of own boundaries and can be quite protective of them. They are aware of others need for boundaries and personal space but have no qualms in transgressing them. **Power imbalance** Uses age, gender, height, weight, standing in the family, genetic gifts, race/skin tone, provided status (baby-sitting, head boy/girl) as opportunities to gain power or control over their siblings.	**Behaviour:** They are dysregulated, avoidant or dissociated. They struggle to remain in their WOT. They cannot regulate to meet a siblings' needs or will try to meet their needs whilst being in a dysregulated state. **Boundaries:** Is unclear about boundaries as they never learnt them. They can be avoidant of others, inconsistent and often chaotic. **Power imbalance** They may respond to their highly controlling sibling with subordination or subordinate their younger sibling or disabled sibling or they may be chaotic or inconsistent in their behaviour.

(Continued)

Table 8.4 (Continued)

Assessment Components: The Child/ren

Factor	Positive		Of Concern	
Child 'A' (name)				
Sibling relationship Child A with child C and child C's views if different	**Presence/absence of a Trauma Bond** **Concerns** Equality in relationships, meeting each child with their own unique needs **Positive attributes** List	Repeat/as above	**Presence/absence of a Trauma Bond** **Concerns** Differential treatment: Favoured **Positive attributes** List	**Presence/absence of a Trauma Bond** **Concerns** Differential treatment: Scapegoated **Positive attributes** List
			Repeat/as above	Repeat/as above
Sibling B's relationship with child C and child C's views if different	Repeat/as above		Repeat/as above	Repeat/as above
Sibling A, B, and C's relationship as a sibling group	Repeat/as above		Repeat/as above	Repeat/as above

Chapter 9

Listening before Listing
Making Sense of Adult and Child Narratives

'Talk to parents and significant relatives' (Becket, 2021). How different would it have been to enable the gathering of much-needed, often missed, information if she had written, 'Listen to parents and significant others.' She goes on to write, 'Parenting assessments *should* already include information about siblings, so review this and think about what aspects you can usefully summarise to include in your sibling assessment' (italics inserted by authors). The problem is this could focus on what was 'done' and not include the circumstances in which it was done, whether what was done was by intention or omission or what was done then did. This information is needed to understand the generational impact of trauma. The children's experiences and subsequent relationships were born in this. Crittenden, poignantly heads her first chapter, 'Yesterday's children are today's mothers and fathers' (2008) and crucially acknowledges, 'Sometimes children's needs would be met best by meeting their parents' personal needs,' and reflects, 'Children rarely live better than their parents. If the parent suffers, so will the child.' Therefore, she recommends, 'Understanding and helping troubled parents to become secure and balanced people is crucial, for the parents themselves, for their children, and for society at large.' This viewpoint is the epitome of model coherence, and yet services are increasingly actively avoiding including this work or actively excluding it from their financial responsibility.

Della, aged 65, described later did not know why her mother did not love her and rejected her. She did not know she was born of rape and was therefore a constant reminder to her mother of that experience. Della parented her own adopted children, without this context, and felt constantly as if she had the wrong parenting handbook. She brought them up through the lens of her own experience of being unloved though she still felt self-love. The impact on her already vulnerable children would depend on how that 'self-love' was developed and how it presents. It could be that she developed resilience and could then model self-worth to her children or, conversely, limit her capacity to express or demonstrate love, raising the risk of misattunement, or fail to consistently and empathically emotionally connect with them.

The chapters in this book have already explored in depth the reasons why some parent(s) or carer(s) do not fully disclose their developmental histories, experiences

DOI: 10.4324/9781003724605-13

of, and beliefs about their caregiving or care receiving. This chapter sets out to explore how to maximise the assessment time with adults, how to elicit information, how to look for gaps and ways to reduce them, and finally how to organise the information in a manner that will allow for analysis.

The Relationship

Meeting with adults and the success of any intervention is based on the relationship with the individual (Ogden et al., 2006). One of the key qualities needed to be a social worker is, 'Their personal skills as individuals: how do they relate to others and how do they understand how others operate' (Dominelli, 2009). The therapeutic alliance, the therapist-client relationship, is accepted as a key foundation to any intervention (Freud, 1912; Friedman, 1969; Fisher, 2026). However, this relationship starts with the professional's level of self-awareness. If there is no true knowledge of self, how is it possible to know anyone else.

It is a requirement for therapists undertaking their core-trainingcore training to undergo their own personal therapy. Most approved courses have an expectation that personal therapy will already have been considered prior to formal training. This places therapists at an advantage over most social workers where, at least in the United Kingdom, there is no formal requirement for personal therapy in that field. There is then, for social workers, the ubiquitous danger of becoming discombobulated, enmeshed, prone to transference and counter-transference issues and vicarious traumatisation (burn-out).(burnout).This view is somewhat endorsed by Dominelli who went on to write, 'Another key quality required by social workers is an emotional dimension. How are they affected by really complicated and sometimes devastating situations that people have to respond to.

Relationships with parents in the context of statutory interventions, be they social work, psychological, psychiatric, or therapeutic have an obvious extra layer of complexity, especially when this relationship and involvement may result in outcomes contrary to the parent or carer's hopes or expectations. Extra care must be taken in these circumstances. The strong relationship required must also be congruent and coherent. The need for model coherency remains the most important component exactly when the odds are against developing an open, honest, and connected relationship despite those adverse factors.

Margaret knew exactly what her story was; after all, she had repeated it so often it was second nature to her. However, whilst she wanted to deal with the impact her story had on her, no matter how many times over the following years she re-established contact, she was unable to proceed with therapy. This suggested that whilst Margaret could develop a relationship with the therapist it was only limited to engagement and the development of a rapport. It just could not progress to a therapeutic alliance. This would be the level of relationship a social worker would need to achieve to support a client to share experiences and beliefs about themselves that would create an understanding of a child's parenting experience. Margaret was consciously aware and capable but, emotionally, less well-equipped.

Jayne and Saul had a child placed with them that was an ill-considered match. There were a number of evident contraindications.

1. Abbey was so close in age to their own born child.
2. Jayne and Saul were first-time foster carers.
3. Their child was an only child.

What was harder to evaluate were the original drivers in the couple's histories and relationship. Neither parent could see how their expectations were born in their past. Yet when provided the opportunity, were both able to relatively quickly self-reflect and then individually make sense of the drives they had previously been unaware or avoidant of. What was harder for them was to acknowledge with each other that they had irrevocably grown apart, and their relationship had reached a crisis point. Their inability to acknowledge this meant the prognosis for the placement was poor, whether they stayed suspended in limbo or managed to share their feelings openly. This is also a crisis point for many practitioners. The instinct to rescue a placement can lead to providing every programme, therapy and support available, often mirroring and repeating the same strategies already used when trying to keep the child in their birth family. Jayne was not going to shift from her position that Abbey was negatively impacting on her daughter, and Saul could not imagine giving up on Abbey even at the cost of losing his wife and daughter.

Safety and Trust

Interventions with children and adults follow the same principle: to develop safety and trust. Again, it is difficult when the outcome may be contrary to parents' or carers' hoped or expected outcome. This task is not achieved through manipulation, deceit, or false promises, but through congruence, honesty, and connecting to the pain the situation is causing each individual. The parent who, by telling the truth, may bring about the removal of their child, the young adult who has sexually harmed a sibling in sharing this information may lead to the loss of liberty and sibling, or the couple who feel irreconcilably different towards a child face the loss of each other and/or the child. The best outcome is when clients feel safe enough and can trust the practitioner to emotionally and psychologically 'hold' them during these often painfully brutal interviews. This is borne out of real relationships which have taken time to develop through deep connections. This takes the one thing most services and practitioners and timescales do not have time. To be coherent, this has to change. A change of this magnitude will take a societal change in priorities and policies.

The Intervention or Assessment

The foundation of building safety and trust through a relationship contains the elements of compassion or empathy. This is not feeling sorry for someone or having sentimental feelings,

One participates completely in the clients communication, comments are in line with the client, that despite the power differentials this is an equal relationship on a common problem (in this instance assessing whether the siblings can stay together or not) that feelings are accepted.

(Rogers, 1961)

After all, their feelings are based on their experiences and the current situation and should therefore be welcomed into the room. Violence and aggression are not feelings. They may well result from feelings that are intolerable, not manageable or contained in their window of tolerance, unprocessed and by being unmetabolised prevent compromise in responses or actions. This usually occurs when the capacity to self-regulate has been overestimated or there has been a failure to provide self, co-regulation, or grounding exercises prior to delving deeper.

The hardest element is to hold a stance of Unconditional Positive Regard (UPR) (Rogers, 1959). This is to hold a person in all their fallible humanness whist accepting one's own fallible humanness and frailty with humility without shaming or judging their core or skewed beliefs. Accepting people as they are enables acceptance of the other's beliefs and views without having to like, condone or agree with those views. The task is then to see if there is capacity to understand where those views were born and if there is capacity for change or movement, or are stuck, ingrained, rigid, and then to determine if the capacity to change is compromised or so entrenched that making the necessary changes is outside of the child's timescales.

Tabitha was a foster carer for 12-year-old Tara. In the waiting room prior to therapy, Tara exited her window of tolerance, flew into a rage directed at Tabitha, kicking, hitting, screaming, shouting, tearing out clumps of Tabitha's hair and becoming a danger to herself and those around her. Tabitha was scared. The school support worker and escort had influenced Tabitha to take control utilising strategies which may have worked in a school environment, but the support worker and escort were unable or unwilling to accept the limitations of their strategies, or to question whether those practices may even be harmful to Tara. When Tabitha was scared she became more physical in her interactions. Tabitha and the school staff could not adequately physically restrain Tara. When Tara's behaviour escalated in response, Tabitha threatened to call the police. Having been alerted, the therapist intervened.

Having empathy for the adult's situation, whilst seeing the negative impact on Tara and maintaining UPR for their situation rather than their methods is a challenge. Essentially there is the danger of becoming complicit, enmeshed or embroiled in ill-fitting strategies. The final requirement is congruence. 'Congruence or genuineness is neither a technique nor an attitude. It is the state of realness, maturity and authenticity existing in persons who accurately perceive their self-experience.' (Natiello, 2001).

To manage the situation, the therapist needed to intervene immediately without shaming, blaming, or inflaming the situation for Tara, Tabitha, or the school workers. Talking directly to Tara, the therapist used a volume that was loud enough to hear, authoritative enough to believe, with prosody to make connection possible, to avoid control or threat, intonation to help modulate affect, rhythm to create a measured flow, a tone that is coherent with the message, a pitch that does not over or under power the situation and content that matches the situation connect with all three. Tabitha's message was incoherent. She was threatening repeatedly to call the police. Tara was not a criminal. She was traumatised, scared, and fighting for her life. She was reliving her past and dissociating. She needed 'bringing back' to the here and now. The message delivered was the one she needed to hear, that she is safe now; she was showing how scared she is, but she is safe now. Tabitha was also hearing the message through this modelling of the required response and noting her unhelpful responses for later processing. At the same time, the therapist was modelling for the school worker who was largely silent but willing to relax her physical holding (restraining) of Tara, thus allowing scope for a cessation of that less helpful intervention.

Following the event, and prior to subsequent 'meltdowns,' both the education workers and Tabitha required psychoeducation on the source and purpose of Tara's presentation, alternative responses and processing of the event(s). The ability to be congruent leads to the individual's ability to reflect on their stance, consider and practice alternatives or to become resistant, in opposition to or rejecting of those views. Either way the potential outcomes become clearer. The practice of Regulate, Relate, Reason before Repair endorses this process (Perry, 2021).

Parent/Carer History

Gathering a full history of the parent's experience is a vital component in understanding the children's experience; indeed, it is the foundation and the building block of the children's experience. When assessing the children's sibling relationship, it is vital to include the parents' sibling relationships in their childhood and present lives. The importance of accessing a clear and detailed chronology that allows the possibility to track and assess the variables across relationships and generations cannot be overemphasised.

Parent/Carer: To Be Repeated for All Key Adults in the Children's Lives

The level of information required on the parent's parent (grandparent, step, substitute et al.) will depend on the type of information that is presented, missing, contradicts, or contraindicates healthy parenting. There is often a struggle to understand the purpose and need to collect and collate this depth of historical information, despite key texts supporting this as a requirement. The *Purple Book* (DOH, 1999) sets out 'Parenting capacity' and 'Family and environmental factors' as key components by including, 'The care and upbringing of children does not take place in a vacuum. All family members are influenced both positively and negatively by the wider family, the neighbourhood and social networks within which they live.' This guidance draws well on writers such as Belsky and Vondra (1989), but they did not include the impact of developmental trauma, and where mental health issues are drawn on from other authors (Aldridge and Becker, 1999; Tucker et al., 1999; Buchanan, 1994), they too did not include the impact of unresolved trauma mimicking the diagnostic criteria for mental illness.

One clear example of this is Ada. Her horrendous and unimaginable life experience that scarred her emotionally, psychologically, psychically, biologically, and physically impacted on her ability to function as an individual and as a parent to her daughter Saffron. Following the assessment when contact is being considered, should her history compromise her seeing her child, what issues would need to be included, what would need to be put in place to alleviate any potential negative impact, to ensure any identified negatives or risks do not outweigh identified potential benefits?

Another is Margaret, who was acutely conflicted, wanting therapy but not being able to take the final step, no matter how many times she contacted the Service over the years. What impact could this level of ambivalence, uncertainty, indecisiveness and fear have on her children or her grandchildren? How would this presentation be received in an assessment?

Preconception History

Della was an adopter whose adoptive children had grown up and left home. Despite this, she was hopelessly bound to her daughter who lived locally. She was so enmeshed in her needs and dependency; the only way out was to consider moving. She described herself as a happy and positive person, an image and disposition she entirely believed.

It only took Della two sessions to realise that the reason she lived with her maternal grandmother, whom she described as loving, was because her mother didn't love her, couldn't bear to look at her, let alone spend any time with her. Her mother was 16 when she became pregnant with Della and was emotionally unready to have a child. Further exploration of her mother's circumstances led to her sharing her knowledge that she was born of rape. Della was the living reminder of that experience for her mother. These circumstances then led to very relevant questions about her grandmother's relationship with and her parenting of Della's mother. Something Della was not ready or able to consider because of her enmeshed relationship with her grandmother.

The information about Lucy and Krystal would be very different to the parents with a 'normative' experience such as Hannah and Devon, but this is akin to comparing internalising and externalising children. When a child is severely externalising to the point that their presentation or behaviour is a danger to themselves or those around them, the need for intervention is often clear without a psychometric.

However, assessment tools are still clinically valuable. They establish baselines, severity, track change and can compare across settings. The tests can help in identifying differences between the siblings. Seeing internalising behaviour is much harder. The adults like Hannah and Devon, or their children may not have externalised, but their experiences were still on a spectrum or a continuum and thus so would their outcomes. By being difficult to see does not mean internalising behaviour has less impact or needs less intervention. It is at least the same or worse. Worse when there has been no obvious outlet, for example, until someone takes their life and the response is, 'We didn't see that coming.' That is not to say that externalising people are not at the risk of the same outcome. Campbell and Hale (1991) in their research on suicide, argue that seeing suicide as a solipsistic act is misleading because it neglects the violent dynamics at work. This may suggest that suicide can be understood as both an internalising and externalising solution.

Suggested below are questions needed to identify the factors that added to any individual positive or negative impact of children's and parents' in-utero experiences and the factors that ameliorated them:

- Attachment quality and critically what caused the attachment to be formed in this way. If the behaviours match the criteria for insecure or disorganised style, the information needs to answer the question: what were they so scared of?
- Temperament.
- Locus of control issues.
- Internalising or externalising behaviour.
- Resilience factors versus adversity.
- Presence or absence of the 5 'P's and 8 'C's.
- Infant period experiences.
- Preschool experiences.
- School-age experiences.
- Adolescent experiences.
- Managing young adulthood.
- Post-school learning, education, employment, travel, calling, purpose, outlook, or ability to manage and cope with challenges.
- Quality and types of relationships, friendships, and support networks. Their experience of ACEs, toxic or enmeshed relationships, co-dependency, scapegoating, favouritism, and/or transition/movement/change.
- Their experience of ACEs, toxic or enmeshed relationships, co-dependency, scapegoating, favouritism.
- Their reactions to times of transition or movement or change.

These formative experiences can offer important clues about how adults present themselves and how they relate, communicate, and choose to share or conceal aspects of their history during assessment. Early experiences often shape presentation, whether through Character Strategies or the presence and influence of Parts. Recognising these differences, which are sometimes evident and sometimes subtle, enables assessors to connect at a deeper level and therefore elicit information that may otherwise have remained hidden. This information will then guide the assessor to reveal more about the children's lived experience than by questions alone.

Character Strategies

Character Strategies (Ogden) or Character Styles (Johnson) are survival strategies that often reflect underlying limiting core beliefs. They are a child's developmental response to maladaptive care receiving messages, abuse, deficits in care, inconsistent or less than optimum parenting.

The concept of Character Strategies was first articulated by Reich (1933) and further developed by Fenechel (1945) and others in the psychoanalytic tradition. Ron Kurtz later reframed them before Pat Ogden incorporated them into Sensorimotor Psychotherapy. Kurtz writes, 'We can think about character patterns in different ways: as strengths or weaknesses, function or malfunction, as reflections of the strategies other creatures use; as adjustment processes to the particular stress of information overload' (2007), but then goes on to state, 'Character patterns are strategies. A defence is a general way of dealing with the world, a way of managing one's experience. People are creative and we find many strategies within one person' (2007). Johnson (1994) argues,

> These strategies result from the child attempting to make sense of, and live with, adversity resulting from their care and that some early attempts at resolving this are based both on limited equipment and limited experience of the world. Furthermore, when the issues are faced in trauma, their early resolutions tend to become rigid and resistant to change. In this view, these early solutions were often quite adaptive given the limitations of the environment and the limitations of the individual's capacities, but they often achieved an imperfect escape from trauma.

Integration is achieved when raised in a secure environment with optimum parenting or a deep and successful therapeutic intervention has been undertaken. Character strategies are then balanced or come back into balance. There are elements of all of them, but none are over-relied upon or used exclusively. Differences are hard to see. The more adversity faced the more heavily one or two may be relied upon. Ogden cites the following nine developmental responses to different care provision. They tend to be on a continuum.

- Sensitive-Withdrawn: a strategy in response to the failure of basic safety between birth and 12 months. Tom's strategy.
- Sensitive-Emotional: a strategy in response to fear, loss, abandonment, and abuse that is also experienced in the first 12 months. Seen in Cicely, Amy, and Ada's presentation.
- Dependent-Endearing: developed between 12–36 months. Webster describes it as a toddler. The challenge is when the toddler's needs are not met by attuned

parents; the response is to adapt in some way. This is seen in Tia and Sonia's presentation.
- Self-Reliant: a response to the failure of needs being met. The child takes responsibility or is given the responsibility for meeting this need on its own. Seen in Cherry, Tia, Becky, Amber, Lacey, Karen and Beatrice's presentation.
- Burdened-Enduring: develops between 2–5 years when the child's developmental task revolves around the expression of will, 'Can I have an impact on my environment?' and/or is obliged to take on responsibilities before developmentally ready. This is often seen in adults who have been child carers or were children who had to keep on keeping on despite the odds stacked against them. Daria, Cicely, Amy, Lisa, and Karen's Strategy.
- Charming-Manipulative: this strategy and Burdened/Enduring are a response to environments that do not allow children to express their will, to have age-appropriate power. This is a presentation seen in many successful adults such as entrepreneurs, salespeople, and politicians but also seen in Harmful Sexual Behaviour, paedophiles, and sex offenders. Charity, Hunter, Joe, Max, and Emmett's presentation.
- Tough-Generous: on becoming more independent were not allowed to be vulnerable or had to learn that generosity was conditional. Seen in Tia.
- Industrious-Overfocused: as a response to wondering if love was given unconditionally or an acknowledgement dependent on how they perform. The bar is often raised as they get close or remains just out of reach and so the child has to keep pushing personal limits. Charity and Karen's presentation.
- Expressive-Clinging: as a response to not knowing what needed to be done to receive attention when love is not given freely by parents. Seen in Cicely's presentation.

Integration requires being raised in a secure environment with optimum parenting or having undertaken a deep and successful therapeutic intervention. Character strategies need to be balanced or come back into balance. Everyone has elements of all of them, but none should be over-relied upon or used exclusively. The more adversity faced the more heavily one or two are relied upon.

Consider the parent who was harder to engage/connect with and what might be their character strategy? What might their missed experience be to build their reliance on this strategy? Might this be presenting part and how would this be ascertained? What impact may it have had on those around them? How could this information support the receptivity of this parent?

Parts

For simplicity and clarity, 'character strategies' and 'parts' have been addressed individually. However, the danger is that this is oversimplifying a very complex subject. In essence, however, they belong to the same body of thought but have been aligned through different hypothetical starting points. The baby, infant, or very young child is in a crisis because they are dependent on their caregiver for survival. In response to less than optimal or abusive care, they have to come up with a solution in order to survive. They take on the 'holding pattern' in their roles, which become character strategies to the outside eye (the assessor perhaps), which is essentially the 'part' doing their job that is evident in the strategy. The parts are undertaking the roles they were given or compelled to take on to survive and carry their burdens. These become visible when extreme or contextualised within roles that appear 'valued' (social role valorisation). Examples are the successful businessperson may in fact be industrious and overfocused, the Local Authority social worker may be self-reliant, the foster carer who never gives up on extremely challenging children may be burdened-enduring, and the politician may be charming and manipulative. So, we see the presentation, but underneath there may also be a 'part.'

The development of parts and how they are presented in daily life can be subtle. Each can be living what is believed to be an authentic life because awareness of past difficult, stressful, or traumatic experiences can be limited. These experiences or parts can be cut off or dissociated from consciousness or repressed or held by a part of self that remains hidden from awareness.

Ogden (2015) and Fisher (2026) discuss the complexity of presentation when they state that 'Different self-states or "parts" may hold different working models with relatively fixed meaning-making and conflicting expectations of the future that are not integrated. This might mean that adults may believe what they are telling you, but this may not mean this is the reality'.

Schwartz (1995) states 'Parts exist from birth, either in potential or in actuality. That is, multiplicity is inherent in the nature of the mind, rather than being the result of the introjection of external phenomena, or the result of fragmentation through trauma.' Because parts are in essence the individual, the individual can be unaware that they are not in homeostasis.

These indicators are essential to understanding individual strengths and resistance to negative affect, vicarious traumatisation, and ability to remain consistent, level, nurturing, empathically attuned and responsive in relationships and what will be passed on generationally. The impact on child rearing then becomes clear.

One difficulty is not in the collection of data; even if there is time and an optimum relationship to do so, it is in the organisation of the data in a manner that allows for cross-referencing from other sources and then the analysis.

Karen's situation could have been missed by the mere collation of data. The important information the practitioner picked up on was her response, 'I'm fine,' a common answer to a well-being question that was not coherent with her current circumstances. Hypothesising and triangulating how to understand her, 'I'm fine,' is needed. The I'm fine from a burdened-enduring character strategy may be met with resistance because this I'm fine will always be fine because it is necessary to carry on, carrying on. If it is a part, it may be a 'manager' whose business or job is to keep people away and is determined to persuade there is no weakness or vulnerability. A good time to request further assessments including psychometrics, to help further understand what is going on.

Psychometrics

The use of psychometrics helps triangulate information gathered from other sources. Every test has its purpose and limitations. Organisations should be aware of those strengths and limitations as they may skew outcomes of interventions either positively or negatively. It is rarely helpful to rely on one metric for accurate results, yet many organisations favour screening tests rather than those that offer more in-depth analysis.

A meta-analysis of psychometric tests available to assess the impact of trauma was published in the *Journal of Trauma and Abuse* identified the most useful as John Briere's battery of psychometrics. They fit with a trauma in a trauma-informed assessment given the context of the majority of the children's and families' experiences. They are excellent for identifying and understanding the impact of trauma on individual children and adults.

Finding a test or tests which fit with the context of each professional's or service's remit is a helpful tool in triangulating information, but care must be taken to avoid the risk of alienating or potentially pathologising an individual. Taylor and Shrive (2023) in their trauma-informed alternative to the Diagnostic and Statistical Manual of Mental Health Disorders provide some helpful alternatives.

One argument against using psychometrics comes from the fear they dehumanise people, that it is something, 'done to,' rather than, 'done with,' individuals. Like any intervention this is dependent on the intent and mindset of the practitioner.

Karen was first asked to fill out a psychometric (Briere's Trauma Symptom Checklist for Children, 1992) on her daughter. This was less stressful for Karen because she was a health professional with concerns for her daughter's well-being. The test for validity was met, the results valid but had to be inaccurate because if correct her child would have been presenting very differently to the description of the behaviour from mum and school. It did not triangulate. Karen believed her scores, or the results would have been invalid. In discussion Karen understood the concept that the scorer can unconsciously score not for their child but a result more accurate for herself. She had no anxiety in undertaking a psychometric on herself (Briere's Trauma Symptom Inventory-2). This highlighted clear issues. Its use, with sensitivity, opened up emerging communication which enabled her to accept and reflect on her own experiences. This did not mean that her child no longer had any issues, or that she was the one with the issues but that both co-existed and could easily be resolved for one without the other. This is why assessments with time and funding provided are needed to provide for the parent's recovery and not just the child's. Particularly where the 'parent' is a foster carer or adopter and the first assessment failed to uncover the previous experiences.

Questions need to be asked before completing the graphs:

What was the context of the parents' own history and the parents' own parents' history?

Consider:

- Gender, cultural heritage, language, faith/belief/religion, financial freedom or hardship, sexuality, disability or ability, educational attainment, resilience or vulnerability, ACEs, neurodivergence, general well-being, physical, emotional, biological, sexual health, habitual behaviour or addiction, interests, hobbies, political and social ideology, fitness, diet, addiction, and fundamentally their identity.

Specifically:

- How did they meet and at what age? Did this have any bearing on their readiness, maturity, energy, financial security or resilience? No single factor will be a rationale for their resilience or vulnerability, but incrementally will build a picture of their situation.
- How did they meet, preconception wishes, hopes and plans, the conception circumstances of each adult, planned, accidental, through rape, entrapment, violence?
- During pregnancy history. Considered or wished for or tried termination? Who was told or not told about the pregnancy? Levels of intrafamilial or extrafamilial stress, domestic control/violence, depression, financial hardship, ill-health, fragility, substance misuse, medical implications made better or worse by conception.
- Cooperation with antenatal services. Desire to engage (both parents), interest, capacity to pay attention, absorb, process, and analyse information, ability to memorise, retain, and recall information.
- Labour and birth issues: uncomplicated/complicated, planned, or emergency Caesarean section or other interventions needed, who wanted or didn't want to be present, was present, who held the baby first, baby to special baby care or emergency treatment. Impact of being present when all went well or badly.
- Family makeup and support.
- Presence or absence of siblings: age range, quality of relationships, type of sibling (full, half, step, adopted, foster, other).
- Deaths or separations and how they are managed. Wartime evacuation or abandonment?
- Type and quality of their relationship. Equal, enmeshed, co-dependent, skewed, controlling, power differentials, support, violent, manipulation, dependent/independent, loyal, vibrant, hopeless/helpless, burdened.

Table 9.1 Psychodynamic Formulation

Child, Sibling, Parent/Carer Psychodynamic Formulation

Parent/Person's name		Date		
Tendency	Positive	Of Concern		Unknown
Focus	Resilience Factors	Adversity/ ACEs/Hyper	Adversity/ ACEs/Hypo	Need/Gaps
History				
Personal history and presentation issues				
Parent/carer history				
Circumstances of conception				
Pregnancy				
Family Support				
Faith				
Given name meaning				
Transitions/movement/change				
Geographic issues				
Support systems: family/friends				
Financial stability				
Accommodation stability/ satisfaction				
Presentation				
Attachment style				
Temperament				
Locus of control				
Internal working model				
Balanced/internalising/externalising behaviour				

(Continued)

Table 9.1 (Continued)

Child, Sibling, Parent/Carer Psychodynamic Formulation

Parent/Person's name   Date

Tendency	Positive Resilience Factors	Adversity/ ACEs/Hyper Of Concern	Adversity/ ACEs/Hypo	Unknown Need/Gaps
Focus				
Sensory processing/ sensorimotor				
Boundaries and limits				
Window of tolerance				
Attachment style				
Belief system				
Regulation				
Chronological vs developmental age				
Presentation				
Common behavioural or presentation markers (honesty, food, response to transition and change, dreams, nightmares, night terrors, routines, toileting, ambivalence, avoidance, dissociation, disassociation, anger, rage, depression, hyper-vigilance, opposition, defiance)				
Denial				
Play				
8 'C's				
5 'P's				
Levels of Stress or Trauma				
Shame				

(Continued)

Table 9.1 (Continued)

Child, Sibling, Parent/Carer Psychodynamic Formulation

Parent/Person's name   Date

Tendency	Positive		Of Concern		Unknown
Focus	Resilience Factors	Adversity/ ACEs/Hyper	Adversity/ ACEs of Concern	Adversity/ ACEs/Hypo	Need/Gaps

Identity
Heritage, faith/beliefs, gender, sexuality, ability/disability (physical, emotional, psychological, physiological, cognitive/educational, somatic), body image, interests
Parts
Character strategies
Safety level vs sense of safety level
General Outlook: optimistic/pessimistic
Tension reducing behaviours
Ability to be socially regulated
Ability to self-regulate
Active interests/Hobbies

Health
Health: general (physical, emotional, psychological)
Health: Exercise/Lifestyle
Health: Diet/Routine
Veiled compliance

(Continued)

Listening before Listing 193

Table 9.1 (Continued)

Child, Sibling, Parent/Carer Psychodynamic Formulation

Parent/Person's name   Date

Tendency	Positive	Of Concern		Unknown
Focus	Resilience Factors	Adversity/ ACEs/Hyper	Adversity/ ACEs/Hypo	Need/Gaps

Education/ employment
School/education
Nursery
Primary
Secondary/High
College/ further education/ apprenticeship.
University
later life learning
employment/satisfaction
Relationships
Birth Parent relationships
Sibling relationships
Grandparent relationships
Foster carer relationships
Adopter Parent relationships
Residential support relationships
Presence of empathic attunement, nurture, consistency, 'Playfulness, Acceptance, Curiosity and Empathy,' 'Regulate, Relate, Reason, Reflect,' 'ACE'

Chapter 10

From Insight to Action

Analysis and Decision-Making

The analysis of the narrative, within an assessment report, is crucial to extrapolate the information which holds the weight of researched, observed, cross-referenced, and reported evidence. This analysis needs to be congruent with and supported by the conclusions and final recommendations. If the information has been collated and presented in as clear a manner as possible, then the analysis will be easier to undertake and present. It will also be simpler to identify patterns, trends and outliers, leading to more accurate and actionable insights.

An assessment finds, collates, processes, presents, analyses information before coming to conclusions and making recommendations. As a result, information is considered many times. It is without apology that over the two volumes information in case examples has been presented in relation to each section to bring the process to life. During the analysis the same will apply but there may be feelings of Déjà vu as some information must be repeated to make sense.

This analysis process takes into account the time usually available to complete an assessment. It could be much longer but is shortened to meet current time pressures.

Eight components are presented here to consider when undertaking this assessment. It is acknowledged that there are innumerable variables that may also need to be taken into account.

1. Gathering comprehensive historical and current data on all family members across various domains within each individual's spheres of influence (e.g., home, foster care, adoption, education, health, contact, et al.) is essential. Include fact-finding about each sibling and family member, identify gaps in the information, and evaluate its current relevance. The task here is to separate fact from opinion, historical versus current information, and objectivity from judgement.
2. Evaluate each sibling's unique trauma level. Although they may have experienced similar situations (e.g., significant harm, contact), the effects, impacts, and their individual responses will differ. Keep in mind a sibling showing fewer signs of distress or behavioural markers, i.e. internalising their distress may be struggling more than the externalising sibling.

DOI: 10.4324/9781003724605-14

3. Develop and critically evaluate hypotheses regarding placement options from a trauma-informed perspective, while avoiding assumptions. Remember a singular hypothesis at the outset amounts to a predetermined decision.
4. Present the cross-referenced or triangulated evidence from information gathered within the child and family sessions, historical records, education, health, therapy, psychometrics and other sources.
5. Assess and analyse the information gathered, the 'so what?' component, for example, from the chronology. Then determine what was the developmental impact on this child, and has this resolved, or are they still going to impact on their placement needs?
6. Clearly identify what is needed and when, whether the conclusion is to place siblings separately or together, to ensure a successful outcome.
7. Recommendations. Resist the inclusion of limiting restrictions, be they financial or resource-led, which may restrain, change or influence the recommendations.
8. Add details of follow-up and reviews needed to ensure developmentally changing needs are met and lead to the exit strategy.

Gathering and Collating the Information

In the early 1990s a Local Authority social worker was requested to undertake a sibling assessment by their team manager. The social worker asked for the format and guidelines, but these, at that time, did not exist. This book represents a culmination of research, experience and literature to endeavour to plug gaps in this trauma-focused work. It was hoped to include in this chapter several examples of the formats used by different Agencies, approved by their local courts, to support the writing of the report on the assessment undertaken but none of the many Local Authorities approached responded. It has therefore not been possible to comment on where such assessment formats exist, how much they differ or how trauma-focused they are.

What can be commented on is too often the problem is that some formats, seen in court proceedings, have been completed using checklist pro formas which have been taken into interviews and worked through systematically, sometimes to the detriment of building a relationship with the individual. One particular pro forma for assessment has been developed utilising emojis to help elicit feelings that are difficult to articulate, but paradoxically replace the need to develop the secure relationship required to explore these complex paradoxical relationships, or even to ascertain the true meanings of the emojis chosen for the individual. Conclusions were then drawn from the interviewer's interpretation of the meaning behind the emoji's grimace or smile without clarification, or when it was attempted was done in a way, often using 'why?' questions which left the child unable to respond and feeling shamed or blamed for not being able to. There is no doubt it will feel that the ability to gather and then use information needed will be subject to many variables and therefore seem inconsistent and unreliable. However, achieving consistency or reliability by routine use of a standard questionnaire or pro forma will make these possible unless before their use vital time is taken to create an empathically connected relationship between the practitioner, those being assessed, and others contributing to the assessment.

This resulting relationship will enable the practitioner to gather information that is more reliable and create a narrative of that information. An assessment is not just about creating a narrative; it is also about the 'So what bit?' So, what does this information mean for this sibling, not just what was done to this sibling but what did it do and, most importantly, what was missing? Then, what are the resulting actual, researched and evidenced consequences for this child and what are the probable consequences.

One father being assessed cooperated by turning up religiously to appointments, but when in session was resistant and verbally restrictive, answered few questions, but questioned much. He appeared compliant but any responses he gave were carefully measured, being vigilant not to criticise his estranged wife too much, but when he did, he balanced it out with his hypotheses about her struggles but was delivered in an inauthentic manner. When he praised her, it was with a backdrop context of the struggles he believed her to have. Exploration of these events led to a smokescreen of questions, challenges or misdirection which were hard to pinpoint. Stepping back and imagining being this man's children gave not only some insight into how they would feel but also what messages would they receive individually and as a group. How would they view family members and the world in general? During the penultimate session having read the report he commented the analysis meant that he could no longer use the report for other purposes. He would not say what those purposes were and requested the analysis be changed. He was not happy that the assessor felt that his response validated the conclusions: that he was veiled compliant and that his attendance was for an ulterior motive. He did not come back for the final goodbye session. It would have been tempting to focus on the content rather than his strategy. It was his evidenced strategy that was the important factor in the assessment.

The 'So what?' question is followed by one important, 'What if?' question. What if you could recommend or action unlimited resources available to meet each sibling's individual needs and sibling group needs? This will always be an interesting question to ask, especially at times of limited resources which often result in limiting recommendations to fit with what is available. Frustrating and sometimes terrifying to be able to identify what is actually needed then find the decision, they have to live together or separately, is based on resources rather than their carefully assessed needs, then having to prioritise these needs or deal with extensive waiting lists.

The voice of the child/ren must never not be overlooked or minimised and must remain the central focus of the intervention. Whilst the ascertainable wishes and feelings of the child or young person should be sought, this does not mean they should be acted upon when the rationale for their wishes and feelings not being actioned is that they are not in the child's best interests. The reasons for this are then laid out within the analysis.

Evaluate Each Sibling's Unique Trauma Level

This is the collation of, and review of, the extended chronology noting the impact of trauma on each sibling's physical and psychological development, their capacity to share, ability to self-regulate or require external regulation. It contains the descriptions of attachment behaviours observed when with everyone known including siblings, parents, carers, other family members, hospital staff, nursery, playgroup or educational staff including the dinner team, contact service workers, neighbours, friendships, voluntary and religious organisations, and the practitioner. Research done by a residential family assessment centre found all but one of the children's views of who, out of all the highly qualified professional staff, was most important to them during their stay and who they would miss most chose the staff in the kitchen.

Based on and using the information in the extended chronology, a summary of each sibling's history, positives and negatives, impact of trauma and resilience factors from preconception, conception, in-utero experiences, birth and through to first birthday. If this child was placed in care from birth or has been in care for any length of time, how many changes of carer, any changes in 'sibling' experiences, i.e., other children in the foster home arriving or leaving, relationship with carer's children, and extended family, important friendships. This needs to be both a factual chronology, what harm, its impact, consequent interventions needed, was done during which developmental stage and, more importantly, an emotional chronology of the quality of any attachments made, who the child remembers, misses most or least and what it was about that relationship that made it so.

This provides information about consistency versus inconsistency, developmental needs provided versus abuse and neglect, age-appropriate attachment and separation behaviours. It is determining and balancing the differences between child development and child psychopathology. One fourteen-year-old spoke of an 'older brother' he loved and missed very much and desperately wanted to see again. This 'older brother' was the teenage son in the first of his five foster homes, for ten weeks, when he was four years old and not remembered or known of by his now eighth social worker doing his assessment.

Lacy and Eleanor were placed together in a short-term foster placement. The rationale for the children being placed together included:

- The children were young and would therefore have been less affected by their experiences.
- Children placed together have more favourable outcomes.
- They could be managed by experienced carers.
- They had a positive relationship.

When the time came to assess the long-term plans, and whether the children should or could be kept together or placed separately, the following information was taken into account.

- The children's history highlighted multiple ACEs and both were showing behaviours consistent with a disorganised attachment. Disorganisation of attachment results from not being able to know or trust whether any interaction precedes or predicts harm, hurt, or hugs not just with parents or carers but also siblings. Their unmet attachment needs now required strong, consistent, authoritative but sensitive and empathic parenting from empathically attuned, physically and emotionally available secure parents.
- The children's mother had made no changes and remained inconsistent and incoherent in her responses, contact and coherence. Children fundamentally require consistency to feel safe.
- In contact, the children targeted each other and their mother to the point that she would end up in tears on the floor whilst her young children assaulted her. Children are equally scared of scared parents as they are of scary parents.
- The very experienced foster carers made it clear that they could not cope with the children together. They had never experienced such distressed and disorganised children. The carers were exhausted. Whilst they certainly had more parenting skills and resilience than the children's mother, they described being and feeling being worn down by the children's presentation. They were in danger of giving up just like the children's mother.
- The sibling relationship was complex. They had been assessed as having a trauma bond. Lacey presented a pseudo-parentified role towards her sister. This resulted in her putting her sister's needs above her own. Eleanor, on the other hand, was in fight mode and manipulated her sister into meeting her needs; paradoxically, not to meet her own needs but to keep her sister away from the carers. Lacey was then preoccupied with meeting her sister's needs, and Eleanor was preoccupied with keeping Lacey away.
- Both children were fighting for survival. They both knew they were individually responsible for their own survival. They were not fighting together. Despite her violent and aggressive, sometimes sexualised outbursts, Lacey actually had more advantageous resources to survive: she could connect with the carers, she could problem-solve, whilst she externalised she also had periods of internalised behaviour, and she was able to respond to empathically attuned carers. Eleanor, on the other hand, was running 'hot' and could not stop fighting. Eleanor, when two years old, dominated her older sister. In nursery, she was a compulsive, serial 'mother-figure' finder. She would latch on to any worker, keeping other children at bay. As soon as that worker had to leave, she would latch on to another and yet no one felt connected to her.
- Eleanor would display hyperkineticism, anger and aggression, opposition, defiance, disproportionate, and opposite reactions to accidents by not noticing

a hurt which made observers wince, or overly responding to minute pain, throwing toys, ignoring limits, spitting at, and hitting those around her. The foster carer also reported that Eleanor often became tense and frozen and more susceptible to aggression whilst Lacey had the ability to play.
- The children could not live with their mother together or separately. They could not live with the current foster carers together, and neither could they live elsewhere together. The carers were more connected to Lacey than they were to Eleanor. The assessment came too late for the carers. They had run dry and were suffering vicarious traumatisation. The children were subsequently placed in separate long-term foster placements. Lacey settled well into her long-term foster placement and responded to therapy. Eleanor was not provided with any therapy and could not settle in this or subsequent placements, resulting in a number of disruptions.
- What, if any contact, should or could happen? What would it look like, what would be the goal and therefore the content, what skills would the supervisor need?

Develop and Critically Assess Hypotheses

All assessments need to be undertaken with an open mind. How can this be done and be truly monitored without a strong supportive and yet challenging supervisor and clinical supervisor? A single hypothesis, for example, is actually a decision and strongly suggests a predetermined view of the outcome. If this is the case, what happens to information that does not fit that hypothesis? Is it looked for, then lost, left out, dismissed, or weighted in a disadvantageous manner? Conversely, what if the hypothesis does not fit comfortably with the practitioner, the management, the organisation, or anyone else but happens to be correct, or the least-worst option?

How does the practitioner make challenges that may be at odds with their organisation's needs or traditional thinking based on old research that siblings should be placed together? Not agreeing with a principle such as placing siblings together, or indeed contact, does not equate to disagreeing with it. A neutral beginning or at least an awareness of any bias is a good starting point to ensure the assessment is done with an open mind, open hypothesising, ensuring the detailed questions listed later are asked and, more importantly, answered to enable and ensure a trauma-informed decision is made. This will reduce the likelihood of future trauma in the short, medium, and long term, not just for the children involved, but also for their parents, carers and workers such as the carers (like those of Lacey and Eleanor) and involved practitioners.

The importance of hypothesising when considering all the placement options from a trauma-informed perspective and avoiding the pitfalls of assumptions relies not just on cognitive processing but also on felt sense, whether a physiological and/or emotional response.

For example: Notice your immediate response, be it positive or negative or curious, to the following statements or conclusions about the success or difficulties in a sibling contact:

- 'The boys were happy to see each other.'
- 'She has a close, secure attachment with her eldest sister.'
- 'All three children played happily together.'
- 'They were sad when the contact ended.'

For each statement, write down and list the answers to the following questions:

- What did the supervisor see to use the words happy, close, secure, happily, together, sad to come to this conclusion?
- What did the supervisor not see?
- Did anyone else see the same interaction and what word was used? Was this 'conclusion' word used by the various witnesses, and did the children themselves use the same word, a similar word, or a totally different word? If not, why not and reasons for difference to be explored.
- Were there any differences of opinion or conclusions from various witnesses and the children themselves?
- Would the different words used by anyone result in any changes to your initial response/opinion?
- Did the other observers or authors have an agenda in coming to their conclusions?
- What experience or training did the other observers or authors have which would make their opinion more or less valid?
- Please delete the indent and add These questions can usefully be kept in mind when reading the case example of Karen later in this chapter

Model coherence requires consideration of all the aspects of any given situation within an assessment, i.e., the 'preceding' hypotheses, the evidence gathered, cross-referencing of evidence throughout before the congruent conclusion or conclusions are arrived at.

Present the Cross-Referenced or Triangulated Evidence

Single source information is less robust than information from multiple sources. Multiple sources that are the same in description or conclusion have to be explored; e.g., a number of teachers from the same school may show similar patterns of concern or may show that there is a concern in one environment. It may be that the child has been labelled. Reliance on psychometrics, questionnaires, protocols or exercises may overfocus on particular elements or medicalise a person. Observations in school may be different from the contact or home environment. Where more sources are found, explored, analysed, and cross-referenced the greater the chance the conclusions and recommendations will hold greater weight. Oftentimes, what is left out are the unknowns; yet, identifying or hypothesising about the unknowns also allows us to know what was previously unknown.

Karen presented as formidable in her presentation despite her daughter's disclosure of sexual abuse. The word 'despite' may suggest a prejudgement of what is 'normal.' However, what it emphasises is the seeming lack of emotional connection or a need to understand the job of protecting her child and meeting her needs – but at that point was an unknown. Of course, there were clues here in her overly cognitive presentation, but it did not evidence that would be how she was with her daughter. The school reported that the child and parent had a lovely relationship, and they evidenced this as a two-way phenomenon and as such may undermine the observed feelings that perhaps Karen lacked emotional attunement. The psychometrics that Karen completed on her daughter enabled it to be seen that she thought her daughter had significant difficulties. However, the difficulties the psychometrics suggested were greater than was initially hypothesised. The usefulness of researched formal psychometrics is that they also show what should be expected and this knowledge helps focus on the problem. If her daughter did have the level of concerns suggested by the test, then it would be expected that she would have a similar range of presentations at school (this of course is not always the case but in this situation, would have been easily identified). To triangulate this problem, the school was contacted, who provided the information that they had seen a change of late in her presentation, but this was more subtle than the psychometrics suggested. A direct school observation was also undertaken that appeared to give weight to the hypothesis that she was internalising and required support, but not to the level in the test. This increased evidence of the daughter internalising then raised the question about Karen's contradictory view of her daughter's externalisation. Karen knew, as soon as this was raised, that she would have to see the situation through a dual lens, both her daughter's negative experience and her own experiences. She agreed to a psychometric on herself that led, within the already robust client-practitioner relationship, to an exploration of her experiences that may have exacerbated her fears for her daughter.

The questions asked in a psycholmetric test are only half the equation. It is also how they are answered, avoided, or received that helps in understanding what is going on for the person. The information gathered helps develop the conclusions and the resultant recommendations. The outcome may have been different if Karen had presented differently and refused the offer of psychometrics. How differently would the recommendations look if Karen refused support, and what would be the implications on the provision of a service or not for her daughter? For her daughter to receive a service to overcome her experiences would be helpful, but the efficacy would be continually compromised if Karen were also not given the opportunity to overcome her own experiences.

Taking care to ensure all questions are answered as fully as they can be helps tailor the recommendations.

Assess and Analyse the Information Gathered

A parent may be depressed. This may impact on a child's presentation, where they may become demanding, oppositional, or aggressive, which then may become a major contributory factor to a parent's depression and lead to the home environment being neglected. Conversely, a child may be struggling with unknown experiences and externalise those experiences in their behaviour. This will then impact on the mother, who, already struggling to cope becomes depressed from the hopelessness of their situation and leads to the home environment becoming neglected. In turn, this impacts on the child, as the lack of her availability will increase their externalising behaviour. Then the question arises: where is child's father, the mother's partner if not the child's father, or their family, friendship, or professional support network? This section is about making sense of the information we see using multiple lenses to avoid missing the source, making judgments, or limiting the efficacy of the assessment.

Gathering and processing the information needed to assess the relationship each sibling has with each other is where many assessments lose their evidential weight. The analyst must carefully identify what was missing for each sibling, what was done to each sibling and what it did to each sibling. These findings are complex for one child; they become more complex with every additional sibling. There may be shared influences such as generational and genetic influences, prebirth conditions and experiences. Yet the impact of the developmental trauma must be mapped for each child both as an individual and as a sibling whether they witnessed harm, participated in it, or witnessed another sibling's participation as a perpetrator, bystander, or denier and how these roles shaped their relationships and beliefs.

Further information should include each child's individual presentation and their experiences within parental, sibling, familial, and educational contexts. The assessment needs to establish their current and future needs, whether they remain together or not. Where siblings do not live together, then contact requires an equal level of consideration; its purpose, content, level of supervision, the experience and training of the supervisor, reliance of the assessor on the 'quality' of the note taking by not actually observing a contact, whether it should continue, be suspended or stopped. This must then have a specified process to review decisions over time.

Important too to ensure supervision, focusing on agency needs, and clinical supervision, focusing on worker's needs, is not a luxury but is necessary to ensure the stance of not only being open and accepting of challenge from others, but also self-challenge. This ensures developing a capacity for reflective and critical thinking and inviting people to become a critical friend with professional curiosity.

At this point, rigorous reflection with cross-referencing and triangulating themes is required. It holds evidence that is factual and accurate as opposed to fanciful, unhelpful hearsay, assumptions, historical, or misrepresentations. The component that is often least presented is where the findings are then considered against cause and effect, or where experiences impact on an outcome, or an outcome is a result of previous experiences. This can be seen in the paradoxical statements: survivors of sexual abuse generally do not go on to sexually abuse. Perpetrators of sexual abuse often have been sexually abused. What are the factors, if any, that increase either outcome and what are the factors that prevent it?

An example of this could be seen in an earlier case study where the father was ordered by the courts to undertake therapy. Therapy is not an assessment. The courts did not want feedback but did require a report on the outcome to be submitted to the Local Authority. When considering this highly complex situation, it can be seen how model coherence will inform thinking.

The family were in court in family proceedings over concerns about the well-being of their surviving children. One danger of this situation is the parents may feel under siege, their stress responses may be activated and they come out fighting the 'outsider' rather than each other, present in an adversarial manner or go into flight mode by shutting down completely or becoming unavailable, all states reducing their capacity to share. In these situations, without empathic, trauma-informed understanding, there will be heightened views of them as perhaps more functional than they are, uncooperative, hostile, and unwilling to work in partnership. In this situation, their stress may overshadow their actual competence.

The parents had separated and were going through an acrimonious divorce. The mother, also ordered to undertake therapy by the courts, shut down and very quickly withdrew. Her passive resistance hid her capacity as a strong and articulate person who also happened to be shrewd in her management of services. The father, unlike the mother who refused to comply with the court-ordered therapy, attended all of his therapy sessions. He was, however, always late and presented in a manner that put the onus of responsibility for change onto the therapist.

The fact that the therapy was court-ordered placed the therapeutic relationship on an unequal footing. The relationship between client and therapist requires trust, collaboration, and autonomy. This can be achieved, but when it is court-ordered it is much harder to accomplish. It was always going to be more challenging for this father because effectively he was being ordered to attend. Taking away his free will and autonomy impacted on trust in the therapeutic relationship and created doubt over what the therapist would, should or could share in the court-ordered report to be sent to the Local Authority. These challenges for the therapist taken to clinical supervision.

There can be therapeutic healing in the assessment process where a connection has been made with the assessor, and the individual starts to make sense of their situation. Also, it can be said that within therapy, the therapist can start to make sense of the client's drives and/or motivations that would have been helpful in an assessment. In a review near the end of the therapy, the report was shared with the father. The father wanted to know who had seen it before him. The answer, no one had, but the better question in response was, 'I wonder what makes you ask that?' The rationale for sharing a report with the client first is based on the fact that this is still part of the individual's process regardless of it being an assessment or an intervention. It is still part of the relationship and the information-gathering process.

There is always the reserved right to change the content of reports in light of new information and be open to challenge. He was unhappy with the report. There were some minor errors for which the therapist apologised, changed, and thanked him for his vigilance, demonstrating a commitment to the process being owned by both. However, he then declared his disappointment that there were so many factors of need reported in the document, which he read as negative. He concurred that he agreed with the positive points. This demonstrated an imbalance in only being able to face the positive and suggested being closed to any of his learning edges. When asked what it was that made it so important to him that the report did not contain any suggestion of imperfection, he replied, 'I won't be able to use the report for other purposes.' When pushed on what that meant, he was unable to share. He failed to attend the final session, suggesting his engagement in the process was to enable him to have evidence for other purposes.

The interpretation and analysis of the results of the gathered assessment information can so easily be skewed or influenced by a number of factors.

For Lacy and Eleanor, there was an overly optimistic hypothesis at the beginning. This resulted in minimising and avoiding negatives to avoid the pain of splitting two very young siblings. Regardless of the evidence, the information presented was biased to match the predetermined belief that children should be placed together. There was also too much hope that there would be a miraculous change, despite evidence to the contrary.

Becky and Tom's relationship was overshadowed by their female foster carer's veiled compliance and her husband's avoidance of engagement with professionals.

Hunter, Faith and Charity's assessment was incomplete because of the lack of information elicited from their previous foster carer. She simply was not able to see the children's behaviour was sexualised, partly due to her religious bias and partly her knowledge that the siblings shared a bedroom, the approval for which was never ascertained. This eventually led to the children's adopter, Hope, being seen as verging on the hysterical and being suspected of Fabricated or Induced Illness (FII), in the USA as Factitious Disorder Imposed on Another, and previously known as Munchausen's Syndrome by Proxy, because no previous concerns had been raised by any other individual or professional. This potential diagnosis could have also been raised as a perfectly rational hypothesis.

Hypotheses are tentative ideas about the reasons for something occurring and are working assumptions. They help keep an open mind and prevent the assessor from becoming fixed on one outcome belief. The stress of looking after two highly traumatised children plus having to fight to be believed actually and paradoxically exposed Hope to an increased risk of adverse mental health more than it did to solve the problem of whether or not the children were sexualised. Two further hypotheses can be presented: If Hope was liked by the assessor, this could have increased the risk of the assessor overlooking evidence of FII; conversely, if she was viewed negatively, it may have increased the risk of her becoming the subject of professional concern. The new evidenced assessment concluded the children should never have been placed together and negated the concerns about the presence of FII.

Future contact, needs to be equally assessed through a trauma-informed lens, arranged, managed, and planned in a way that is coherent and consistent with the outcome of the assessment. This assessment includes the impact of contact, including both positives and negatives observed on attachment behaviours, separation, and reunion experiences, behaviour before, during, and after contact with family members, other people, and most importantly each other in sibling contact.

The Conclusion

There is a paradox in the time needed from starting the assessment to reaching the conclusion. Delay is contraindicated and is why it was enshrined in the Children Act 1989, Section 1(2), where it states, 'Delay in determining questions about a child's upbringing is likely to prejudice their welfare.' However, assessments involving multiple siblings, where trying to ascertain wishes and feelings, complex, often non-verbal, or counter-intuitive communication scripts are all wrapped up in ambivalent or disorganised behaviour, where groomed or even coerced messages may mean that a longer assessment is not negative but paradoxically positive. Rushing a complex assessment can equally bring about negative consequences. Important information can be missed or historical information copied and pasted without first determining its present relevance or it lacks depth or evidence in the analysis. Delay, over-optimistic views or being risk averse can all add to the trauma practitioners are trying to lessen, i.e. type 4 trauma, or in other words, practice guidelines, timescales, procedures, and practitioners can become part of the problem. Children need certainty and if this book shows anything, it should show the consequences of unprocessed anxiety brought on by uncertainty. Doing what seems like the worst thing – slowing things down – is paradoxically far less damaging when the information gleaned by slowing down is then shared with the right people as soon as possible.

Further, as presented earlier, a conclusion that is made because of resource or financial deficits is not an authentic assessment. Living in a world of finite resources that are continually reducing means that decision makers often have to make pragmatic and difficult decisions on resource limits, but that is separate and unrelated to the conclusion of the assessment and the final recommendations.

Becky and Tom were prime examples of children who were denied a sibling assessment. They were living in a harm-filled situation that also required assessing. The mantra of whatever you do, do not do nothing echoes here. The involved social workers could see the situation was dire. They could see Emmett presented as avoidant, entitled and domineering. They could see Cicely was able to say the right thing in some situations but complained bitterly in others. Even on the basis of just this inconsistency it was evident she could not provide these siblings with what they needed. Even their own birth children 'poured petrol on the flames.' The agency wanted the placement to continue but because of the social workers' conflicted feelings and desire to 'do no harm' the agency felt stuck and unable to see how the future could be any better, and so maintained the status quo. The outcome, however, was far more painfully tragic and did not resolve the harm done, now being done and caused further, type 4 trauma. The alternative would have been painful and awful but far less damaging. The children should never have been placed together and certainly should not have been placed, nor remain in this obviously dysfunctional placement. Questions to be answered include what could have been done differently, when and why not?

Recommendations

Congruence and alignment are required between the final recommendations and the original letter of instruction, brief given and assessment type. Where the assessment goes beyond the brief, the reasons for this should be made clear with separate bullet points outlining the rationale that made this necessary.

Recommendations are best presented in a concise, bullet-pointed list. They should be clear, measurable, and having read the narrative should bring no surprise to the reader:

- Placement needs of each sibling based on their individual profile.
- Details of not just the knowledge and skills needed but also the ability to effectively and consistently apply these are required to show how each individual child's detailed needs now, and in the future, will be met.
- How complementary or distinctly different each sibling's needs are.
- How complementary are the knowledge, skills, ability, and experience the carers will need to have to enable them, not just as individuals but together, to meet the individual and joint needs of the siblings.
- Where the siblings' needs or the potential carers' abilities are so diverse and distinct to be too great a challenge to achieve, the explanation for this needs to be clearly stated.
- Or, would it be possible to achieve these abilities as part of a package of training and at least weekly support for the carers and therapy for each child?
- Or, each sibling's needs will be met in separate foster or adoptive homes, and decisions made, following a separate assessment, about how contact will be arranged to ensure that, at a minimum, no further harm will be done, hopefully ensuring the siblings will at least have a relationship more akin to close cousins.
- Or, the information gathered is such that it would not be possible to place these siblings together because their experiences together have resulted in their needs being too diverse, too competitive, too dynamic; the potential to do each other psychological harm exists, repetition of previously or ongoing physical and/or sexual behaviour harm is indicated, their alliances to parents or others are too diverse to place them together, and whether, at this time, contact between the siblings or others is contraindicated.

- Consideration is given to what is needed to enable a no-contact decision to be reviewed. When success in the work or therapy indicates this is possible, interventions should be put in place to facilitate this. Timescales for reviewing the great deal of work and therapy are needed, with each sibling, to even consider contact as positive or healing. Contact, if possible can then start, continue, change, or stop.

Review Cycle and Exit Strategy

Therapists and social workers are familiar with reviews of interventions. These reviews must include the need for re-assessments for a number of reasons. It may be that what is needed is not just one assessment or review but cycles of assessments for reviews to help ensure that the child, family, and team around the child maintain a focus on the success or otherwise of the recommendations and targets, particularly in paradoxical complex situations or where a large sibling group has been assessed or re-assessed. This is challenging and difficult to do when the review is running across multiple purposes or agencies: criminal, family, safeguarding, children in need, housing, refuge. Feedback, within an agreed timescale, may then need to be tailored for different audiences with differences between confidentiality and need-to-know understood and agreed.

A review is an integral part of the intervention. It is placing the written hypotheses, evidence, and believed to be the best or hoped for outcome in the public domain. This is not to demonstrate expertise or a diktat but more helpfully to be an opportunity to examine, scrutinise, and share the findings and recommendations, progress or further needs uncovered.

Common errors of reviews include:

- Being undertaken before the participants have had the opportunity to read available reports.
- Significant parties have not been invited.
- The wrong people have been invited to match the purpose of the review.
- Children have not been invited when they should not have been and/or without knowing what to expect.
- Children have not been invited when they should or could have been.
- There were no introductions. A manager or senior manager is present when ordinarily this would not be expected.
- There was no agenda, or the agenda trimmed to fit someone's available time.
- Participants were not previously asked for their agenda items or agenda not shared until the meeting.
- The chair is not experienced or skilled enough to manage the paradoxical complexity of the information or the participants.
- An individual dominated the review.
- There is confusion between who is a decision maker and who is an advisor.

- The felt 'frisson' was not acknowledged. This is often a 'felt sense' when someone enters a meeting and it is clearly evident there has been a pre-meeting, where participants or a particular participant objects to another's perspective or presence. This can be presented as passive aggressive or in an attempt to hijack the individual. Resolution of this can include acknowledgement, 'Oh my something is going on here, let's explore what I missed,' or, 'I can feel the tension in the room, perhaps we could explore that first,' or, 'A senior manager is present, could we start with their concerns?' If this frisson is not addressed, the child, young person, family member, or indeed other professionals can be left with other unprocessed feelings triggered by the unresolved frisson which then inform their recommendations and decision making.
- Individuals were not enabled to share their perspectives.
- Information shared was narrative and process-heavy rather than specific and targeted.
- The voice of the child was not sought or represented.
- The voice of the child had been sought but weighted in a manner that was inconsistent with the well-being of the child.
- Participants, especially children and family members, have not been adequately prepared before the review.
- The exit strategy was not discussed.
- Participants, especially children and family members, have not been adequately, or not at all, debriefed after the review.
- There were no outcomes, recommendations or actionable items.
- Actionable items failed to have an identified person responsible for each action.
- Actionable items failed to have a timescale or completion date agreed upon.
- There was no summary of the outcomes.
- The participants were not thanked.
- There were no contemporaneous or comprehensive minutes, or a participant was asked to take minutes rather than arranging a minute-taker.
- Timescale for minutes to be distributed or signed off has not been agreed.
- Where required, a date for a follow-up review was not agreed or set.
- Review dates were autocratic, set by an individual or organisation without reasonable notice or checking the availability of others.
- Reviews were cancelled or rearranged at the last minute.

A Challenging Review

Entering a meeting the author of a therapeutic report that laid out specific and serious concerns about the safety of siblings within a chaotic adoptive family felt a 'frisson' of discomfort. The feeling was felt so the practitioner stated, 'That's a strong feeling, what did I miss?' the participants of the very large meeting either looked down or toward a senior manager, to which the practitioner stated, 'Wow, that's real hard for people, maybe this should be the starting point?' The senior manager then challenged the author on the findings of the report. The author heard and accepted the challenge then stated the counter evidence. It became clear that the organisation did not want to hear the concerns. The author named this fact, 'It seems as if you do not accept the findings.' The receiving organisation agreed and then demanded a rewrite. The author responded, 'I cannot do that. I stand by my findings and recommendations, and they are my professional view.' The senior manager again tried to force a rewrite. The author with no other option and no support from the other, thus far, mute participants stated, 'My concern is that this family situation has the components of a serious case review.' The manager shouted, 'You cannot say that!' which elicited the response from a head teacher, 'Yes, he can say that. This is the level of concern we have.' This singular response freed up other professionals to share their concerns which had previously been shut down.

A Positive Review

Hunter's social worker had canvassed and agreed the TAC dates. The therapist submitted the progress report three weeks before the review. Hunter, now aged 16 was prepared for the review by the therapist, had been asked what if anything he would like to share and similarly his thoughts were sought by his social worker. The therapist checked out if he wanted to hear his therapist's views and on receiving the affirmative, shared the information carefully, mindfully processed Hunter's responses and the meaning behind those responses. Hunter was told who would be at the meeting and asked if he wanted to attend. He declined, which was also processed. He was informed that his mother would be at the meeting. This was also processed. HIs mother was also prepared by the therapist and separately by the social worker.

The review was chaired by the social worker, introductions were made, and the purpose of the meeting clarified. The social worker confirmed the previous minutes had been agreed and went through the previously agreed actionable items. All the named people assigned the actions confirmed the actions had been completed where they had been or cited reasons why they had not. New targets were set for the completion of unresolved actions.

All participants were enabled to share both Hunter's progress, achievements and positive attributes with targets set on how to enhance these positives. They were then asked to share their concerns. A discussion ensued on how to try to reduce those concerns. The greatest concern was about whether or not he was accessing pornography through Wi-Fi enabled tech and if he was, what was the nature of that pornography. The concern was based on his levels of secrecy, accessing tech when he should not, being vague and using charming or manipulative behaviour to avoid the truth. The concerns were not just about Hunter, but the impact this could have on his sister Charity. Some members wanted an AIM Technology Assisted Harmful Sexual Behaviour Assessment to be undertaken. Whilst there was an argument for this action, it needed to be balanced against the following;

- Actual evidence of him doing this.
- His mother's current ability to supervise.
- Hunter's age and need to access technology.
- The concerns were based on past behaviour and that no evidence existed to confirm this was his current behaviour.
- Charity was aware of Hunter's secrecy. Had talked openly to her brother and her mother about her concerns that he may be using his tech in a manner that may hurt other people or himself and told him he was stuck and needed to move on.
- His mother kept and would keep the TAC informed.
- The assessment would need to be undertaken by another unknown individual which was likely to trigger his attachment responses in a negative way. An example would be that under stress he was more likely to manipulate new people or ingratiate himself with new people. In addition, the outcome of the assessment would not enhance the TAC's knowledge of Hunter, but this would be kept under review.

Alternatives were discussed. It was agreed that Hope, his adoptive mother, social worker and therapist would all feedback their shared concerns and help Hunter process this in a cognitive, physiological, emotional and psychological manner. Hope was going to share her concerns that he was struggling and wanted to help him but make sure that Faith and Charity were protected. The social worker stated that he would talk to Hunter about the TAC's concerns in a cognitive way to help him reflect on what he was trying to tell people. The therapist agreed to explore with Hunter and his mother, who was currently included in sessions with him, what he was experiencing and why he was drawn to leaving his mother in doubt about his desires and intentions. Dates were agreed to undertake the proposed interventions and a date to feedback the findings. The process, despite differences of opinions was collaborative, open and planned, utilised many members of the TAC, with feed back to the whole team agreed for future decision making.

The exit strategy dovetails into the therapeutic process of endings, which starts at the beginning. All interventions should build in a structure that helps the child, young person, or adult maintain awareness of the number of sessions remaining. Having a countdown method, even if it increases after review, enables the future focus always to be on ending and thus helps prevent over-reliance and dependency whilst simultaneously providing the opportunity to develop autonomy. The creation of a psychodynamic formulation also highlights the work that needs to be addressed and undertaken. Further, it keeps the process of the therapeutic journey transparent and accessible to the individual, family, and involved services. Oftentimes, this also helps the individual not feel so damaged but have hope for a pain-free future and to share important information towards the end of the intervention.

Can You Hear Me, Hold Me, and Help Me?

Candice is reminded by the assessing dual-qualified therapist/social worker that this is the last assessment session.

Candice: 'Yeah fucking thank god for that.'
Therapist: Reflects her relief.
Candice: 'Err, umm, err…(confused)…fuck off.'
Therapist: Clarifies this is her last chance to share any worries, concerns or hurts.
Candice: 'Oh by the way you're not coming to school with me…I'll tell you that now, I'll tell you straight you are not coming to school with me and if you do, I'll snap and I'm sorry you can't come to my school and you're not coming anyway.'
Therapist: Acknowledges her fear and confirms that they agreed they did not think it would be helpful to go to her school because it would be too much for her and would not be fair.
Candice: 'Go out of the room, go out, oh just fucking go out ohhhh (she dissociates a moment, then cries) go out!'
Therapist: Reflects her pain and reiterates this was her time to share anything she had not been able to say.
Candice: 'I want to go home but the judge won't let me…and why? I just want you to fucking go.'
Therapist: 'This is so hard for you, and it seems so unfair to you.' 'Candice, all the grown-ups are worried that you have been hurt by someone, but they don't know how or by whom.'
Candice: 'Yes but I just want to go home and live with my mum and dad (she cries a little) I want to see my sisters.'
Therapist: 'Do you think you would be safe?'
Candice: '(screams) Yes I would, my mum does keep me safe…so fuck off and go out.'
Therapist: 'It seems like you want to go home real bad.'
Candice: 'Yes, but I know my mum, she doesn't like me, I wish you would fuck off and leave me alone.'
Therapist: 'There is an even harder question, but I'm not sure you could answer it.'
Candice: 'Go on then.'
Therapist: 'The adults are worried that someone had hurt or made you feel uncomfortable, or even in a way that felt nice but was touching in a sex way.'
Candice: 'I didn't do anything, I didn't do it though (she leaves the room and returns a while later crying). I don't want you to talk to me anymore cos you upset me, but I didn't even do any sex, I didn't do any of them, I just want to go back with my mum'…'My sisters are allowed home, but I've got to stay in this shit hole, my sisters are allowed home.'
Therapist: 'And that feels really unfair to you.'
Candice: 'It won't be fair to me.'

Therapist: 'I wonder if they would be safe if they went home?'
Candice: 'Yes, because my mum likes them.'
Therapist: 'I'm wondering what mum likes about them?'
Candice: 'Because, because she does, she doesn't like me, and I just want to go back home.'
Therapist: 'That is such a sad thought.'
Candice: '(screams) Why you are being nasty to me now? You are (screams) go out, go out, go out (sobs) please I just want to go home and be a family again, I want to go home, and I want you to fuck off and get out get out now.'
Therapist: 'You can leave the room at any time, Candice, but I will be here for the hour.'
Candice: 'No, no, no, you're fucking going now or I'll fucking drag you out (she leaves the room and returns shortly). I'm really sorry but I want to go back home to my mum, my mum does keep me safe.' (Candice gets stuck in a cycle of wanting to go home, seeing her sisters and for the therapist to go before leaving the room again.)
Candice: (Returns with a picture of her sisters held close to her chest) 'I want to go back to these, I want to go back to them but I know my sister hates me (she strokes the picture)…they're not my sisters anymore, are they?'
Therapist: 'That's what it feels like to you.'
Candice: '(Silent scream) they're not my sisters anymore.'
Therapist: 'You feel like you've lost everything.'
Candice: 'Yes…they're not my sisters, are they? (sobs), I think, I think I've lost everything…I've even lost my sisters.'
Therapist: 'And nobody seems to see how much that hurts you.'
Candice: (She holds the picture tight and cries.)
Therapist: 'You will always remember them no matter what happens.'
Candice: 'No…they won't, they're not my sisters, are they? They're not…I'll miss them, they're not my sisters any more…my friggin social worker won't let me see my sister…tell the judge I want to go home…I'll die, I'll die if I can't go home, nobody likes me, people want me to die, my sister hates me, hates me…I didn't have sex with them and now I'm in this shit hole and you made me cry and I want to go home and I won't see them ever again.'

Candice becomes increasingly more stuck, repetitive and incoherent. She lacks self-assuagement strategies to calm down and cannot let the assessor help her. She uses exit strategies to speak to the staff. She stays for the hour, but kicks the assessor on her way out at the end (she did well to confine it to that).

Providing lifelines to children is acknowledging that sometimes they may need to return to therapy and that is not a failure, a bit like a car overheating, needing a service or an Ministry of Transport test; that is the natural rhythm of life, that some days are harder than others and that recovery is not linear.

Part V

Sustaining the Work
Supervision, Well-being, and Organisational Care

Chapter 11

Boiling Frogs and Full Up Jugs

Metaphors for Vicarious Trauma

The comment about 'boiling a frog' came from a young person who had been sexually exploited. She made the comment whilst she was trying to make sense of the intense, compulsive almost addictive quality of the relationship she had with the man who was exploiting her. She remembered a science lesson where the teacher said that a frog in cold water would die if the water was gradually heated because it would not notice the rising temperature until it was too late to escape. Alternatively, if the frog was put into water which was too hot it would immediately jump out and would survive. She could not recall the purpose of this lesson but for the first time it made sense to her. This was exactly her experience of being groomed. Had she known what the outcome would be she would have 'got out' straight away or not 'got in.' It's like boiling a frog – a perfect metaphor for vicarious trauma.

Studies have examined the number of care workers and therapists who have experienced victimisation during their childhood. Their own need for recovery prompted engagement in therapy and/or working in a caring profession such as nursing, social work and foster caring. The positive aspects of their own recovery through their own experience of therapy and/or experiencing positive relationships leads them to offering their own recovery experiences as a base for understanding their clients' needs and feelings and then using this to enable them to help another victim recover from their experiences of harm (Barr, 2006; Stanley et al., 2007; Straussner et al., 2018).

What does this research imply or conclude? That practitioners who are 'wounded healers' should not be doing the job they are in. Or that there will be 'wounded healers' already in those jobs who may need extra support and supervision to ensure they are not just experts from their own experience who, by not having had their own wounds healed, become 'healers who wound.'

In 1995, a study on ACEs found 87% of practitioners had more than one ACE, followed by more than 70 papers on the topic by 2015, asking as few as 14 questions, one with 200.

More specifically, a study from Public Health Wales (Bellis et al., 2016) found that those who had experienced more than four ACEs (i.e. 14% of the population), in comparison to those who had not had these experiences, were:

DOI: 10.4324/9781003724605-16

- 4x more likely to be high-risk drinkers.
- 6x more likely to have had or have caused unintended teenage pregnancy.
- 6x more likely to smoke cigarettes or e-cigarettes.
- 11x more likely to smoke cannabis.
- 14x more likely to have been the victim of violence over the last 12 months.
- 15x more likely to have committed violence against others over the last 12 months.
- 20x more likely to have been incarcerated.

At a conference on ACEs in July 2019 organised for professionals working in the caring professions organised by a charity supporting survivors of incest (CISters Childhood Incest Survivors), the audience was asked to complete a standard ACEs questionnaire, which gave the following results:

	Less than Four (%)	More than Four (%)
USA study	87	13
Wales	86	14
Event	83	17
Cisters	15	85

'One must come to terms with and integrate one's own shadow (darkness) in order to relate authentically compassionately to others' (Jung, 1973). Jack Brookes (2017) commented in his blog Lost in Care, 'Certainly, in my experience, children's home staff and children's social workers are almost exclusively wounded healers.' Unfortunately, if true, this is not good news, although it could be if it raised awareness that many are not sufficiently healed. Is he right that many professionals, carers, or parent substitutes are either in denial about their own trauma or unable to acknowledge the impact it still has on them in the here and now? Perhaps this explains the sometimes breathtakingly unempathetic and unsophisticated understanding professionals can have. To accept a child's past experiences can have such a profound and troubling impact on current thoughts/feelings and choices/actions needs practitioners accepting this truth about themselves. To be able to acknowledge siblings do not really know why they feel how they feel or do what they do, because it is often an unconscious process, means practitioners confronting their own defences and drives. This is very painful.

What is not reported at nearly the same level is the number of resilience factors for those who have experienced any number of ACEs and have not become healers who wound but healers who help. There is concern that Main and McLinn's resilience questionnaire has taken on a life of its own when it was only to prompt reflection and conversation on experiences which may help protect most people (about three out of four) with four or more ACEs from developing negative outcomes. White (2017) also invites thinking about resilience and not just ACEs. Using the OFSTED recommended Strengths and Difficulties questionnaire, or the more sophisticated The Child and Adolescent Needs and Strengths (CANS) questionnaire (Lyons n.d.), could help in assessing the impact on an individual rather than assuming everyone experiencing the same number of ACEs has the same outcome. Research also shows that despite the number of ACEs, resilience for a child comes from that child being in a relationship with someone: a neighbour, a friend, a professional who made the child feel valued, confirmed for the child that the child was ok, it was what was happening that was not, and prevented the trauma from continuing. This genuine, empathic relationship, even if very short term, reduces the toxic effects of the trauma on the brain, endocrine, immune, emotional and behavioural systems.

There is a need to consider what can be done to support 'caring professionals' who have experienced ACEs. Clearly, they cannot (and should not) be excluded from working within any of the caring professions. The research does not clarify if the health consequences of ACEs, obesity, heart problems, and diabetes, mentioned in the Wales study, effect career choice and if it does will this increase the risk of vicarious trauma. It is essential for managers and supervisors to be well-informed about vicarious trauma, recognise vulnerability to it among their team members, and provide trauma-informed supervision accordingly. This approach ensures supervisors can effectively support their staff while addressing related issues. In the United States the National Association of Social Workers Code of Ethics (2017) includes social workers have an ethical responsibility to ensure that their personal problems, including behavioural or health issues, do not interfere with their work and it is professionals' obligation to advocate for work environments which provide the necessary support to protect and maintain the well-being of practitioners. This would result in the provision of higher-quality services to clients and more effective interventions.

Any trauma-informed caring organisation must therefore provide trauma-informed supervision. Several authors, such as van der Kolk, Rothschild, and Briere, have introduced the term, 'wounded healers' to highlight the awareness of practitioners whose trauma history has led them to work in a caring profession (van der Kolk, Rothschild, and Briere). CISters, a charity supporting survivors of childhood sexual harm, has introduced the term, 'healers who wound,' based on their lived experiences of harm caused by practitioners whose own wounds have not healed and who consider themselves experts based on their personal experiences. They share their own recovery journey as the only way forward. Members of CISters, experts from their own experience, advocate for organisations to exercise caution when recruiting or using practitioners or volunteers who, in interview, present themselves as experts from their own experience, ensuring there is a process in place to ensure these individuals are truly 'wounded healers' and not 'healers who wound.'

Transference and countertransference issues are present in every therapeutic relationship. These may be more challenging or complex for the wounded healer. This necessitates a high level of self-awareness and consultation with an informed supervisor to monitor for any indicators of vicarious trauma (Wilson and Lindy, 1994; Rothschild, 2015; Pearlman and Saakvitne, 1995; Sedgewick, 2016). In the context of clinical supervision, it is important to observe when the focus shifts from addressing the client's feelings, arousal, and behaviours to emphasising issues related to the practitioner's own trauma history. For example, a client's mention of previous suicidal ideation may become a focal point during assessment, therapy, or supervision, influenced by the practitioners' personal experiences with suicide within their family history. Similarly, if a practitioner frequently discusses deviant sexual arousal patterns observed in the client during their own supervision or therapy, it may be driven by the practitioner or therapist's need to address their own arousal patterns or those of an abuser.

From being a survivor Jo went on to train as a therapist. At the end of her own therapy she described herself as a precious piece of porcelain that had been smashed in her childhood. She said her therapy had enabled her with some very special glue to stick herself back together again so that anyone looking at her would never know she had been smashed. With a wry smile she then added, with some annoyance, that she knew she would never hold hot water and would have to continually look out for this to avoid it melting her glue and her then falling to pieces. A year later, she said she still watched out for hot water but could now hold hotter water than before and looked forward to this progress continuing. She knew her life would never be 'hot water' free. The therapist shared with her an anecdote from the world champion golfer, Seve Ballesteros, who was asked by an interviewer what his worst golf shot was. His reply, 'Getting out of bunkers.' He was then asked if he spent a lot of time practicing getting out of bunkers. His immediate reply: 'No, I spend a lot of my time practicing how to avoid bunkers.' Applying this non-abuse example of a lifelong strategy normalised strategic survival behaviour helped her supervisee to relax and know that practicing did and would help her.

Another survivor who went on to train as a social worker described the harm done to her as being like having an ankle broken in childhood, which would prevent her from ever running the marathon. She was not bothered whether this would happen or not, but was significantly annoyed that the choice of whether or not to run in a marathon had been taken away from her. She was always quick to notice any injustice or lack of choice in her caseload and would immediately offer her support to right that wrong, whether or not it was the priority need in a safeguarding situation.

Despite receiving monthly supervision, both experienced significant levels of vicarious trauma within two years of being in practice. They blamed themselves for their lack of experience, knowledge and coping skills but kept these feelings secret just as they had done as children, and did not share this in supervision fearing blame, shame and disapproval. In effect, keeping these feelings, and their feeling of annoyance with their clients who made them feel like this, secret from their supervisors meant the extent to which this now trauma was impacting on them now was resulting in vicarious trauma and feeling how they had felt then as children.

Both took on more and more responsibility for the well-being of their current client group offering more time to some, less time to others, with increasingly rigid or chaotic boundaries. This in turn led to their clients feeling less and less safe, less contained, more fearful and therefore more and more dependent.

During supervision, both reported increased frustration and dissatisfaction due to their perception of their clients' diminishing competencies. They also noted that their clients did not acknowledge the additional effort they were putting into their work. The supervisor's trauma-informed training had included transference and countertransference issues. The supervisor was aware that raising these in the wrong way, for both the practitioner and their clients, too fast or without a great deal of empathy would reinforce the feelings of shame, blame and responsibility. As a result, this would repeat childhood solutions of a sudden and rigid introduction of boundaries causing their clients to experience empathic disruption, feel abandoned and adrift, threaten to withdraw from the therapy and the practitioner to withdraw from or miss supervision. The supervisor was also aware a change of supervisor was often sought, the supervisor then being blamed for causing the overwhelming destabilisation in the practitioner. Experience and knowledge led to a gentle exploration of the issues separating the need for supervision from the need for individual therapy enabling the practitioners to continue with both being mindful of the potential for vicarious trauma and that this would be an ongoing issue in their supervision.

A social worker's supervisor focused on the timescale for an assessment being undertaken by the practitioner, which was nearing the end of the allotted time and detailed the work still needing to be done within that period. This sharp refocusing, without knowledge of the practitioner's history and without empathy, led to the practitioner becoming focused on the timescale and pressurising the client to cooperate. Like a straw breaking the camel's back, one question too many, too quickly led to the client becoming angry and physically assaulting the social worker. She then required several weeks of sick leave to recover and left both practitioner and supervisor wondering if she should continue in her career. A criminal charge of assault and an unwillingness to engage with another practitioner resulted in care proceedings and the children being placed in foster care.

It's useful to note some vicarious trauma 'red flag' comments made by practitioners such as:

- 'I have the solutions from my own solutions.'
- 'I know this person better than anyone else does.'
- 'I am not appreciated the way I should be.'
- 'I'm willing to deal with any crisis no matter how busy I am.'
- 'Why does he/she not realise how much I have done for him/her.'
- 'No one understands the impact of this work on us.' Note the word us is used and not the word me.
- 'I need to cancel supervision again because I am just too busy.'

- 'All we have time for in supervision are management issues and checking files are up to date.'
- 'I know I'm just back from holiday; the next holiday can't come soon enough.'

These comments are often shared within chats with colleagues and not in supervision. These red flags indicate unaddressed transference and countertransference issues that are important predictors or indicators of vicarious trauma.

One way of preventing vicarious trauma and increasing self-protection is using cling film or bubble wrap. The idea for this metaphor came from the exercise, 'Loving and Caring Water' undertaken with children to explain family relationships. The exercise requires a cup to represent each family member and a jug full of coloured water to represent hurting. Another jug with differently coloured water represents loving. The hurt child pours their choice of the amount of hurting and loving water into the parent's cup then into the child's cup to represent the amount of loving and hurting done by that parent. To stop more hurting and to preserve the loving already received, the child stretches a sheet of cling film over their cup. While the cling film stops more hurting, it also stops more loving. To take it off means more hurting. Coming into foster care requires another sheet or even sheets of cling film. Children in care often hope that one day someone will love or like them enough to make it safe to remove the cling film. Practitioners at risk of vicarious trauma often seek a similar method of self-protection which decreases the capacity to be coherently empathically attuned to their clients, colleagues, or others.

A therapist, previously a social worker, with a history of childhood trauma is assigned to help a deeply troubled child. The practitioner's ability to attune to this child's feelings and needs comes from his high level of acquired skill to use attunement to predict whether a smile would predict hurt or hugs to preserve his own safety as a child. The practitioner recognises the child's need to be loved as being very similar to his own unmet needs. His need to let the child experience a high level of understanding by him increasing his attunement results in him removing his cling film. The child's hurt is then added to the practitioner's own and vice versa. Both then experience each other's trauma in a way that overwhelms them both. The practitioner experiences vicarious trauma. The child, as she did for her parents, takes care of the practitioner's needs reaffirming for her it is her role to take care of someone who hurts her. If not resolved this would reinforce it was and will be her role in future relationships where she is hurt.

The metaphor of the bubble wrap comes from the look of bubble wrap as having many air pockets which can be burst, but still the fabric of the bubble wrap holds. It enables a practitioner to use empathic attunement which recognises and deeply connects with the child's unmet needs. Doing this may pop a few 'bubble pockets' but the 'wrap' holds and is still protective, allowing the child to experience the practitioner's empathy without the risk of the child's and practitioner's hurt being shared, protecting both from further trauma and increasing their ability to self-care.

Self-care is important for individuals working with trauma in any capacity. A very common coping strategy for those living with the consequences of trauma is continuous self-blame. Phrases beginning with I should have are common. 'I should have seen it coming,' 'I should have done something to stop it,' 'I should be over this by now,' and 'Of course it's my fault.' It's a long therapeutic journey to resolve this and crucially to understand the difference between empathy, attunement, and sentimentality to avoid being overwhelmed with self-blame, use the same coping strategies and to avoid becoming a helpaholic (Miller, 2018). The word 'should' is another red-flag indicator for vicarious trauma. In trauma-informed therapy or supervision it is replaced with the word 'could' to enable curiosity and reflection.

A young adult, after her father's conviction for multiple sexual and violent offences, chose to remain living at home with her mother to continue her college course. Her relationship with her mother was extremely fraught and unpleasant, making it very difficult for them to be in the same room together. She repeated several times, 'How different my mother is from my dad. I miss him so much. I do, I just miss him.' When asked what she missed, her immediate answer was, 'His empathy.' The narcissistic and solipsistic behaviours that informed his parenting and the likelihood of him having any empathy was virtually zero. Instead of just believing what she said, this was gently explored with her by asking, 'Tell me some of the ways he was empathic,' inviting curiosity. She replied, 'He always knew what I was thinking, he always knew how as I was feeling, he just had to look at me and he knew. He could get right inside my head and change my thoughts and sadness. He was so empathic.' This sounded like empathy but, of course, was not. It was him using his ability to intensely attune, using this attunement to manipulate her to meet his needs first and foremost without thinking or caring that what he was doing would cause her significant harm. Had he been empathic he would have been putting his needs aside, first and foremost, to meet her needs.

Whenever she attempted to have a conversation with her, her mother would immediately cry and with sentimentality say, 'It was awful, what he did was terrible.' She did not stop there and continued saying, 'I know. I know. I can't sleep at night. I'll never get over this. I don't know what I'd do without you,' and with each sentence becoming more and more distressed, expecting her daughter to take care of her rather than vice versa. Her mother was neither attuned nor empathic to her daughter's needs, making the missing of the 'empathic' father, and what he offered, more intense. By not separating out empathy, attunement, and sentimentality there are so many potential pitfalls for a practitioner to fall into: accepting her missing of her father and arranging contact to help her feel better, being caught up in mother's very evident distress, minimising the girl's levels of distress because she continues at college and appears resilient, feeling sorry for the dad having a whingeing wife like her.

'Symptoms' of becoming a helpaholic, a healer who wounds or indeed sometimes of a wounded healer, are seen in someone thinking pain and suffering are bad, saying I should do more to alleviate these, I must be the best helper possible, I must never make mistakes, I cannot be weak, demanding or tearful, I must put others' needs before having fun, If I am not perfect I am a failure, If I don't help no one will and that will be terrible, If I take care of myself my clients will suffer. by becoming over-involved in trying to solve their problems for, not with. Effectively caught in the Karpman drama triangle by self-blame, shame and feeling responsible (Karpman, 1968; West, 2020).

'The problem with us helpaholics is that we are as sneaky and self-deluded as any other 'holic.' We convince ourselves that we really are happy doing what we are doing! Not too different from, 'I have my drinking under control, so I'll just have this one glass of wine and then another, and another.' Or, I'll just eat a couple of cookies then eat the whole bag. Helpaholics see someone who needs help. And before even being asked, the helpaholic is coming up with great ideas, strategies, new ways to solve the problem, because the helpaholic is sure help is needed. It feels natural and cannot not help. By being born a pleaser, I like to do things for people. It feels good until it doesn't help and self-blame returns (Miller, 1991).' Perhaps listening to Maya Angelou (1969) would be helpful in avoiding becoming a helpaholic, 'Never make someone a priority when all you are to them is an option.'

Effective supervision, particularly clinical supervision rather than management, is essential in the current environment. This regular oversight is crucial to mitigate or manage the risk of vicarious trauma. Every Child Protection or Part 8 Enquiry has commented on the poor quality or lack of supervision. As long ago as 1985 Blom-Cooper, in the A Child in Trust inquiry he chaired into the death of Jasmine Beckford, made the following recommendations about the purpose and content of supervision needed to help practitioners and protect children:

> The supervisor must ensure the practitioner has the knowledge and skills to carry out the task, objectively monitor the activities of the practitioner, be aware of the attitudes of the practitioner towards the case and correct, if necessary, the way in which they affect the handling of it, support the practitioner both emotionally and practically and set aside a regular, uninterrupted period for discussion with each practitioner.

Every Inquiry into the death of a child has commented on the paucity or non-existence of adequate supervision and yet, for example, the Adoption Support Fund barely accepts these findings and funds less than the minimum requirement, if at all.

Everyone needs to take responsibility for their own well-being through self-awareness and self-monitoring. It is important to recognise when being affected by personal issues or external factors which can cause unintentional empathic disruptions or missteps. Such matters should be addressed in supervision or therapy as needed (Wilson, 1994). Employing the 'jug' metaphor can be useful in acknowledging the past cannot be changed but it is possible to resolve its consequences. This enables working with relational, empathic depth to avoid becoming overwhelmed or experiencing vicarious trauma.

Every agency, Local Authority and professional organisations are required to have a supervision policy in place to ensure practitioners know they do not just have a right to supervision, but it is right to have supervision. Supervision meets the needs of the practitioners. It is not about what the practitioner is doing; it is about how the practitioner is doing. Supervision is not a management meeting to ensure the needs of the Agency, Local Authority, or professional organisation are met. Doing the right thing by insisting on supervision meets practitioners' needs. Doing things right meets the service user's needs. A challenge for all to avoid doing things right to meet the needs of the organisation or inspectors.

'Social workers, indeed all professionals, have an ethical responsibility to ensure that their personal problems, including behavioural health issues, do not interfere with their work. However, it is the profession's obligation to advocate for work environments that provide the necessary support to protect and maintain the well-being of social workers, efforts that would likely result in the provision of higher-quality services to clients and more effective programmes (Code of ethics of the National Association of Social Workers. Washington, DC: Author; 2017). In the UK there is no explicit reference to the responsibilities of employers in the British Association for Social Works (BASW) Code of Ethics. What BASW has is an emphasis on the responsibilities of employers in their Good Practice Tool Kit.

So, remember the 'frog' to ensure self-care, well-being, and needs are met. Not just for practitioners, but also for those worked with, to ensure there is an end to what is started and avoid adding to 'jugs' that are already full to overflowing.

Chapter 12

When the Work Gets In

Vicarious Trauma, Clinical Supervision, and Self-Care

The following extract taken from Volume 1 is repeated here because of its continuing importance and to underline its significance. Experienced social workers with many years post-qualifying experience, who later undertook therapeutic training, often fared better when engaged in relational work. Their earlier grounding provided essential exposure to the realities of the lived experiences of children, and their practice was shaped by the need to rely on empathic connection. They came to understand the impact of trauma, not just on the children and families they worked with, but also on colleagues and on themselves. By contrast, it is not uncommon to see newly qualified social work practitioners, or even experienced practitioners become undone and emotionally overwhelmed when attempting to impose a task-led model on deeply relational work. This difficulty is often compounded when their supervision is not clinical supervision and mirrors that same task-driven emphasis, focused narrowly on agency requirements and inspection demands. Conversely, practitioners whose training is rooted primarily in therapy may excel in building individual relationships yet struggle to contextualise a child's experience within the complexity of family or family of origin. Those who seek to operate from only one approach, whether purely therapeutic or purely systemic, risk finding themselves unanchored, adrift in a vessel without rudder, sail, engine, or oars.

Teddy had been a social worker for fifteen years before qualifying as a therapist. He worked tirelessly for another fifteen years in that role before one day he found he could not get out of bed. He lost his drive, was emotionally numb and could not find meaning, was physically and emotionally exhausted, overwhelmed by the most mundane and routine of life tasks and could not get to work. He later reflected, 'In hospital, the mental health workers looked at me in abject fear. I think they realised that the person they were looking at could be them.' Teddy had been a robust and resilient individual with a wide network of support and friends but worked alone and that aloneness was for him and is for others where the risk can increase. He never worked again.

An essential method for preventing vicarious traumatisation is to maintain a high level of self-awareness. 'Despite common misperceptions supervision cannot replace training and self-awareness …. otherwise, early burnout is inevitable' (Pross, 2006). Regular self-examination, reflective team discussions and supervision are important, even crucial, for individuals involved in assessment, planning, and therapeutic interventions. This helps prevent over-identification with clients, which can lead to loss of professional detachment and over-involvement and/or detached avoidance, which can result in denial of the trauma experienced by clients or its impact on practitioners.

The advantage therapists often had over social workers is that it is a course requirement to have personal therapy as part of their training. In recent years, some organisations are reducing or even removing this requirement, a significant error of judgement which reduces the robustness of the training. Personal therapy allows the practitioner to 'see,' acknowledge, and work on their own weak links, their tender spots, and thus work to shore themselves, bubble wrap themselves, against the vagaries inherent in working with survivors of trauma. 'What I cannot tolerate in myself I cannot tolerate in someone else,' and continues, 'With integration,' (a state more likely to reached with personal therapy), 'I enable differentiation of my various aspects to be cultivated, including states of mind. If I am not open to parts of myself, to these varied states, I will not be open to receiving them from my client' (Siegel, 2010).

Therefore, it is critical to keep in mind the metaphor of the frog from the previous chapter. Ensuring that all practitioners are well and their needs are met is crucial, not only for their own well-being but also for those they work with. This approach helps ensure and safeguard the completion of tasks and prevents any further trauma from occurring during their meetings, sessions, and day-to-day business, especially when practitioners are already feeling overwhelmed.

One of the concerns heard from workers is that more time is spent in 'supervision' on management issues to meet the agencies or inspectors' needs rather than on clinical issues extrapolated in clinical supervision. Although logged as supervision, the focus is on targets, policy, procedures, timescales, recording, and external expectations. Where there is case discussion, its focus often shifts to case management. The focus is on, 'What are you doing rather than how are you doing?' or the essence of the intervention rather than the practicalities of the intervention. The impact of the work can only then be shared with colleagues or partners which, whilst providing much-needed discharge of distress and letting off steam, is not clinical supervision and does not lessen the likelihood of the worker experiencing vicarious trauma. It may well vicariously traumatise the partner or colleague who feels helpless to help when hearing not just what was done did to the client but also what it is doing to the practitioner. Similar to the way children who are relying on support from each other when experiencing, witnessing, or recovering from trauma without an adult, parent, carer, or mentor present try to meet their own and their sibling's needs. An 'enlightened witness' is needed to achieve well-being and resilience and avoid vicarious trauma (Miller, 1988).

Just as it is the knowledge, skill and empathic connection that enables those training practitioners to demonstrate how to ask the correct questions in the right way, so too does the supervisor need to recognise arousal symptoms, externally manage the window of tolerance if and when needed and use the same skill set as the worker. The supervisor so too needs to be supervised in a coherent manner, commonly referred to as clinical supervision of clinical supervision. It is hoped that managers will have developed and used these skills, when they themselves were practitioners working with troubled and traumatised clients and can now transfer these into their role as supervisors. This is not just to encourage self-awareness and growth but is needed when difficult, intrusive and personal questions need to be asked to deepen trust and professional development. Being dependable, boundaried and consistent, the key components of a safe professional relationship, need to be transferred into supervision to ensure there is no blurring or crossover from a supervisory role into a therapeutic one.

How much does a supervisor need to know about themselves and their supervisees? Is the following often complex and paradoxical information known? If not why not and what stops this from being possible?

- Their motivation for this work: status, usefulness, affection, acceptance, putting the world to rights, recognition, anger, their own history.
- Their ability to recognise and deal with the following paradoxes and conflicting issues personally and professionally.
- Being dependable and creating dependency.
- Listening to and talking to others.
- Consent real and consent false or compromised.
- Individual rights and family rights.
- Individual needs and family needs.
- Individual children's needs and siblings' needs.
- Own survival strategies and their clients' strategies.
- Shame, blame and empathic curiosity.
- Attunement and empathy.
- Curiosity and nosiness.
- Punishment and treatment.
- Hopeless and hopeful.
- Denial and awareness.
- Secrecy and openness.
- Collusion and partnership.
- Compliance and cooperation.
- Control and safe boundaries.
- Power and trust.
- Being externally driven and internally aware.
- Good self-care or an 'aholic,' alcoholic, shopaholic, foodaholic, helpaholic, workaholic.
- Hearing about trauma and managing its professional and personal impact.
- Ability to trust and be trusted.
- Willingness to and ability to listen.

- Attitudes to abuse, abusers and failure to protect.
- To meet needs and be needed?
- Fears of and history of assault/trauma.
- Ability to deal with own issues related to assault, recognise and know how to manage their own triggers to avoid being hi-jacked into empathic disruption.
- Ability to work with individuals and their system or context.
- Own needs identified and willingness to work on these in supervision and do not use avoidance by diverting to management or organisational needs.

Clarity is also needed between practitioners experiencing vicarious trauma, those under stress or high stress, and those who are self-aware and ensuring their own well-being, are coping but experiencing stretch. The following helps differentiate vicarious trauma from coping but stretched:

Vicarious Trauma	*Coping but Stretched*
Requires management	Requires clinical supervision
Uses cling film	Uses bubble wrap
Uses attunement script	Uses empathy script
Disorganised attachment behaviours	Secure attachment behaviours
Chaotic or inconsistent work	Boundaried and consistent
Externally driven	Internally aware
Identification with	Differentiation from
'Off' for noticing unmet needs	'On' for noticing unmet needs
Unprotected core	Protected core
Unaware of using self-disclosure	Aware of use of appropriate-self disclosure
About me	About you
Chaotic changing boundaries	Flexible boundaries
Rigidity	Therapeutic stretch
Feels hopeless	Feels motivated
Feels unappreciated/disrespected	Happy in role. Personal vs Professional
Avoids colleagues	Available with appropriate boundaries
Numb or flat	Appropriate energy
Social withdrawal	Enjoys life, has fun
Nightmares, sleep disrupted	Good quality sleep
Alterations in sensory experiences (flashbacks)	Integrated
Dysregulates or uses Trauma Reducing Behaviour	Self regulates
No time or energy for self	Boundaried self-care
Adrenalin driven volunteering	Says no, recognises enough to do
Rapid exhaustion	More tired than usual
Disconnection from loved ones	Shares experience with loved ones
'Self' motivated curiosity	Client motivated curiosity
Karpman triangle operating	'Dented circle'

Vicarious Trauma	Coping but Stretched
Disrupted frame of reference	Notes frame of reference, wobbles
Changes in world view	Questions world view
Diminished self-capacities	Notices when on the edge of capacity
Impaired ego resources	Own needs are as important as clients
Disrupted schemas	Safely reviews schemas

Some years ago, it was usual in a manager's course, misnamed a supervisor's course, for the trainer to divide the large group into three small groups, each being given a card with their group's task on it, a sheet of flipchart paper, and a pen. The task for each small group was (1) to be a child listing the qualities in a parent they needed to ensure they had the best chance of becoming a healthy, happy, functioning adult; (2) a child listing the qualities in their social worker/therapist needed to ensure the best chance of becoming a healthy, happy, functioning adult; and (3) to be a practitioner listing the qualities in their supervisor which would ensure the best chance of becoming a healthy, happy, functioning worker. Each group thought all were given the same task. The completed three sheets of flipchart were put on the wall, and the large group was then invited to determine which list applied to which task. The lists were always remarkably similar. The only difference was the child wanting their social worker to have a supercar was missing from the adults' list.

The skills are transferable, as is vowing not to behave in the way an abusive parent did but to emulate a parent's positives, and, as is the case for parenting, accepting practitioners' skills are not finite and ensuring both the practitioners and the supervisors learning is lifelong. Practitioners need to know about the impact of trauma on the children, their families, and themselves. Supervisors need to know about the impact of vicarious trauma on their practitioners and themselves and work effectively to ensure all practitioners are functioning in an ever-widening window of tolerance. By doing this also protects their colleagues, their own children and families and the children and families they provide a service to.

When working with siblings, the issue of self-care and being able to see the situation through the eyes of each sibling becomes even harder. A practitioner responsible for a sibling group needs clinical supervision to oversee and ensure practice is egalitarian; one child's difficulties are not overshadowing another child's resilience, the volcano in the corner is not obliterating the sound of the earthquake or tsunami the other siblings represent. It is a hard task to remain balanced when there is a less challenging or more connected sibling responding positively and when there is a sibling who is raging and directing that rage at the practitioner or others.

Would a different practitioner with every sibling be easier? What if one confident practitioner can shout the needs of 'their child' above the needs of a less vocal colleague? What if the division mirrors the disunion and split between the siblings, when the practitioners find it harder to 'see' the needs of all the siblings, or one sibling is scapegoated as only a perpetrator, another seen only as a victim? Where each sibling has their own practitioner adding someone with group oversight, a line manager and clinical supervisors would this make the work even more complex to process and communication challenging.

Managers/supervisors must model being self-aware, noticing their own body reactions, emotions, thoughts, and fantasies. By maintaining their own well-being, demonstrated by words, actions, peer support, training, their own supervision, and having unrelated-to-work interests. To remain empathically curious without blame or shame when the going is tough or mistakes are made means the supervision offered is not just meeting the supervisor's own intellectual and emotional needs or the organisation's issues. Everyone needs to be aware of the signs of vicarious trauma for individuals and their team members. This is crucial to ensure the mirroring clearly shows it is possible to be part of a happy, functioning, boundaried group of practitioners and siblings.

> Engagement in this work thus poses some risk to the therapist's own psychological health. The therapist's adverse reactions, unless understood and contained, also predictably lead to disruptions in the therapeutic alliance with clients and to conflict with professional colleagues. Therapists who work with traumatized people require an ongoing support system to deal with these intense reactions. Just as no survivor can recover alone, no therapist can work with trauma alone.
> (Herman, 1992)

Although Judith Herman is referring to therapists, her comment refers to everyone whose work involves assessing and working with traumatised siblings, not just in their lives before intervention but they do not experience further trauma as a result of assessments or interventions which incorrectly resulted in siblings living together or apart.

And finally to repeat van der Kolk (1996), 'Our brains can take in new information when our bodies feel safe but if we become fixated on the trauma, then our ability to take in new information safe. But is we become fixated on the trauma, then our ability to take in new information is lost, and we continue to construct and re-construct the old realities'

Sound advice not just for parents ensuring the health, safety, practical and emotional growth of their children but for everyone working in the complex paraxdoxfull field of trauma and the many additional paradoxes present when working with siblings.

References

Aldgate, J. and Simmonds, J. (1988) *Direct Work with Children: A Guide for Social Work Practitioners. Child Care Policy and Practice.* London: B. T. Batsford Ltd and BAAF.

Aldridge, J. and Becker, S. (1999) *Children as Carers: The Impact of Parental Illness and Disability on Children's Caring Roles.* Loughborough: Young Carers Research Group, Department of Social Sciences, Loughborough University.

Angelou, M. (1969) *I Know Why the Caged Bird Sings.* New York: Random House.

Bannister, A. (2003) *Creative Therapies with Traumatized Children.* London: Jessica Kingsley.

Barber, J.G. and Delfabbro, P.H. (2004) *Children in Foster Care.* London: Routledge.

Barr, A. (2006) 'Exploring the impact of trauma on children in care', paper presented at the COSCA Research Dialogue Conference, Edinburgh, 15 March.

Beckett, S. (2018) *Beyond Together or Apart: Planning for, Assessing and Placing Sibling Groups.* London: Coram BAAF.

Beckett, S. (2021) *Beyond Together or Apart: Planning for, Assessing and Placing Sibling Groups: Good Practice Guide.* 2nd edn. London: Coram BAAF.

Belsky, J. and Vondra, J. (1989) 'Lessons from child abuse: The determinants of parenting', in Cicchetti, D. and Carlson, V. (eds.) *Child Maltreatment: Theory and Research on the Causes and Consequences of Child Abuse and Neglect.* Cambridge: Cambridge University Press, pp. 153–202.

Blaustein, M.E. and Kinniburgh, K.M. (2010) *Treating Traumatic Stress in Children and Adolescents: How to Foster Resilience Through Attachment, Self-Regulation, and Competency.* New York: Guilford Press.

Bray, M. (1997) *Sexual Abuse: The Child's Voice — Poppies on the Rubbish Heap.* 2nd edn. London: Jessica Kingsley Publishers.

Briere, J. (1992) *TSCC: Trauma Symptom Checklist for Children: Professional Manual.* Florida: PAR.

Brookes, J. (2017) 'Lost in care', *The Attachment Theory Blog*, 12 January. Available at: https://martinbrookes.medium.com/who-cares-988aa0987a26 (Accessed 18 March 26)

Brown, H. and Craft, A. (1989) *Thinking the Unthinkable: Papers on Sexual Abuse and People with Learning Difficulties.* London: FPA Education Unit.

Brown, R. and Ward, H. (2013) *Decision-Making Within a Child's Timeframe: An Overview of Current Research Evidence for Family Justice Professionals Concerning Child Development and the Impact of Maltreatment.* London: Childhood Wellbeing Research Centre.

Buchanan, A. (ed.) (1994) *Caring for Children: Families and Services*. Chichester: Wiley.

Burnell, A. and Vaughn, J. (2008) 'Remembering Never to Forget and Forgetting Never to Remember: Re-Thinking Life Story Work', in Luckock, B. and Lefevre, M. (eds.) *Direct Work: Social Work With Children and Young People in Care*. London: BAAF, pp. 223–233.

Cairns, K. (2002) *Attachment, Trauma and Resilience*. London: BAAF.

Calder, M., Harold, G.T. and Howarth, E. (2004) *Children Living With Domestic Violence: Towards a Framework for Assessment and Intervention*. Lyme Regis: Russell House Publishing.

Campbell, D. and Hale, R. (1991) 'Suicidal Acts', in Holmes, J. (ed.) *Textbook of Psychotherapy in Psychiatric Practice*. London: Churchill Livingstone.

Centers for Disease Control and Prevention. (2010) 'Adverse childhood experiences reported by adults — Five states, 2009', *Morbidity and Mortality Weekly Report*, 59(49), pp. 1609–1613.

Coram. (2024) *Sibling Time Activity Day Pilot: Evaluation Report*. Available at: https://www.coram.org.uk/wp-content/uploads/2024/04/Sibling-Time-Report-April-2024.pdf (Accessed: 26 August 2026).

Cozolino, L. (2006) *The Neuroscience of Human Relationships: Attachment and the Developing Social Brain*. London: Norton.

Crittenden, P. M. (2008) *Raising Parents: Attachment, Parenting and Child Safety*. Cullompton: Willan Publishing.

Department for Education (2013) *Statutory Guidance on Adoption*. London: Department for Education. https://assets.publishing.service.gov.uk/government/uploads/system/uploads/attachment_data/file/270100/statutory_guidance_on_adoption.pdf (Accessed: 10 July 2025).

Department for Education (2018) *Working Together to Safeguard Children: A Guide to Interagency Working to Safeguard and Promote the Welfare of Children*. London: Department for Education. Available at: https://assets.publishing.service.gov.uk/government/uploads/system/uploads/attachment_data/file/942454/Working_together_to_safeguard_children_inter_agency_guidance.pdf (Accessed: 10 July 2025).

Department of Health and Social Security. (1988) *Report of the Inquiry into Child Abuse in Cleveland 1987 (Cm 412)*. London: HMSO.

Dominelli, L. (2009) *Introducing Social Work*. Cambridge: Polity.

Fahlberg, V. (1994) *A Child's Journey Through Placement*. London: BAAF.

Fisher, J. (2023) *Embracing our Fragmented Selves: A Workbook for Trauma Survivors and Their Therapists*. London: PESI.

Freud, S. (1912) 'The dynamics of transference', in *The Standard Edition of the Complete Psychological Works of Sigmund Freud, Vol. XII (1911–1913)*. London: Hogarth Press, pp. 97–108.

Friedman, L. (1969) 'The Therapeutic Alliance', *International Journal of Psycho-Analysis*, 50, p. 139.

Garbarino, J., Brookhouser, P.E. and Authier, K.J. (1987) *Special Children, Special Risks: The Maltreatment of Children With Disabilities*. New York: Aldine De Gruyter.

Gordon, M. (2009) *Roots of Empathy: Changing the World Child by Child*. New York: Thomas Allen and Son Ltd.

Herman, J.L. (1992) *Trauma and Recovery*. New York: Basic Books.

Humphreys, C. and Kiraly, M. (2010) 'High frequency family contact: A road to nowhere for infants', *Child & Family Social Work*, 16(1), pp. 1–11.

Johnson, S.M. (1994) *Character Styles*. London: W. W. Norton and Company.

Jung, C. G. (1973) *Letters of C.G. Jung: Volume I, 1906–1950*. Edited by G. Adler and A. Jaffé. Translated by R.F.C. Hull. London: Routledge.

Karpman, S. (1968) 'Fairy tales and script drama analysis', *Transactional Analysis Bulletin*, 7(26), pp. 39–43.

Kenrick, J. (2009) 'Concurrent planning: A retrospective study of the continuities and discontinuities of care and their consequences', *Adoption & Fostering*, 33(1), pp. 5–18.

Kurtz, R. (2007) *Body-Centred Psychotherapy: The Hakomi Method*. Mendocino, CA: LifeRhythm Press.

Levy, T. and Orlans, M. (1998) *Attachment, Trauma and Healing: Understanding and Treating Attachment Disorder in Children and Families*. Washington, DC: Child Welfare League of America.

Lord, J. and Borthwick, S. (2008, 2014) *Together or Apart? Assessing Siblings for Permanent Placement*. 2nd edn. London: Coram BAAF.

Lyons, J. S. (n.d.) *Child and Adolescent Needs and Strengths (CANS)*. Chicago: Praed Foundation.

Malatesta, C.Z., Jonas, R. and Izard, C.E. (1987) 'The relation between low facial expressivity during emotional arousal and somatic symptoms', *British Journal of Medical Psychology*, 60, pp. 169–180.

Maslow, A.H. (1954) *Motivation and Personality*. New York: Harper & Row.

McMahon, L. (1992) *The Handbook of Play Therapy*. London: Routledge.

Miller, A. (1988) *Banished Knowledge: Facing Childhood Injuries*. New York: Nan A. Talese/Doubleday.

Miller, M. (2018) *Confessions of a Recovering Helpaholic*. Texas: Peoplebiz.

Miller, J.B. (1991) *The "Helpaholic" Syndrome: How to Stop "Helping" and Start Loving*. New York: Paulist Press.

Morgan, S.R. (1987) *Abuse and Neglect of Handicapped Children*. Boston: College-Hill Publication.

Munby, J.L. (2010) *Family Justice Council Debate on Contact for Babies in Care Proceedings*. Available at: https://www.judiciary.uk/wp-content/uploads/JCO/Documents/FJC/Transcript_of_baby_contact_debate.pdf. (Accessed 11 August 2015).

Natiello, P.M. (2001) *The Person-Centered Approach: A Passionate Presence*. Ross-on-Wye: PCCS Books.

National Association of Social Workers (2017) *Code of Ethics of the National Association of Social Workers*. Washington, DC: NASW Press. Available at: https://www.socialworkers.org/About/Ethics/Code-of-Ethics/Code-of-Ethics-English (Accessed: 26 August 2025).

National Institute for Health and Care Excellence (NICE). (2015) *Looked-after Children and Young People*. Public Health Guideline [PH28]. Available at: https://www.nice.org.uk/guidance/ph28 (Accessed: 11 August 2025).

Oaklander, V. (1978) *Windows to Our Children: A Gestalt Therapy Approach to Children and Adolescents*. Utah: Real People Press.

Owen, P. and Curtis, P. (n.d.) *Techniques for Working with Children: A Guide for Professionals*. Manchester: North West Children's Services.

Ogden, P. and Fisher, J. (2015) *Sensorimotor Psychotherapy: Interventions for Trauma and Attachment*. London: W.W. Norton.

Ogden, P., Minton, K. and Pain, C. (2006) *Trauma and the Body: A Sensorimotor Approach to Psychotherapy*. London: W.W. Norton.

Orkney (1992) *Inquiry into Removal of Children in Orkney*. Scottish Office.

Pearlman, L.A. and Saakvitne, K.W. (1995) *Trauma and the Therapist*. London: W.W. Norton.

Perry, B.D. and Szalavitz, M. (2006) *The Boy Who Was Raised As a Dog: And Other Stories from a Child Psychiatrist's Notebook*. New York: Basic Books.

Perry, B.D. and Winfrey, O. (2021) *What Happened to You? Conversations on Trauma, Resilience, and Healing*. London: Bluebird.

Pike, A., Kretschmer, T. and Dunn, J. (2009) 'Siblings: Friends or Foes?' *The Psychologist*, 22(6), pp. 494–496.

Pross, C. (2006) 'Burnout, vicarious traumatization and its prevention: What is burnout, what is vicarious traumatization?', *Torture*, 16(1), pp. 1–9.

Putnam, F.W. (1997) *Dissociation in Children and Adolescents: A Developmental Perspective*. London: Guilford Press.

Quinton, D., Rushton, A., Dance, C. and Mayes, D. (1997) 'Contact between children placed away from home and their birth parents: Research issues and evidence', *Clinical Child Psychology and Psychiatry*, 2(3), pp. 393–413.

Radford, L. and Hester, M. (1995) *Domestic Violence and Child Contact in England and Denmark*. Bristol: Policy Press.

Redgrave, P. (1987) *Child's Play: "Direct Work" With the Deprived Child*. Manchester: Boys and Girls Welfare Society and Manchester Free Press.

Reich, W. (1933) *Character Analysis: Foundations for Students and Practicing Analysts*. Berlin: International Psychoanalytical University.

Rogers, C.R. (1951) *Client-Centered Therapy: Its Current Practice, Implications and Theory*. Boston: Houghton Mifflin.

Rogers, C.R. (1961) *On Becoming a Person: A Therapist's View of Psychotherapy*. London: Constable.

Rose, R. (2017) *Innovative Therapeutic Life Story Work: Developing Trauma-Informed Practice for Working with Children, Adolescents and Young Adults*. London: Jessica Kingsley Publishers.

Rose, R. and Philpot, T. (2005) *The Child's Own Story: Life Story work with Traumatised Children*. London: Jessica Kingsley Publishers.

Rothschild, B. (2015) *The Wounded Healer*. London: Norton.

Schofield, G., Beek, M., Ward, E. and Sellick, C. (2011) *Care Planning for Permanence in Foster Care*. Norwich: Centre for Research on the Family and Child, University of East Anglia.

Schofield, G. and Simmonds, J. (2009) 'Contact for infants subject to care proceedings', in *The Child Placement Handbook: Policy, Research and Practice*. London: BAAF.

Schofield, G. and Simmonds, J. (2011) 'Contact for infants subject to care proceedings', *Family Law*, June.

Schwartz, R. (1995) *Internal Family Systems Therapy*. New York: Guilford Press.

SCIE (2010) *Promoting the Quality of Life for Looked After Children and Young People*. London: Social Care Institute for Excellence.

Scott, D., O'Neill, C. and Minge, A. (2005) *Contact Between Children in Out-of-Home Care and Their Birth Families*. Sydney: NSW Department of Community Services.

Sedgewick, D. (2016) *The Wounded Healer: Countertransference from a Jungian Perspective*. London: Routledge.

Siegel, D.J. (1999) *The Developing Mind: How Relationships and the Brain Interact to Shape Who We Are*. London: Guilford.

Siegel, D.J. (2010) *The Mindful Therapist: A Clinician's Guide to Mindsight and Neural Integration*. London: WW Norton.
Siegel, D.J. and Bryson, T.P. (2011) *The Whole-Brain Child*. New York: Delacorte Press.
Sinclair, I., Baker, C., Wilson, K. and Gibbs, I. (2004) *Foster Children: Where They Go and How They Get On*. London: Jessica Kingsley Publishers.
Stanley, N., Manthorpe, J. and White, M. (2007) 'Depression in the profession: Social workers' experiences and perceptions', *British Journal of Social Work*, 37(2), pp. 281–298.
Stern, D.N. (1977) *The First Relationship: Infant and Mother*. Cambridge, MA: Harvard University Press.
Straussner, S.L.A., Senreich, E. and Steen, J.T. (2018) 'Wounded healers: A multistate study of licensed social workers' behavioral health problems', *Social Work*, 63(2), pp. 125–135.
Summit, R.C. (1983) 'Beyond belief: The child sexual abuse accommodation syndrome', *Child Abuse and Neglect*, 7, pp. 177–193.
Taylor, J. and Shrive, J. (2023) *Indicative Trauma Impact Manual (ITIM) for Professionals: A Non-Diagnostic, Trauma-Informed Guide to Emotion, Thought, and Behaviour*. 1st edn. Great Britain: Victim Focus.
The Children Act (1989) London: HMSO.
The Scottish Office. (1992) *Report of the inquiry into the removal of children from Orkney in February 1991*. Edinburgh: HMSO.
Tucker, C., Jenkins, C., McHale, S. and Crouter, A. (2008) 'Links between older and younger adolescent siblings' adjustment: The moderating role of shared activities', *International Journal of Behavioural Development*, 32(2), pp. 152–160.
Tucker, S., Farmer, P. and Mutch, A. (1999) *Young Carers and Their Families: A Survey into the Needs of Young Carers in Nottingham*. Nottingham: Nottingham Young Carers Project/Barnardo's.
Van der Kolk, B., McFarlane, A.C. and Weisaeth, L. (eds.) (1996) *Traumatic Stress*. New York: Guilford Press.
Ward, H., Brown, R., Westlake, D. and Munro, E. (2010) *Infants Suffering, or Likely to Suffer, Significant Harm: A Prospective Longitudinal Study*. London: DCSF.
Waterhouse, R. (2000) *Return to an Address of the Honourable the House of Commons Dated 14th February 2000 for the Report of the Tribunal of Inquiry Into the Abuse of Children in Care in the Former County Council Areas of Gwynedd and Clwyd Since 1974: Lost in Care – Summary of Report with Conclusions and Recommendations in Full*. London: The Stationary Office.
West, C. (2020) *The Karpman Drama Triangle Explained: A Guide for Coaches, Managers, Trainers, and Therapists*. London: CWTK.
White, S. C. (2017) 'Relational wellbeing: Re-centring the politics of happiness, policy and the self', *Policy & Politics*, 45(2), pp. 121–136.
Wilson J.P. and Lindy, J.B. (1994) *Countertransference in the Treatment of PTSD*. New York: Guilford Press.
Wolkind, S. (1988) 'Emotional signs', in Bainham, A. (ed.) *Parents and Children*. London: Routledge, pp. 82–87.
Woodhouse, T. (2015) 'Subcutaneous, subcortical, subconscious and subterranean: The most toxic boy in the world's search for mum', in McCarthy, D. (ed.) *Deep Play: Exploring the Use of Depth in Psychotherapy with Children*. London: Jessica Kingsley Publishers.

Wrench, K. and Naylor, L. (2013) *Life Story Work with Children Who Are Fostered or Adopted: Creative Ideas and Activities*. London: Jessica Kingsley Publishers.

Zeitlin, H. (1983) *The Natural History of Psychiatric Disorder in Childhood*. MD Thesis University of London.

Index

abuse: emotional 134; neglect 8–10, 55, 190, 199, 217–218; physical 31, 35; sexual 49, 62, 89, 92, 108, 135, 160, 202–204; thresholds 135, 217–218
achieving best evidence (ABE) 37, 86
adolescence 29
adoption placement decision-making 29, 41–42, 50–55, 89–93
Adverse Childhood Experiences (ACEs) 3, 60, 93, 215
adversity 185–187
aggression, risk of 121, 125, 149, 153, 168
alcohol 27–28, 67, 107, 134, 167, 227
Aldgate, J. 68
Aldridge, J. 184
amygdala 78
analysis: parenting 48, 61; weighing the evidence 43, 49, 98–99, 101, 125, 195–197, 180, 189
Angelou, M. 223
assessment: concurrent 92; family 89, 197; framework 61; inter-sibling dynamics 34, 36, 37, 43; sibling 4, 5, 9, 16, 34, 38, 47, 50, 76, 83, 86, 89, 93, 106, 177, 178, 195, 205–207
attachment, assessment 81–194; relational patterns 35
attention deficit disorder (ADD) 81
attention deficit hyperactivity disorder (ADHD) 80
autism spectrum condition (ASC) 57
avoidance 52, 88, 124, 152, 191, 204

Bannister, A. 73
Barber, J.G. 14
Barr, A. 226
Beckett, S. 4, 25

belief 39, 43, 44, 67, 75, 92–93, 96, 136, 143, 182, 186, 205
best interests, decision-making, balancing needs and risk 24, 26, 30, 31, 36
bias: mantra-based 205; professional 51, 94; systemic 94, 205; values 48
blame 37, 93, 96, 98, 220, 227
boiling frogs 216
Bray, M. 66
Briere, J.N. 189, 228
Brookes, J. 217
Brown, H. 26
Brown, R. 27
Buchanan, A. 184
Burnell, A. 73

Cairns, K. 38
Calder, M. 116
Campbell, D. 185
capacity: adult's 84, 86; carer's 11, 28, 41, 48, 51–52, 181; parent's 4, 48, 87, 182; professional's 71–73, 181; sibling's 197
care proceedings 32, 219
character strategies: burdened-enduring 117, 130, 145, 166, 172; charming-manipulative 73, 115, 117, 130, 144, 145, 166; expressive-clinging 117, 130, 145; sensitive-emotional 115, 130, 144; sensitive-withdrawn 115, 130, 144; tough-generous 49, 116, 144, 186
child: development 143, 197; psychopathology 49, 197, 200–201
Child and Adolescent Needs and Strengths (CANS) 217
The Children Act 13, 29, 58, 163, 205
Cleveland Inquiry 98

clinical supervision 48, 68, 73, 99, 100, 203, 218, 222, 224–229
coercive control 96
coherence: model 200, 220; narrative 198
competence: Gillick/Fraser 19
compliance 15, 220, 226; false 70; inspection 69; safety in 7, 70; veiled 204
conclusions, no foregone 93–157
contact 24, 194, 197–199, 202, 205, 221; sibling 6, 17, 21–23, 30, 34–43, 49, 200, 205, 206
context: adoption 51, 55; child's 87, 189; contact 24, 228; environment 10; parent's 189; professional 219; siblings 87, 106, 107, 170
Coram 16, 18
Cozolino, L. 28
Crittenden, P.M. 179
culture: context 123; family 123, 133, 159; gang 159; professional 16, 103, 190
curiosity: professional 37, 92, 127, 155, 203, 222, 227, 228

decision-making 208, 210
defiance 191, 198
development 7–10; professional 226
disability 105, 107, 114
disagreement 76
dissociation 68, 75, 124
domestic violence 9, 15, 25, 36, 96
Dominelli, L. 179, 232
8 (11) c's 126, 127, 153, 154

empathic parenting 198
empathy 25, 44, 54, 103
evidence, cross-referencing 207; tri-angulated 200–207

fabricated or induced illness (FII) 204
Fahlberg, V. 67
family disruption 24
fault lines 83, 92
formulation: psychodynamic 95, 190–195
Freud, S. 179
Friedman, L. 179

Garbarino, J. 29
Gordon, M. 25
grief and loss 32, 41–42, 54–55, 79, 86, 127, 153

harmful sexual behaviour-sibling-specific assessment 6, 24, 31, 35, 39, 59, 87, 186, 209
healing: contact 207; therapeutic 203
Herman, J.L. 229
Humphreys, C. 13, 14
hypotheses 6, 8, 40, 93–95, 98, 195, 199–200, 204

identity: cultural 24, 25, 34; gender 108; sexual 49, 67
impact of contact 9, 94, 205
Independent Fostering Agency (IFA) 86
insight 89, 94, 100
integration 26, 47, 71, 185, 213, 225
internal working model (IWM) 108, 134

Johnson, S.M. 165, 167
Jung, C.G. 216

Karpman, S. 222, 227
Kenrick, J. 14
Kurtz, R. 185

lens 105
Levy, T. 67
life story work: therapeutic life story 65, 67–70, 72–76, 88, 159
listening before listing 178
Lord, J. 6
Loss 7–10, 23, 86, 150

McMahon, L. 66, 70, 71
Malatesta, C.Z. 27
mantra based practice 205
mantra to map 3–12
Maslow, A.H. 60
meaning making 36, 187
mental health 66, 83; child 108, 135; parental 7, 25, 84, 107, 133, 134, 166, 183, 204
metaphors 35, 42, 78, 125, 153; boiling frogs, full-up jugs 215, 223, 225; bridges or battlegrounds 24–33
Miller, M. 221
model coherency 66, 92, 105, 179
Morgan, S.R. 29
multidisciplinary working 3, 48, 50
Munby, J.L. 14

Natiello, P.M. 181
National Association of Social Workers 217, 223

National Institute for Health and Care Excellence (NICE) 15
neurobiology 19
neurodevelopment 25
neurodivergence 104, 107, 114, 134, 143, 157, 189
neurological 43, 76, 114
neuroscience 17

Oaklander, V. 65
observation 42, 100–105, 194, 200, 201; behavioural 19, 197, 205; contact 8, 15, 16, 19, 27, 202
OFSTED 72
Ogden, P. 72, 179, 185, 187
oppositional behaviour 110, 123, 153, 168, 202
Orkney 98
outcomes 7, 12, 16, 19, 25, 27, 47, 50, 51, 57, 58, 94, 111, 112, 124, 184, 188, 208
Owen, P. 65

paradoxes 4, 25–26, 28, 30, 32, 50, 57, 76, 86–89, 93, 114, 195, 198, 202–204; contact 35, 43; organisational 68, 207, 226; sibling 12, 25, 26, 30, 34, 35–43, 72, 76, 89, 94, 198, 207, 229
paramount principle 3, 25
parenting 10, 15, 16, 25, 55, 78, 84, 90, 178, 179, 183, 185, 186, 221, 228; good enough 15, 17, 49, 52, 55, 58, 60; plus 60; pseudo 89
parts 26, 101, 114, 127, 143, 155, 184, 186, 187, 192, 225
Pearlman, L.A. 217
Perry, B.D. 9, 182
Pike, A. 5
placement 3; breakdown 5, 15, 23, 32, 37; disruption 8–10, 24, 32–33, 38, 92, 199; matching 50–60; permanence 11, 51; stability 47–62, 86
play therapy 84
professional: conflict 61, 229; curiosity *see* curiosity; wellbeing 217, 223, 225, 227, 229
projection 67, 100
Pross, C. 224, 234
psychometrics 93, 104, 183, 188, 195, 200, 201; Trauma Symptom Checklist for Children (TSCC) 188; Trauma Symptom Inventory 2 (TSI-2) 188

psychopathology 25, 49, 104, 107, 114, 134, 143, 157, 197
Putman, F.W. 37

Radford, I. 15
Rapport 103, 179
recommendations 15, 42, 61, 84, 93, 102, 194, 196, 201, 205–209, 222
reflection 96, 101, 202, 216, 221
regression 11, 12, 32, 120, 147
regulation 191; emotional 140; self 79, 111, 113, 142; social 27, 67, 71, 142, 181, 197
repair 170, 182
resilience 7, 25, 34, 36–37, 42, 47, 72, 96, 107–108, 136, 184, 188, 225; protective factors 9, 51–57, 107, 134, 190–193, 216
review 7, 16, 19, 39, 70, 72–73, 87, 94, 104, 178, 195, 197, 202–203, 207–210; clinical 224–229; judicial 1, 4
rights 13–23, 26, 112, 141, 226
risk 5, 10, 13–23, 57, 59, 71, 75, 83, 84, 124–125, 152, 161, 204–205, 220, 229; assessment 77; dynamic 83; emotional 94, 178, 224; formulation 95, 190–193
Rogers, C.R. 181
Rose, R. 67
Rothschild, B. 217
rupture 162, 173

safeguarding 20, 25, 29, 34, 35, 68, 78, 96, 122, 150, 207, 217
safety planning 18, 34, 38
scapegoating 5, 10, 87, 108, 134, 135, 161, 162, 171, 177, 184, 229
Schofield, G. 13, 15
Schwartz, R. 187
Sedgewick, D. 217
sexual: development 96, 114, 143, 164, 165; harm 57, 108, 136, 156, 206, 217
sibling: dynamics: assessment *see* assessment; contact 34, 36, 37, 43, 95; harmful dynamics 21, 22, 28, 35–37, 108; protective roles 88, 168, 172, 176; together or apart 5, 35, 36, 41, 47, 74, 76, 94, 98, 229; *see also* contact
Sinclair, I. 13
Social Care Institute for Excellence (SCIE) 15
social work judgement 47, 50, 194, 225
special guardianship orders (SGO) 3

Stanley, N. 215
Stern, D. 25
Straussner, S.L. 215
Stress: assessment markers 47, 98, 106, 110, 112, 118, 120, 126, 127, 133, 139, 154–160, 166, 168, 194, 204
substance misuse 110, 128, 138, 156, 189
Summit, R. 29
supervision 73, 100, 202, 218, 222; clinical *see* clinical; containment 48; decision 19, 100, 102, 202; reflective 41, 53, 54, 95, 102, 202, 224

Taylor, J. 188
temperament: 9, 25, 77, 109, 137, 175, 184, 190
therapeutic alliance 104, 179, 206, 229; life-story work *see* life story work
trafficking 167
transference and counter-transference 67, 100, 179, 217, 219, 220
transition 10, 28, 32, 42, 51, 92, 122, 150, 163, 184, 190, 191

trauma: cumulative impact 7; developmental 10, 51, 54, 56, 183, 202; trauma informed assessment 89, 90, 93, 94, 97, 188, 195; type 1–3 126, 154; type 4 205, 206
Tucker, S. 5, 183

vicarious trauma/traumatisation 15, 179, 187, 199, 215, 217–225, 227–229
voice of the child 196, 208

Ward, H. 15, 25
Waterhouse, R. 66
wellbeing 25, 30, 116, 203
West, C. 222
window of tolerance 68, 75, 91, 95, 112, 141, 181, 191, 226, 228
Wolkind, S. 10
Woodhouse, T. 32
Wrench, K. 67, 68, 71

Zeitlin, H. 67

For Product Safety Concerns and Information please contact our EU representative GPSR@taylorandfrancis.com
Taylor & Francis Verlag GmbH, Kaufingerstraße 24, 80331 München, Germany

www.ingramcontent.com/pod-product-compliance
Ingram Content Group UK Ltd.
Pitfield, Milton Keynes, MK11 3LW, UK
UKHW020443240426
470322UK00023B/521